SpringBoard®

Level 2

Mathematics with Meaning™

THE COLLEGE BOARD
inspiring minds™

The College Board is a mission-driven not-for-profit organization that connects students to college success and opportunity. Founded in 1900, the College Board was created to expand access to higher education. Today, the membership association is made up of more than 5,900 of the world's leading educational institutions and is dedicated to promoting excellence and equity in education. Each year, the College Board helps more than seven million students prepare for a successful transition to college through programs and services in college readiness and college success—including the SAT® and the Advanced Placement Program®. The organization also serves the education community through research and advocacy on behalf of students, educators and schools.

For further information, visit www.collegeboard.com.

ISBN: 0-87447-865-0
ISBN: 978-0-87447-865-5

4 5 6 7 8   11 12 13 14
Printed in the United States of America

Acknowledgments

The College Board gratefully acknowledges the outstanding work of the classroom teachers and writers who have been integral to the development of this revised program. The end product is a testimony to their expertise, understanding of student learning needs, and dedication to rigorous but accessible math education.

Virginia Bohme
School Specialist
University of Arizona
Mathematics Department
Tucson, Arizona

Tammy Buckshi
Mathematics Teacher
Iredell-Statesville Schools
Iredell County, North Carolina

Marcia Chumas
Math Department Chair
East Mecklenburg High School
Charlotte, North Carolina

Betty Davis
Mathematics Teacher
Boston Latin School
Boston, Massachusetts

Wendy L. DenBesten
Mathematics Teacher
Hoover High School
Fresno Unified School District
Fresno, California

Karen Flowers
STEM Coach, Mathematics
Nashville Public Schools
Nashville, Tennessee

Megan Gerstenzang
Mathematics Teacher
Gibbons Middle School
Westborough Public Schools
Westborough, Massachusetts

Shawn Harris
Mathematics Instructor
Ronan Middle School
Ronan, Montana

Melinda Herman
Mathematics Teacher
Christ Presbyterian Academy
Nashville, Tennessee

Marie Humphrey
Mathematics Teacher
David W. Butler High School
Matthews, North Carolina

Andrew Kearns
Math Department Chair
Dr. Michael M. Krop Senior High
Miami-Dade County Public Schools
Miami, Florida

Dean Packard
Mathematics Teacher
Tucson High Magnet School
Tucson, Arizona

Aaron Smith
Mathematics Curriculum Specialist
Duval County Public Schools
Duval County, Florida

Jill Stevens
Mathematics Teacher
Trinity High School
Euless, Texas

Andrea Sukow
Instructional Specialist, SpringBoard
Math Coordinator, retired
Metro Nashville Public Schools
Nashville, Tennessee

Sue Swanda
Mathematics Teacher, retired
Charlotte-Mecklenburg Schools
Cornelius, North Carolina

Judy Windle
Instructional Specialist, SpringBoard
Mathematics Teacher, retired
Charlotte-Mecklenburg Schools
Charlotte, North Carolina

Special thanks also go to the writers and teachers whose excellence in creating the previous Mathematics with Meaning™ program provided the strong foundation on which this program rests.

Sandy Campo
Mathematics Consultant
Providence, Rhode Island

James R. Choike
Professor of Mathematics
Oklahoma State University
Stillwater, Oklahoma

Jill Gough
Mathematics Teacher
The Westminster Schools
Atlanta, Georgia

Sam Gough
Mathematics Teacher
The Westminster Schools
Atlanta, Georgia

Christopher Kribs-Zaleta
Associate Professor of Mathematics
University of Texas at Arlington
Arlington, Texas

Guy Mauldin
Mathematics Teacher
Science Hill High School
Johnson City, Tennessee

Chris Sollars
Mathematics Teacher
Alamo Heights High School
San Antonio, Texas

J. T. Sutcliffe
Mathematics Teacher
The St. Mark's School of Texas
Dallas, Texas

Assessment Advisors

The assessment advisors provided valuable input during the development of the Math Standards Review to ensure the format of this practice was aligned with national and state assessment formats. We especially thank Beverly Whittington for her work on rubrics.

Margaret Bambrick
K-12 Mathematics Specialist
Volusia County Public Schools
DeLand, Florida

Gail Burton
Middle School Math Teacher on
    Assignment
Volusia County Public Schools
DeLand, Florida

Patra Cooks
SpringBoard Coordinator for Math
Hillsborough County Public Schools
Tampa, Florida

Johnnie Ebbert
Mathematics Teacher
Volusia County Schools
DeLand. Florida

Vicki Ewing
District Resource Teacher for
    Promise /former Middle School
    Math Teacher
Hillsborough County Public Schools
Tampa, Florida

Bonnie Fenwick
Mathematics Teacher
Volusia County Public Schools
Port Orange, Florida

Nicki Junkins, Ed. D.
Director of K-12 Curriculum and
    Program Accountability, retired
Volusia County Public Schools
DeLand, Florida

Beverly Whittington
Mathematics Consultant
Bordentown Township, New Jersey

Program Reviewers

The following reviewers contributed immeasurably to this revised edition, and we gratefully thank them for all their suggestions for improvements and clarifications.

James Choike
Professor of Mathematics
Oklahoma State University
College Board, Mathematical
    Sciences AAC
Stillwater, Oklahoma

Kristi Connally
Mathematics Teacher
Broward County Public Schools
Ft. Lauderdale, Florida

Landy Godbold
Mathematics Teacher
The Westminster Schools
Atlanta, Georgia

Janice Martin
Mathematics Teacher/Principal,
    retired
Charlotte-Mecklenburg Schools
Charlotte, North Carolina

Julie Skalka Martin
Mathematics Curriculum
    Coordinator
Metropolitan Nashville Public
    Schools
Nashville, Tennessee

Karen Martinez
Mathematics Teacher and Coach
Broward County Public Schools
Ft. Lauderdale, Florida

Jerry McMahon
Mathematics/Computer Science
    Teacher
Charlotte-Mecklenburg Schools
Charlotte, North Carolina

Joanne Patchin
A. P. Mathematics Teacher
Palm Beach County Public Schools
West Palm Beach, Florida

Carla Richards
Title I Math Coach
Franklin Special School District
Franklin, Tennessee

Sandra Ammons Sullivan
Mathematics Teacher
York County School District #2
Clover, South Carolina

Research and Planning Advisors

We also wish to thank the members of our SpringBoard Advisory Council, the SpringBoard Math Trainers, and the many educators who gave generously of their time and their ideas as we conducted research for the program. Your suggestions and reactions to ideas helped immeasurably as we planned the revisions. We gratefully acknowledge the teachers and administrators in the following districts:

Broward County Public Schools
Fort Lauderdale, Florida

Cherry Creek School District
Cherry Creek, Colorado

Chicago Public Schools
Chicago, Illinois

DeKalb County School System
DeKalb County, Georgia

Duval County Public Schools
Jacksonville, Florida

Guilford County Schools
Greensboro, North Carolina

Hillsborough County Public Schools
Tampa, Florida

Hobbs Municipal Schools
Hobbs, New Mexico

Indianapolis Public Schools
Indianapolis, Indiana

Miami-Dade County Public Schools
Miami, Florida

Metropolitan Nashville Public Schools
Nashville, Tennessee

The City School District of New Rochelle
New Rochelle, New York

Orange County Public Schools
Orlando, Florida

School District of Palm Beach County
Palm Beach, Florida

Penninsula School District
Gig Harbor, Washington

Pinellas County Schools
Largo, Florida

San Antonio Independent School District
San Antonio, Texas

Spokane Public Schools
Spokane, Washington

Volusia County Schools
DeLand, Florida

Editorial Leadership

The College Board gratefully acknowledges the expertise, time, and commitment of the math editorial team.

Betty Barnett
Educational Publishing Consultant

John Nelson
Director of Curriculum and
   Instructional Products, SpringBoard

Contents

Level 2

Unit 2 Equations, Inequalities, and Linear Relationships

Contents *continued*

Contents *continued*

Resources

To the Student

Welcome to the SpringBoard program. We hope you will discover how SpringBoard can help you achieve high academic standards, reach your learning goals, and prepare for success in future mathematics studies. The program has been created with you in mind: the content you need to learn, the tools to help you learn, and the critical thinking skills that help you build confidence in your own knowledge of mathematics.

The College Board publishes the SpringBoard program. It is also the publisher of the PSAT/NMSQT, the SAT, and the Advanced Placement exams—all exams that you are likely to encounter in your student years. Preparing you to perform well on those exams and to develop the mathematics skills needed for high school success is the primary purpose of this program.

Why Do You Need Mathematics?

Knowledge of mathematics helps prepare you for future success in college, in work, and in your personal life. We all encounter some form of mathematics daily, from calculating the cost of gasoline and its impact on monthly household budgets to calculating materials needed to build a new hotel.

The foundation of SpringBoard is the College Board Standards for College Success, which set out the mathematics skills and knowledge that you should master to succeed in high school and in future college-level work. The standards follow these broad areas of mathematics concepts, procedures, and processes.

- Operations and Equivalent Representations
- Algebraic Manipulation Skills
- Quantity and Measurement
- Proportionality
- Relations, Patterns, and Functions
- Shape and Transformation
- Data and Variation
- Chance, Fairness, and Risk

In the middle school years, your study of mathematics begins with a basic understanding of fractions and the operations performed with them. Your study continues with the development of a deep understanding of the rational numbers, their different representations, and the connections between these numbers and other number systems and operations. You will need a broad understanding of addition, subtraction, and multiplication with rational numbers, along with computational fluency with whole-number operations.

As you continue your studies, you will examine ratios and rates, which will allow you to make comparisons between numbers. Ratio and rates represent proportionality. Understanding the concept of proportionality is critical to future success in your study of algebra and the rest of the high school mathematics curriculum.

Strategies for Learning Mathematics

Some tools to help you learn are built into every activity. Throughout the unit activities, you will see suggested learning strategies. Each of these strategies is explained in full in the Resources section of your book. As you learn to use each strategy, you'll have the opportunity to decide which strategies work best for you. Suggested learning strategies include:

- Reading strategies
- Writing strategies
- Problem-solving strategies
- Collaborative strategies

Reading strategies help you learn to look at problem descriptions in different ways, from marking the text to highlight key information to turning problem information into questions that help you break the problem down into its separate parts. Sample reading strategies are included; you will want to try them all to see which ones work best for you.

Writing strategies help you focus on your purpose for writing and what you're writing about.

Problem-solving strategies give you multiple ways to approach the problem, from learning to identify the tasks within a problem to looking for patterns or working backward to see how the problem is set up.

You'll use *collaborative strategies* with your classmates as you explore concepts and problems in group discussions and working with partners.

Building Mathematics Knowledge and Skills

Whether it's mathematics or sports or cooking, one way we learn something really well is by practice and repetition. To help you learn mathematics, the SpringBoard program is built around problem solving, reasoning and justification, communication, connections between concepts and ideas, and visual representation of mathematical concepts.

Problem Solving   Many of the problems in this book are based on real-life situations that require you to ***analyze*** the situation and the information in the problem, ***make decisions***, ***determine the strategies*** you'll use to solve the problem, and ***justify*** your solution. Having a real-world focus helps you see how mathematics is used in everyday life.

Reasoning and Justification   One part of learning mathematics, or any subject, is learning not only how to solve problems but also why you solved them the way you did. You will have many opportunities to predict possible solutions and then to verify solutions. You will be asked to explain the reasoning behind how you solved the problem, the mathematics concepts involved, and why your approach was appropriate for solving the problem.

Communication   When learning a language, saying words out loud helps you learn to pronounce the words and to remember them. Communicating about mathematics, orally and in writing, with your classmates and teachers helps you organize your learning and explain mathematics concepts and problem-solving strategies more precisely. Sharing your ideas and thoughts allows you and your classmates to build on each other's ideas and expand your own understanding.

Mathematics Connections   As you study mathematics, you will learn many different concepts and ways of solving problems. Reading the problem descriptions will take you into the real-life applications of mathematics. As you develop your mathematics knowledge, you will see the many connections between mathematics concepts and between mathematics and your own life.

Representations   Artists create representations through drawings and paintings. In mathematics, representations can take many forms, such as numeric, verbal, graphic, or symbolic. In this course, you are encouraged to use representations to organize problem information, present possible solutions, and communicate your reasoning. Creating representations is a tool you can use to gain understanding of concepts and communicate that understanding to others.

We hope you enjoy your study of mathematics using the SpringBoard program. We, the writers, are all classroom teachers, and we created this program because we love mathematics. We wanted to inspire you to learn mathematics *and* build confidence that you can be successful in your math studies and in using mathematics in daily life.

How To Use This Book

Middle School Mathematics 2 has five units starting with a basic understanding of Integers and Rational Numbers. Linear Relationships are introduced, followed by Two-Dimensional and Three-Dimensional Geometry. The book concludes with a last unit on Data and Probability.

Preview of the Unit sets the purpose for the unit and gives a snapshot of what you'll learn.

Unit Overviews outline the big ideas of what you'll learn in this unit and show how the content is connected from unit to unit.

- **Academic Vocabulary** lists key math terms you'll find in the unit.
- **Essential Questions** focus on key math questions that help you make connections in mathematics.
- **Embedded Assessments** preview the built-in assessments that measure your understanding of the math in the unit.

Getting Ready provides a quick look at what you already know.

- Your answers to questions help pinpoint skills that may need work.
- Questions help you recall earlier learning and refresh skills.

Real World Activities provide context for learning new math concepts and skills. Activities require active participation in groups, in pairs, or independently.

- **Suggested Learning Strategies** are listed on each page to help you "learn how to learn." Find the ones that work best for you.
- **My Notes** space provides a grid for taking notes, creating representations, or working out problems.

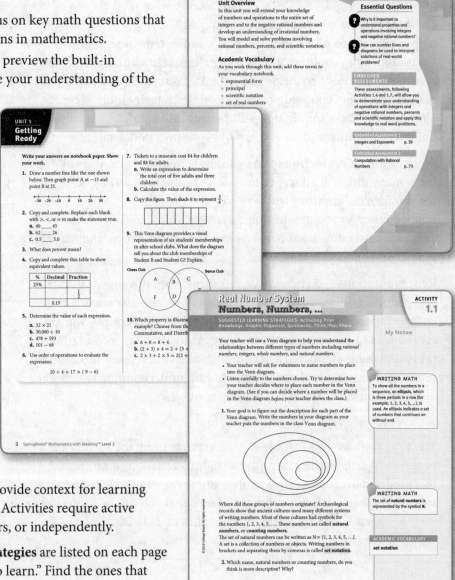

Special Features focus on vocabulary, how to read and write math, connections between mathematics and other subjects, and practice questions to review learning.

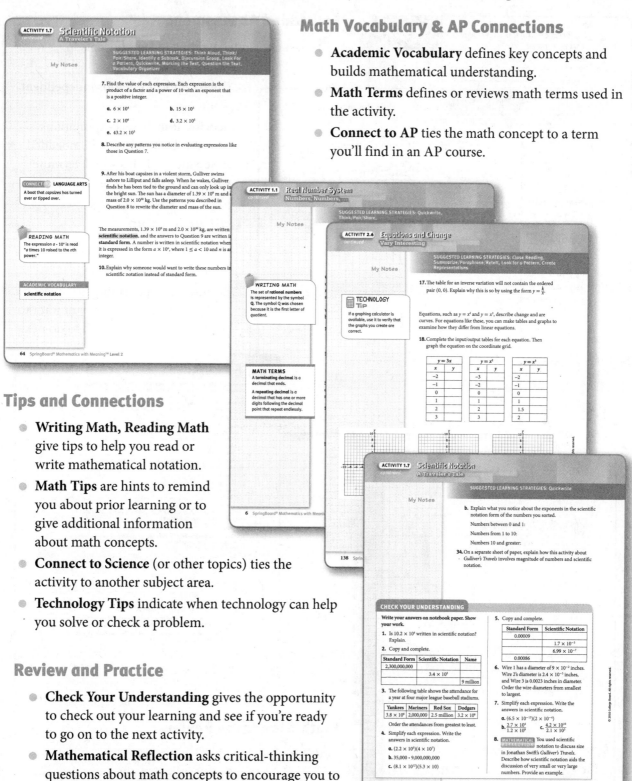

Math Vocabulary & AP Connections

- **Academic Vocabulary** defines key concepts and builds mathematical understanding.
- **Math Terms** defines or reviews math terms used in the activity.
- **Connect to AP** ties the math concept to a term you'll find in an AP course.

Tips and Connections

- **Writing Math, Reading Math** give tips to help you read or write mathematical notation.
- **Math Tips** are hints to remind you about prior learning or to give additional information about math concepts.
- **Connect to Science** (or other topics) ties the activity to another subject area.
- **Technology Tips** indicate when technology can help you solve or check a problem.

Review and Practice

- **Check Your Understanding** gives the opportunity to check out your learning and see if you're ready to go on to the next activity.
- **Mathematical Reflection** asks critical-thinking questions about math concepts to encourage you to make connections between concepts.

Checkpoints for Learning provide opportunities to demonstrate your understanding of the "big math ideas" in the unit and to reflect on your progress.

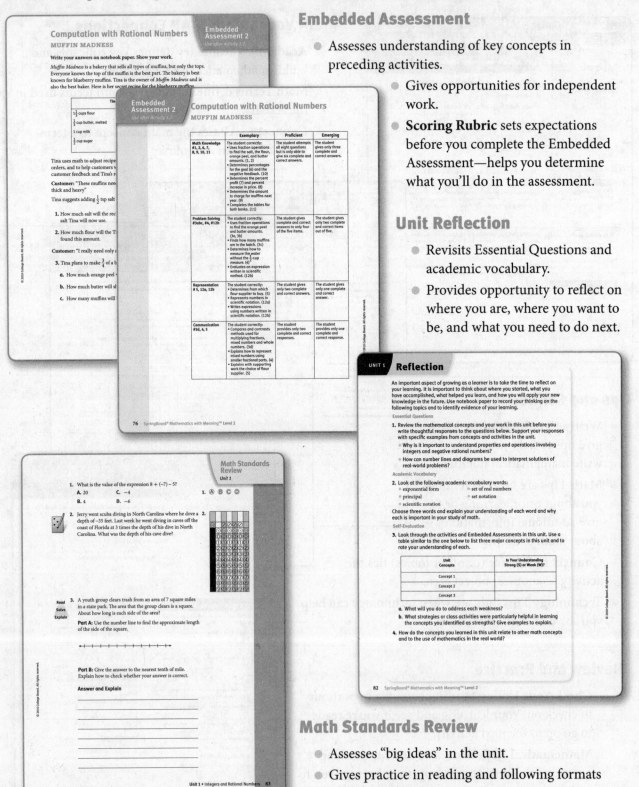

Embedded Assessment

- Assesses understanding of key concepts in preceding activities.
  - Gives opportunities for independent work.
  - **Scoring Rubric** sets expectations before you complete the Embedded Assessment—helps you determine what you'll do in the assessment.

Unit Reflection

- Revisits Essential Questions and academic vocabulary.
- Provides opportunity to reflect on where you are, where you want to be, and what you need to do next.

Math Standards Review

- Assesses "big ideas" in the unit.
- Gives practice in reading and following formats of high-stakes tests.

Integers and Rational Numbers

Unit Overview

In this unit you will extend your knowledge of numbers and operations to the entire set of integers and to the negative rational numbers and develop an understanding of irrational numbers. You will model and solve problems involving rational numbers, percents, and scientific notation.

Academic Vocabulary

As you work through this unit, add these terms to your vocabulary notebook.

- exponential form
- principal
- scientific notation
- set of real numbers
- set notation

Essential Questions

? Why is it important to understand properties and operations involving integers and negative rational numbers?

? How can number lines and diagrams be used to interpret solutions of real-world problems?

EMBEDDED ASSESSMENTS

These assessments, following Activities 1.4 and 1.7, will allow you to demonstrate your understanding of operations with integers and negative rational numbers, percents and scientific notation and apply this knowledge to real word problems.

Write your answers on notebook paper. Show your work.

1. Draw a number line like the one shown below. Then graph point A at −15 and point B at 25.

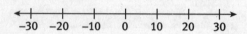

2. Copy and complete. Replace each blank with >, <, or = to make the statement true.
   a. 40 _____ 45
   b. 62 _____ 26
   c. 0.5 _____ 5.0

3. What does *percent* mean?

4. Copy and complete this table to show equivalent values.

%	Decimal	Fraction
25%		
		$\frac{1}{2}$
	0.15	

5. Determine the value of each expression.
   a. 32×21
   b. $30,000 \div 10$
   c. $478 + 593$
   d. $101 - 68$

6. Use order of operations to evaluate the expression:

$$20 \div 4 + 17 \times (9 - 6)$$

7. Tickets to a museum cost $4 for children and $8 for adults.
   a. Write an expression to determine the total cost of five adults and three children.
   b. Calculate the value of the expression.

8. Copy this figure. Then shade it to represent $\frac{3}{4}$.

9. This Venn diagram provides a visual representation of six students' memberships in after-school clubs. What does the diagram tell you about the club memberships of Student B and Student G? Explain.

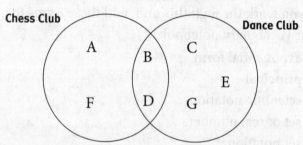

10. Which property is illustrated by each example? Choose from the Associative, Commutative, and Distributive properties.
   a. $6 + 8 = 8 + 6$
   b. $(2 + 3) + 4 = 2 + (3 + 4)$
   c. $2 \times 3 + 2 \times 5 = 2(3 + 5)$

Real Number System
Numbers, Numbers, ...

SUGGESTED LEARNING STRATEGIES: Activating Prior Knowledge, Graphic Organizer, Quickwrite, Think/Pair/Share

Your teacher will use a Venn diagram to help you understand the relationships between different types of numbers including *rational numbers, integers, whole numbers,* and *natural numbers.*

- Your teacher will ask for volunteers to name numbers to place into the Venn diagram.
- Listen carefully to the numbers chosen. Try to determine how your teacher decides where to place each number in the Venn diagram. (See if you can decide where a number will be placed in the Venn diagram *before* your teacher shows the class.)

1. Your goal is to figure out the description for each part of the Venn diagram. Write the numbers in your diagram as your teacher puts the numbers in the class Venn diagram.

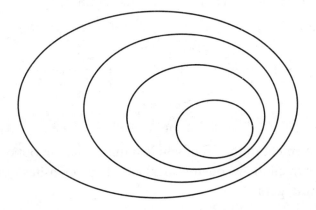

Where did these groups of numbers originate? Archaeological records show that ancient cultures used many different systems of writing numbers. Most of these cultures had symbols for the numbers 1, 2, 3, 4, 5, …. These numbers are called **natural numbers**, or **counting numbers**.

The set of natural numbers can be written as N= {1, 2, 3, 4, 5, …}. A set is a collection of numbers or objects. Writing numbers in brackets and separating them by commas is called **set notation**.

2. Which name, natural numbers or counting numbers, do you think is more descriptive? Why?

My Notes

WRITING MATH

To show all the numbers in a sequence, an **ellipsis**, which is three periods in a row (for example, 1, 2, 3, 4, 5, …), is used. An ellipsis indicates a set of numbers that continues on without end.

WRITING MATH

The set of **natural numbers** is represented by the symbol **N.**

ACADEMIC VOCABULARY

set notation

My Notes

WRITING MATH
The set of **whole numbers** is represented by the symbol **W**.

Notice that 0 is not in the set of natural numbers. Most ancient cultures did not have a concept of the number 0. The Mayans were one of the first to use the concept of 0. Adding 0 to the set of natural numbers forms the set of **whole numbers**.

3. Consider the set of whole numbers and the set of natural numbers. Describe the relationship between the two sets.

4. Use set notation to represent the set of whole numbers.

In mathematics, numbers that are **opposites** are the same distance from zero and have different signs. The numbers −3 and 3 are examples of opposites. On the number line, these two numbers are the same distance from 0 in opposite directions.

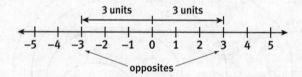

MATH TERMS
The set of **integers** is the set containing all natural numbers, their opposites, and zero.

5. Each element in the set of whole numbers has an opposite. Together, all the whole numbers and their opposites form the set of **integers**.

   a. What is the opposite of 52?

   b. What is the opposite of −312?

   c. What is the opposite of 0?

WRITING MATH
The set of **integers** is represented by the symbol **Z**. This symbol was chosen because in German *Zahlen* is the word for numbers.

6. The set of natural numbers was represented using the notation {1, 2, 3, 4, 5, ...}. Consider the difference between the set of natural numbers and the set of integers.

   a. How would you describe this difference?

   b. Write the set of integers using set notation.

SUGGESTED LEARNING STRATEGIES: Graphic Organizer, Think/Pair/Share, Group Presentation, Quickwrite

<blockquote>
My Notes
</blockquote>

Venn diagrams can be used to compare the set of whole numbers and the set of integers.

7. Place each number in the appropriate region of the Venn diagram.
$5, -1, 0, 3, -12, -11, 15, 23, 2, -9$

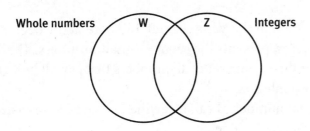

Whole numbers   W   Z   Integers

<blockquote>
CONNECT TO HISTORY

The set of numbers known as **integers** was used by ancient Chinese mathematicians more than 2000 years ago. They performed computations by manipulating counting rods—short rods approximately 10 centimeters long—on a table or counting board. Red rods represented positive numbers and black rods represented opposite or negative numbers.
</blockquote>

8. Write one or more sentences summarizing the results in the Venn diagram in Item 7.

9. Complete this sentence that describes the relationship of the sets in Item 7:

Every _____ is a(n) _____,

but not every _____ is a(n) _____.

10. The Venn diagram below also can be used to compare the set of integers and the set of whole numbers.

a. Place the names of these sets in the Venn diagram and explain why you placed them there.

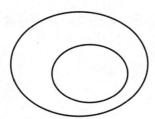

My Notes

b. Compare and contrast the two Venn diagrams. Which do you think is a better representation of the relationship between the two sets? Explain your reasoning.

One of the areas in the Venn diagram we used at the beginning of this activity represents the set of **rational numbers**. The set of rational numbers is the set of all numbers that can all be written as a ratio of two integers.

A rational number, x, can be defined using symbols as $x = \dfrac{a}{b}$, where both a and b are integers and $b \neq 0$. Any rational number may be represented as a fraction, as shown, or as a decimal.

11. Explain why b cannot be 0.

> **WRITING MATH**
>
> The set of **rational numbers** is represented by the symbol Q. The symbol Q was chosen because it is the first letter of *quotient*.

12. If rational numbers are defined as fractions, why can a rational number be represented by a decimal?

Some decimals are *terminating decimals*. To show that these decimals are rational numbers, it must be possible to express these numbers as the ratio of two integers in fraction form.

> **MATH TERMS**
>
> A **terminating decimal** is a decimal that ends.
>
> A **repeating decimal** is a decimal that has one or more digits following the decimal point that repeat endlessly.

13. Write each decimal as a ratio of two integers. Express the answer as a fraction.

    a. 0.35   **b.** 0.004

14. Can all terminating decimals be written as fractions? Justify your answer.

My Notes

Some decimals are *repeating* decimals. To show that these decimals are rational numbers, it must be possible to express these numbers as the ratio of two integers in fraction form.

15. Rewrite each rational number as a decimal. Describe any patterns you observe with the quotients.

    a. $\dfrac{1}{3}$ **b.** $\dfrac{4}{9}$ **c.** $\dfrac{5}{6}$

> **CONNECT TO AP**
>
> In advanced math courses you will learn why a repeating decimal can be expressed as a fraction.

16. Now explore some numbers with nines. Study these equalities and describe any patterns that you observe.

$$0.\overline{41} = \frac{41}{99} \qquad 0.\overline{352} = \frac{352}{999} \qquad 0.\overline{8} = \frac{8}{9}$$

17. Consider the numbers in Items 15 and 16. Would these be considered rational numbers? Why or why not?

> **MATH TERMS**
>
> A **subset** of a set is another set whose elements are all in the original set. Every set is a subset of itself.

18. Explain why natural numbers, whole numbers, and integers are all **subsets** of the set of rational numbers?

> **TECHNOLOGY TIP**
>
> Look at what your calculator shows as a value for π. How is it different from the one on this page?

Irrational numbers are numbers that cannot be written as the ratio of two integers. Some examples are decimals that do not terminate or repeat. These include *pi*, represented by the symbol, π, and the square root of 2, $\sqrt{2}$.

- An approximate decimal value of *pi* is
  3.14159265358979323846426433832795...
- Pi is often represented by the rounded decimal, 3.14. Pi cannot be expressed as a fraction, $\frac{22}{7}$ is close, but is not exact.
- The approximate decimal value of $\sqrt{2}$ is
  1.41421356237309504880168872420 97...
- This decimal also does not terminate or repeat and a fraction cannot be written to equal its value.

> **WRITING MATH**
>
> A symbol that is sometimes used to represent the irrational numbers is $\overline{\mathbf{Q}}$. This symbol means "not rational."

SUGGESTED LEARNING STRATEGIES: Quickwrite, Think/
Pair/Share, Graphic Organizer, Group Presentation, Self
Revision/Peer Revision

My Notes

19. Are all square roots irrational? Explain using at least two examples.

ACADEMIC VOCABULARY

The set of **real numbers** is represented by the symbol **R**.

The set of **real numbers** includes all rational and irrational numbers.

20. For each number, place a check in the box for any set of which the number is a member.

Number	Natural Numbers	Whole Numbers	Integers	Rational Numbers	Irrational Numbers	Real Numbers
0.25						
3						
$\sqrt{3}$						
0						
$\sqrt{64}$						
-3						
3.14						
$0.\overline{4}$						
π						
$5\frac{2}{5}$						

21. Create a Venn diagram to illustrate the relationship between real numbers, rational numbers, irrational numbers, integers, whole numbers, and natural numbers.

My Notes

Some properties can be helpful when you are solving equations and evaluating expressions with real numbers.

22. Write what you recall about the commutative property. Give an example using only whole numbers in your explanation.

23. Write the meaning of the associative property in your own words. Give an example using only integers in your explanation.

24. Two students, Nick and Nathaniel, used the distributive property to make mental math easier. Look at each student's work and explain what each student did.

Nathaniel: $4(100 + 21) = 4 \times 100 + 4 \times 21$

Nick: $3(108) = 3 \times 100 + 3 \times 8$

25. Which property states that when you add a number and its opposite, the sum is zero? Write a problem using rational numbers that are not integers to illustrate this property.

26. What do the identity properties state and does this hold true for all real numbers? Give examples to justify your answer.

SUGGESTED LEARNING STRATEGIES: Quickwrite, Think/ Pair/Share

My Notes

27. List any properties of real numbers that were used to evaluate each expression.

   a. $26 \times 1 = 26$

   b. $2(a + b) = 2a + 2b$

   c. $14 + 30 + 26 = 30 + 14 + 26$

   d. $2 \times (13 \times 5) = (2 \times 5) \times 13$

28. How does using properties of real numbers make it easier for you to do mental math?

CHECK YOUR UNDERSTANDING

Write your answers on notebook paper. Show your work.

Name one number for each description.

1. A whole number but not a natural number.

2. An integer but not a whole number.

3. An integer and a natural number.

4. An irrational number.

5. A rational number but not an integer.

Write the property illustrated in each example.

6. $5 + 0 = 5$

7. $2(3 + 6) = 6 + 12$

8. $2 + 3 + (-2) = 2 + (-2) + 3$

9. $(2 \times 4) \times 5 = 2 \times (4 \times 5)$

10. **MATHEMATICAL REFLECTION** Describe the set of numbers with which you are most comfortable and explain why. Describe the set of numbers with which you are least comfortable and explain why.

Adding and Subtracting Integers
Changing Elevations

My Notes

Ms. Flowers, a math teacher at Rachel Carson Middle School, plans a field trip for her students every year. On the first day of school, each student recommends a place where the class should go on the annual trip.

1. If your teacher were to plan a field trip for your class this year, where would you like to go? Write your choice below and explain why this would be a good choice for your class trip.

When the students report to math class, many have ideas about where they would like to go. Marcus wants the class to go to Death Valley this year. The other students think that Death Valley would not be a pleasant place to visit so they tell Marcus to convince them this is a good choice. In his research, Marcus finds that Death Valley is very interesting and could be called "a land of extremes."

He was surprised to learn that Death Valley has some high mountains and some very low canyons. He noticed that some elevations in Death Valley are above sea level and are listed as positive numbers, while some are below sea level and are listed as negative numbers. He also noticed that the online atlas listed sea level as 0 feet. For a moment he was confused about what these numbers meant, but then remembered that last year he learned that these numbers are called **integers**.

2. In the chart below, list what you already know about integers and what more you would like to learn about them. When you are finished, your class will make a chart showing everyone's information.

What I know about integers:	What I want to learn about integers:

My Notes

SUGGESTED LEARNING STRATEGIES: Visualize, Create Representations, Quickwrite, Look for a Pattern, Group Presentation, Think/Pair/Share

3. Marcus found that one of the lowest elevation points on Earth is in Death Valley. Some of Earth's lowest locations and their elevations are listed below.

Lake Assal (Africa): -509 ft.

Qattara Depression (Egypt): -435 ft.

Laguna del Carbón (Argentina): -344 ft.

Death Valley (United States): -282 ft.

Valdes Peninsula (Argentina): -131 ft.

Graph the integer for each elevation on this number line.

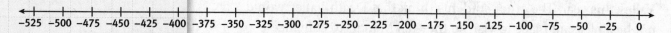

4. Death Valley also has some higher points of elevation. They include:
- Shoshone, with an elevation of 1585 feet
- Dante's View, with an elevation of 5500 feet
- Butte Valley, with an elevation of 4400 feet

Graph the integer for each elevation on this number line.

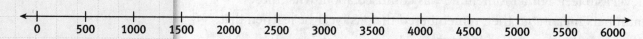

5. Look back at the number lines in Questions 3 and 4. What do you notice about the order of the integers on the number line?

6. Using your generalization from Question 5, order the integers in each set from least to greatest.

    a. $-1360, -282, -435$

    b. $-410, -505, -509, -180$

    c. $-266, -227, -410, -433$

SUGGESTED LEARNING STRATEGIES: Quickwrite, Look for a Pattern, Interactive Word Wall, KWL, Think/Pair/Share

My Notes

The students began thinking about elevation. They reasoned that there must be places as far above sea level as there are below sea level.

7. For example, the elevation of the Salton Sea in California is −227 feet and Jamestown, Louisiana is approximately 227 feet above sea level. Graph the integer for each location.

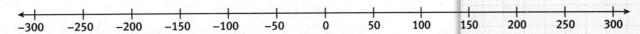

8. Describe the position of these two integers in relationship to zero.

9. Telescope Peak is the highest point in Death Valley. Its elevation is 11,049 feet.

   a. If a student begins a hike at sea level, and hikes to the top of Telescope Peak, how far above sea level will he be?

   b. If a diving bell begins a dive at sea level, and dives to a point below sea level that is as far from sea level as Telescope Peak, how far below sea level would it be?

   c. What are the two distances in questions 8 and 9 called?

10. Why are the distances of the hike and the dive with their changes in elevation an example of two integers with the same *absolute value*?

11. Write the absolute value of each integer.

Integer	23	−46	1659	0	−79,865
Absolute Value					

My Notes

12. Evaluate each expression.

 a. $|-128|$ b. $|56|$ c. $|0|$

The students in Ms. Flower's class were starting to get excited about their field trip, but Lindsay was concerned that they would not be able to stay warm at night. When camping, even when it is very hot during the day, it can be very cold at night. Lindsay decided to do some research on sleeping bags.

The temperature rating of a sleeping bag describes the lowest outside temperature at which the bag will keep a sleeper warm.

13. Look at each situation below and decide if the sleeping bag is the correct bag for the temperature of the camping location based on the rating of the bag.

Location	Sleeping Bag Rating	Outside Temperature	Will sleeper be warm?
Alamosa, Colorado	+35	60°	
Yellowstone National Park	0	−10°	
St. Cloud, Minnesota	−10	−3°	
Bartlett, New Hampshire	−20	15°	
Fairbanks, Alaska	+15	−4°	

14. List the locations for which the sleeping bags are not rated for the temperature and explain why.

15. How did being able to compare integers help you know which sleeping bag would keep a sleeper warm? Explain below.

My Notes

You can use inequalities to compare integers.

16. For each pair of integers, write two inequalities comparing the integers using the given inequality symbol.

Integers	<	>
35, 60		
0, −10		
−10, −3		
15, −20		
15, −4		

Inequalities can also be graphed on a number line.

READING MATH

Read the symbol > as "greater than."

Read the symbol < as "less than."

Read the symbol ≥ as "greater than or equal to."

Read the symbol ≤ as "less than or equal to."

EXAMPLE 1

Graph the inequality: $x < 2$.

Step 1: *Graph the integer in the inequality on the number line.* Since 2 is the integer, locate 2 on the number line.

- If the inequality sign is < or >, graph the point as an open circle because the integer *is not* part of the solution.
- If the inequality sign is ≤ or ≥, graph the point as a closed circle because the integer *is* part of the solution.

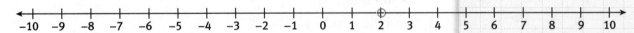

Step 2: *Think about the group of numbers the inequality is describing and draw an arrow on the number line to represent them.*

Since the numbers described in the inequality are less than 2, the arrow goes to the left because that is where all numbers less than 2 are.

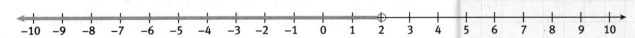

Solution: The number line above is the graph of $x < 2$.

My Notes

TRY THESE A

Graph each inequality.

a. $y < 6$

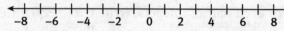

b. $s > -5$

c. $b \geq -2$

d. $a \leq 7$

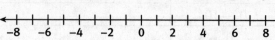

MATH TIP

Integers without signs are considered to be positive.

Some of the students were excited about going hiking on their field trip. Ms. Flowers knew that thinking about hiking could help the students understand adding and subtracting integers. She explained adding and subtracting integers using ideas related to hiking.

- The first number in a problem is where you start your hike.
- The operation sign in the middle of the problem tells you whether you are going to face in the positive direction or the negative direction.
- The sign of the second number tells you if you are going to step backward (−) or forward (+).
- The answer to the integer problem is where your hike ends.

EXAMPLE 2

Find the sum: $-4 + (-2)$

Use this number line to follow along with this example.

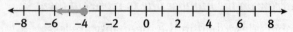

Step 1: *Start at −4.*

Step 2: *Face the positive direction (right).*

Step 3: *Since the 2 is negative, take 2 steps backward (to the left).*

Solution: The answer is −6.

Adding and Subtracting Integers
Changing Elevations

SUGGESTED LEARNING STRATEGIES: Create Representations, Use Manipulatives

My Notes

TRY THESE B

Illustrate the move for each problem. Then record your answer:

a. $-5 + (-3) =$ _____

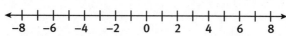

b. $6 + (-6) =$ _____

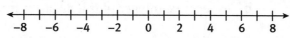

c. $5 + (-3) =$ _____

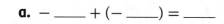

d. $6 + 2 =$ _____

17. Work with a partner. For each problem, roll a number cube twice. Use the numbers you roll to make a problem. Then use the number line to solve the problem. Look for patterns while you work.

WRITING MATH
Parentheses are placed around a signed number to make a problem easier to read.

a. $-$ _____ $+ (-$ _____$) =$ _____

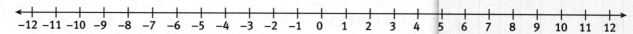

b. $-$ _____ $+$ _____ $=$ _____

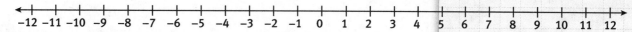

c. _____ $+ (-$ _____$) =$ _____

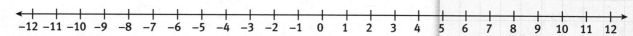

d. _____ $+$ _____ $=$ _____

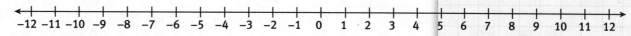

18. What patterns did you notice about integer addition as you worked?

My Notes

19. Use the patterns that you noticed to write rules about adding integers. Include an example in your explanation.

 a. A positive integer plus a positive integer.

 b. A negative integer plus a negative integer.

 c. A negative integer plus a positive integer.

 d. A positive integer plus a negative integer.

 e. An integer and its opposite

Now consider subtracting integers.

> **EXAMPLE 3**
>
> Find the difference: $-4 - (-2)$
>
> Use this number line to follow along with this example.
>
>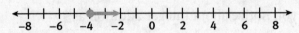
>
> Step 1: *Start at −4.*
> Step 2: *Face the negative direction (left).*
> Step 3: *Since the 2 is negative, take 2 steps backward (to the right).*
> Solution: The answer is −2.

SUGGESTED LEARNING STRATEGIES: Create Representations, Use Manipulatives

My Notes

TRY THESE C

Illustrate the move for each problem. Then record your answer.

a. $-5 - (-3) =$ _____

b. $-6 - 2 =$ _____

c. $5 - (-3) =$ _____

d. $6 - 2 =$ _____

20. For each move that you illustrated in Try These C, show a different move that starts at the same integer and has the same answer as the original problem. The first one is done for you.

a. $-5 - (-3) = \boxed{-5 + (+3) = -2}$

b. $-6 - 2 = \boxed{}$

c. $5 - (-3) = \boxed{}$

d. $6 - 2 = \boxed{}$

My Notes

21. How did you find each move in Question 20?

22. Use the patterns that you noticed to write rules about subtracting integers. Include an example in your explanation.

a. A positive integer minus a positive integer.

b. A negative integer minus a positive integer.

c. A negative integer minus a negative integer.

d. A positive integer minus a negative integer.

SUGGESTED LEARNING STRATEGIES: Use Manipulatives, Group Presentation, Think/Pair/Share

My Notes

23. Work with a partner. For each problem, roll a number cube twice. Use the numbers you roll to make a problem. Then use the number line to solve the problem.

a. $-\rule{1cm}{0.4pt} - (-\rule{1cm}{0.4pt}) = \rule{1cm}{0.4pt}$

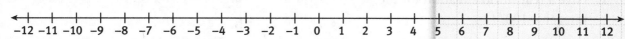

b. $-\rule{1cm}{0.4pt} - \rule{1cm}{0.4pt} = \rule{1cm}{0.4pt}$

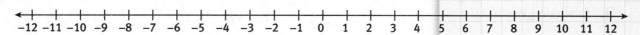

c. $\rule{1cm}{0.4pt} - (-\rule{1cm}{0.4pt}) = \rule{1cm}{0.4pt}$

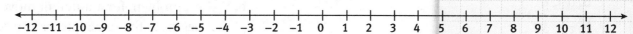

d. $\rule{1cm}{0.4pt} - \rule{1cm}{0.4pt} = \rule{1cm}{0.4pt}$

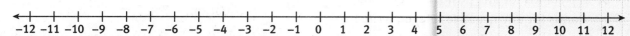

24. For each problem, you will need to add and subtract. You can use the rules you found or number lines to help you add and subtract the integers.

a. $-3 + 6 + (-3) =$

b. $4 - 6 + (-6) =$

c. $-5 + (-2) - 2 =$

25. Describe a situation that matches each equation.

a. $-6° + 6° = 0°$

b. $\$75 + (-\$75) = \$0$

CHECK YOUR UNDERSTANDING

Write your answers on notebook paper. Show your work.

1. Give a real world situation for the integer -100.

2. Order these integers from least to greatest:

   $$0, -132, 458, -789, 984$$

3. Evaluate $|36|$.

4. Give two values that make these inequalities true.

   a. $0 < d$

   b. $z < 37$

   c. $-12 > f$

5. If p stands for any positive integer and t stands for any negative integer, write two inequalities comparing p and t.

6. Graph the inequality $y < 5$ on a number line.

7. Simplify each problem. Use a number line if necessary.

   a. $-3 - (-8)$

   b. $-4 - 6$

   c. $6 - (-6)$

   d. $7 - 3$

8. $-8 - 2$

   a. Use a number line to illustrate this problem and find its solution.

   b. Write a problem for a different move that begins at the same integer and has the same answer.

9. Describe a situation that matches this equation. $-7 + 7 = 0$

10. **MATHEMATICAL REFLECTION** What relationship exists between addition and subtraction? Explain using integer models.

Multiplying and Dividing Integers
Cruising Altitude

SUGGESTED LEARNING STRATEGIES: Shared Reading, Activating
Prior Knowledge

Ms. Flowers and the students in her math class are still not sure
where they want to go for their field trip. Robbie suggested that
they examine the idea of going to Hawaii. The students were excited
about this possibility.

One student, Thane, was uncertain about flying. He did not
know much about flying so he decided to do some research. He
learned that when a passenger jet *ascends* from ground level, it
could take as little as 10 minutes to reach the cruising altitude of
30,000 feet. He also found out that when a passenger jet *descends*,
it could take about the same amount of time to reach ground
level again.

My Notes

> **MATH TIP**
>
> *Ascend* means to move upward
> and *descend* means to move
> downward.

1. If a jet reaches its cruising altitude in the least amount of time,
   what is the distance the jet climbs vertically per minute during
   the ascent? Label your answer in units.

2. Would it make sense for this rate of ascent to be thought of as a
   positive integer or a negative integer? Explain your thinking.

3. What is the vertical distance the jet descends per minute during
   the descent if it takes 15 minutes for the jet to reach ground
   level? Label your answer in units.

4. Would it make sense for this rate
   of descent to be thought of as a
   positive integer or a negative
   integer? Explain your thinking.

When Thane thought about
this situation, he realized he
could make a sketch of the
jet's ascent and descent
using number lines.

My Notes

5. For what mathematical operations could Thane's diagram be a model? Explain your choices.

When Thane showed his diagram to Ms. Flowers, she showed him a diagram she made of the same situation. She told him that each triangle stands for 1000 feet. Her diagram looked like the ones at the left.

6. How is the diagram Ms. Flowers made similar to the one Thane made?

7. Write a number sentence for each part of their diagrams.

8. Write the number sentence illustrated by each diagram. Each counter stands for 10. The first two have been done for you.

a. 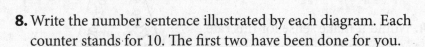 $2 \times 30 = 60$

b. $2 \times -30 = -60$

c.

d.

My Notes

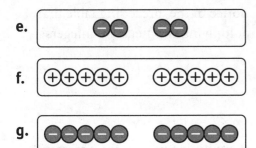

e.

f.

g.

9. From your work in Question 8, what can you say about the sign of the product of a positive integer and a positive integer?

10. From your work in Question 8, what can you say about the sign of the product of a negative integer and a positive integer?

Thane wondered how to find the answer to a problem with two negative factors. Ms. Flowers gave Thane this table.

11. Complete the unshaded part of the table below. Then look for patterns to help you complete the shaded area.

×	3	2	1	0	−1	−2	−3
3							
2							
1							
0							
−1							
−2							
−3							

My Notes

12. What patterns did you notice in the preceding table that would help you when multiplying two negative integers?

13. What rule can you use to multiply two negative integers?

14. Using what you know about multiplying integers, draw a diagram using + and − counters for each division problem and give the answer.

   a. $10 \div 2 = $ _____

   b. $15 \div 3 = $ _____

   c. $-18 \div 6 = $ _____

   d. $-10 \div 5 = $ _____

15. What similarities are there between multiplying integers and dividing integers?

Thane wondered if dividing a negative integer by another negative integer had the same rule as multiplying two negative integers so he decided to make a table to investigate this idea.

My Notes

16. Complete this table. Look for patterns in dividing integers.

Division Problem	Quotient	Related Multiplication	Related Product
−18 ÷ 3	−6	−6 × 3	−18
−18 ÷ 2			
−18 ÷ 1			
−18 ÷ (−1)			
−18 ÷ (−2)			
−18 ÷ (−3)			

17. Why do you think that division by zero is not in the table above?

18. What did you observe about dividing a negative integer by a negative integer? What rule could you write for dividing a negative integer by a negative integer?

19. What is the relationship between multiplication and division?

My Notes

In his research Thane learned that as a plane ascends, the air outside the plane gets colder. In general, the temperature of the Earth's atmosphere decreases by 5 degrees for each increase of 1000 feet of altitude.

20. Use this information to find the temperature change from sea level to 6,000 feet above sea level. Include a diagram and number sentence.

Diagram:

Number Sentence:

CHECK YOUR UNDERSTANDING

Write your answers on notebook paper. Show your work.

1. Evaluate $\dfrac{2 \times 3 \times (-6)}{-9}$.

2. If an airplane descends at a rate of 500 feet per minute, write and evaluate an expression with integers to show how far will it descend in 6 minutes.

3. Copy and complete the number statement by replacing the circle with <, >, or =.

   a. $3 \times (-3) - 1 \bigcirc 3 \times (-3) + 1$

   b. $0 \div (4) + 9 \bigcirc 0 \div (-10) + 9$

4. Divers can descend 7 feet per second. If the diver starts at sea level, what is the depth after 5 seconds of diving? Express your answer as a negative integer.

5. Find the mean of the following cold temperatures at Yellowstone Park: $-10°$ F, $-23°$ F, $-5°$ F, $-18°$ F, and $-9°$ F. (*Hint:* Find the mean by dividing the sum of the values by the number of values.)

6. If a football team gained 5 yards per play for 3 plays and then lost 2 yards per play for 4 plays, write and evaluate an expression with integers to show their total gain or loss.

7. $-3 \times 2 \times (-5) \times (-6) \times 4 =$

8. Between low tide and high tide the width of a beach changes by -17 feet/hour. What is the total change in 3 hours?

9. **MATHEMATICAL REFLECTION** Why are patterns useful in mathematics?

Powers and Roots
Squares and Cubes

SUGGESTED LEARNING STRATEGIES: Activating Prior
Knowledge, Think/Pair/Share, Quickwrite, Group Presentation,
Visualize, Create Representations

My Notes

Dominique Wilkins Middle School is holding its annual school
carnival. Each year, classes and clubs build game booths in the
school gym. This year, the student
council has asked Jonelle's math
class for help in deciding what size
the booths should be and how they
should be arranged on the gym floor.
The class will begin this work by
reviewing some ideas about area.

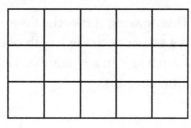

The rectangle above has been divided into squares. Assume that
the length of each side of a small square is 1 cm.

1. Find the area of the rectangle. Explain your method.

Before deciding on how to arrange the booths, the student council
needs to know the area of the gym floor, so several class members
went to the gym to measure the floor. They found that the length of
the floor is 84 feet and the width of the floor is 50 feet.

2. Find the area of the gym floor and write an explanation to the
student council telling what your answer means. Include units
in your answer.

The class is now going to focus on the area of squares since this is
the shape of the base of many of the game booths.

3. Do you need to know both the length and width of a square to
be able to determine its area? Explain your answer. Then draw
a diagram as a model.

My Notes

4. Write a rule, in words, for finding the area of a square.

This drawing shows the floor space of one of the carnival booths. It is a square with the length of one side labeled with the letter *s*. The *s* can be given any number value since the booths are going to be different sizes.

s

5. Complete this table of the areas of some different size booths. The length of a side in feet is represented by *s*, as in the drawing above. Include units for area in the last column.

Length of Side (in feet)	Calculation	Area of the Square
$s = 3$		
$s = 6$		
$s = 8$		
$s = 9$		
$s = 11$		

> **WRITING MATH**
> Sometimes a dot is used as a symbol for multiplication. $3 \times 2 = 6$ and $3 \cdot 2 = 6$ are both ways to show 3 times 2 equals 6.

For each calculation in Question 5 you found the product of a number times itself. The product of a number times itself can be written with a **base** and an **exponent**. For example $5 \cdot 5$, can be written as 5^2.

> **ACADEMIC VOCABULARY**
>
> A number written with an exponent is in **exponential form**.

6. Label the diagram using the terms **base** and **exponent**.

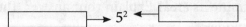

Numbers in this form are said to be in **exponential form**.

7. What are some ways in which this can be read?

SUGGESTED LEARNING STRATEGIES: Quickwrite, Self Revision/Peer Revision, Group Presentation, Interactive Word Wall, Look for a Pattern, Think/Pair/Share

My Notes

When you find the value of the expression 5^2, you are squaring the number 5. The number 25 is called the "square of 5."

8. Why do you think the number 25 is called the square of 5? Draw a model in the My Notes space as part of your explanation.

9. The table below gives some booth sizes in exponential form. Write each expression as a product with the base used twice as a factor and in *standard form.*

Exponential Form	Product Using the Base as a Factor Twice	Standard Form
5^2	$5 \cdot 5$	25
2^2		
1^2		
7^2		
15^2		

10. If you know the area of the floor of a square booth, how can you find the side length of the booth?

Finding the side length of a square is called finding the **square root**. The **square root** of 36 is written as $\sqrt{36}$.

11. Complete each table. All numbers are in standard form.

Number	2	3	4	5	7	10	n
Square							

Number	4	9	16	25	49	100	n^2
Square Root							

WRITING MATH
The symbol $\sqrt{}$ is called a radical sign. It is used in expressions to show square roots.

My Notes

12. What patterns do you notice in the tables you made in Question 11?

13. Think about what you have discovered about the area of a square and finding the side length of a square. Write a sentence to explain what the *square root* of a number means.

14. The carnival booth sizes are assigned according to the number of members in the club or class. To help decide what size booths are needed, complete this table.

Club or Class Size	Area of Square Booth's Floor	Side Length of Booth's Floor
1–30 members	36 ft²	
31–60 members		8 ft
61–90 members		9 ft
91–120 members	121 ft²	
121–150 members	144 ft²	

The area of each booth floor you worked with in Question 14 is called a **perfect square**.

15. What do you think is meant by the term *perfect square*?

Several of the classes would like to make booths with floors that have areas that are not perfect squares. One class wants to have a booth with a square floor that has an area of 18 ft².

16. Why would it be difficult to find the exact square root of 18?

SUGGESTED LEARNING STRATEGIES: Use Manipulatives, Self Revision/Peer Revision, Think/Pair/Share, Create Representations, Identify a Subtask

My Notes

17. Use this number line and the method described in Parts a–f to determine the approximate side length of a square booth with a floor area of 18 ft^2.

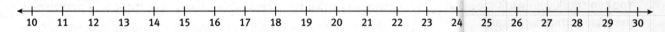

a. Which perfect square is less than 18 but closest to 18? Mark this integer on the number line.

b. Which perfect square is greater than 18 but closest to 18? Mark this integer on the number line.

c. What is the square root of the first integer you marked? Write the square root above the integer on the number line.

d. What is the square root of the second integer you marked? Write the square root above that integer.

e. Put an X on 18. The X should be between the two perfect squares. Is the X closer to the smaller or the larger perfect square?

f. Above the X you put on 18, write a decimal number to the nearest tenth that you think is the square root of 18.

g. Check your estimate by squaring it to see how close you are. Try another decimal number if your check is not close to 18.

18. Using the method you used in number 17 estimate the square root of each integer.

a. 42

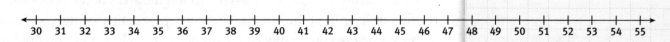

b. 98

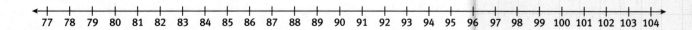

SUGGESTED LEARNING STRATEGIES: Summarize/
Paraphrase/Retell, Visualize, Group Presentation, Think/
Pair/Share, Look for a Pattern

My Notes

TECHNOLOGY TiP

You can check your work in the table with a calculator. Multiply your approximate square root by itself or use the x^2 key.

19. Choose a number from the table below and find its approximate square root. Check by multiplying your approximations to determine how close each square root approximation is. Place your answer on the class table below. Continue with other numbers until the class table below is complete. Then use values in the class table to complete this table below.

Number	Square root
1	1
2	
3	
4	2
5	
6	
7	
8	
9	3
10	
11	
12	
13	
14	
15	
16	4

The student council is very happy with the work the class has done on the carnival so far. The class has found the areas of the floors and the side lengths of the booths. One concept remains for the class to review before completing all the needed work. The booths do not just take up floor space; they also have volume.

My Notes

The diagram at the right represents a cubic foot. Its dimensions are
1 ft • 1 ft • 1 ft.

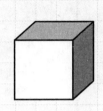

20. Build a solid with dimensions of 2 units • 2 units • 2 units.

 a. What is the name of the solid you just built?

 b. What is true about its edge lengths?

21. Aaron says that to find the volume of a cube he uses the formula
 $l \cdot w \cdot h$. Jonelle says that the formula she uses is l^3. Who uses the
 correct formula? Justify your answer.

22. Use a formula from Question 21. Complete this table to show
 the volume of each cube in exponential form and in cubic feet.

Length of an Edge of a Cube (in feet)	Calculation for Finding Volume of Cube	Volume of the Cube (in exponential form)	Volume of the Cube (in cubic feet)
2			
4			
5			
6			
8			
9			

23. The exponent used in each exponential expression of volume
 in Question 22 is the same. This exponent is used for the
 volume of a cube. Using this exponent is known as **cubing a
 number**. What is the exponent used in cubing a number?

My Notes

24. If you know the volume of a cube you can determine the length of the edge of the cube. The volumes of four cubes are given in this table. Find the length of the edge of each cube.

Volume of the Cube (in cubic units)	Length of the Edge (in units)
1	
8	
27	
64	

The operation you use to find the volume of a cube when you know the edge length is called cubing. The operation you use to find the edge length when you know the volume is called finding the **cube root**. The symbol used for cube root is $\sqrt[3]{}$.

25. Complete each table. All numbers are in standard form.

Number	2	3	4	5	n
Cube					

Number	8	27	64	125	n^3
Cube Root					

26. What patterns do you see in the tables above?

27. Think about what you have discovered about the volume of a cube and finding the edge length of a cube. Write a sentence to explain what the *cube root* of a number means.

WRITING MATH

The index of 3 in the radical sign $\sqrt[3]{}$ shows a **cube root**. $\sqrt[3]{8}$ is read "the cube root of 8."

SUGGESTED LEARNING STRATEGIES: Self Revision/Peer Revision, Group Presentation, Think/Pair/Share, Activating Prior Knowledge, Summarize/Paraphrase/Retell, Visualize, Use Manipulatives

My Notes

28. Some of the booths at the carnival will be cubical. Find the lengths of the edges of the booths listed in this chart.

Volume of the Cubical Booth	Length of each Edge of the Booth
216 ft³	
343 ft³	
729 ft³	
1000 ft³	

29. Exponents other than 2 and 3 can be used. Bases can be numbers other than whole numbers. Complete this table of expressions using other exponents and bases.

Number (in exponential form)	Product Using the Base as a Factor	Number (in standard form)
2^4		
1^9		
9^1		
$\left(\frac{1}{4}\right)^3$		
$(-4)^2$		
7^0		
$(3m)^2$		

MATH TIP

The exponent tells how many times to use the base as a factor. When the exponent is 0, the value of the expression is 1.
$35^0 = 1$, $575^0 = 1$, $n^0 = 1$

30. One of the games to be played at the carnival is *Expression Bingo*. Jonelle's class will play the game first since they have worked so hard to plan for the carnival.

- To start playing, choose nine numbers from the list of *Expression Bingo* Numbers and write them in any order on this bingo card.

Expression Bingo Numbers	
5	6
7	8
10	11
19	21
23	24
25	90
91	92
93	94
95	325
350	375
400	425

My Notes

ORDER OF OPERATIONS

1. Grouping symbols
2. Exponents
3. Multiplication and division
4. Addition and subtraction

- Next evaluate each expression below using order of operations rules. After you have evaluated the first problem, check to see if your answer is on your bingo card. If so, shade that box. If not, move on to the next problem.

$2^0 + 3 \cdot 6$	$6 - 2 + \sqrt{4}$	$1^2 - 6 + (-2)^4$
$5^3 \cdot 3^1$	$4(2 + 3)^2 - 7$	$6 \cdot (5 + 3) \div 3 - 2^3$
$5^2 \cdot 2^4$	$19 + 36 \div 3^2$	$250 - (3 \cdot 5)^2$

- The winner is the player with the most shaded boxes on his or her card. If no player completes a row, column, or diagonal, the winner is the player with the most shaded boxes on his or her card.

CHECK YOUR UNDERSTANDING

Write your answers on notebook paper. Show your work. Be sure to include units in your answers if appropriate.

1. Write $3 \cdot 3 \cdot 3 \cdot 3$ in exponential form.

2. Evaluate the power 4^3.

3. In science we find that some cells divide to form two cells every hour. How many cells will be formed from one cell after 7 hours?

   Copy and replace ○ with =, >, or <.

4. $1^9 \bigcirc 1^0$

5. $3^4 \bigcirc 4^3$

6. If you know that $9^3 = 729$, describe how to find 9^4 without having to multiply four 9's.

7. This figure has an area of 196 in.^{2} and is made up of four small squares. What is the side length of a small square?

8. Evaluate each expression.

   a. $\sqrt{81}$ **b.** $\sqrt[3]{27}$

9. What is the volume of a cube with a side length of 6 cm?

10. What are two whole numbers that can be substituted for n to make this statement true?

    $$9 < \sqrt{n} < 11$$

11. **MATHEMATICAL REFLECTION** As the length of the edge of a cube increases, what happens to the area of a face and the volume of the cube? Explain using diagrams.

Integers and Exponents
RAISE THE ROOF

Write your answers on notebook paper. Show your work.

Camp Shady Groves is holding a summer campout. The campground is 160 feet long by 90 feet wide. The table at the right has the data used to determine the size tents needed for their campers. All tents at Shady Groves have square bases.

Number of Campers	Side Length of Square Base
1–2	7 ft
3–4	9 ft
5–7	11 ft
8–10	12 ft
11–12	15 ft

- There are 6 groups with 1–2 campers.
- There are 5 groups with 3–4 campers.
- There are 8 groups with 5–7 campers.
- There are 3 groups with 8–10 campers.
- There are 3 groups with 11–12 campers.

1. Write a note to the director of Camp Shady Groves to help her planning. Include the area of the campground, the area covered by the groups' tents, and the area that will be free for other activities. Be sure to show your work.

2. The Grizzly Group wants to bring its own tent. Its base has an area of 49 ft². Use the map (at the right) of the area they have reserved to decide whether their tent will fit.

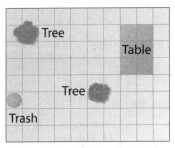

Each square on this grid represents 1 square foot.

3. Three camping groups are holding a fund raiser during the campout to buy a new water purifier and solar shower that cost a total of $200. Campers will pay 50 cents a ticket to play games and buy snacks. Use the information below to determine how much money these three groups made or lost. Show your work.

- The Wolf Pack paid $25 for the supplies to run their Water Game station. They sold 275 tickets.
- The Busy Bunch sold healthy treats. It cost them $205 to make them. They sold 402 tickets.
- The Cougar Crew lost $6 each of the three nights of the jamboree with their Pin The Tail on the Skunk game.

4. The record of expenses and income for this year's jamboree for the Organized Otters is shown at the right. How many tickets will the Organized Otters need to sell to make sure that the four groups earn the $200 needed?

Expenses	Income
−20	25
−15	40
−45	50
−10	5
−8	25

5. Members of the Granola Gang were popping popcorn over the campfire. Each packet was 2 in^3 before it was popped and doubled in size three times while popping.

a. Show this increase as a product of the same factor.

b. Write this increase in both exponential and standard form

6. List the subsets of the real numbers used in this assessment.

	Exemplary	Proficient	Emerging
Math Knowledge # 1, 2, 6	The student correctly: • Finds the area of the campground, the area covered by the groups' tents, and the area that will be free for other activities. (1) • Determines using the map whether the Grizzly Group's tent will fit. (2) • Lists the subsets of the real numbers used in the assessment. (6)	The student attempts all three items answering only two questions correctly and completely.	The student is able to answer only one question correctly and completely.
Problem Solving #2, 3, 4	The student correctly: • Determines the length of the side of the square given its area. (2) • Determines how much money each group makes. (3) • Finds how many tickets need to be sold to earn the $200. (4)	The student attempts all three items answering only two questions correctly and completely.	The student is able to answer only one question correctly and completely.
Representation #5	The student correctly: • Shows the increase as a product of the same factor. (5a) • Shows the increase in exponential and standard form. (5b)	The student represents values in two of three forms: standard form, exponential notation, or as a product of the same factor.	The student represents values in one of three forms: exponential notation, standard form, or as a product of the same factor.
Communication #1	The student correctly explains how the area of the campground, the area occupied by the tents, and the remaining area were determined. (1)	The student explains how the area of the campground, the area occupied by the tents and the remaining area were determined, but explanation is incomplete.	The student's explanation contains conceptual misunderstandings.

Computation with Rational Numbers
Set a World Record

SUGGESTED LEARNING STRATEGIES: Marking the Text, Summarize/Paraphrase/Retell, Create Representations, Use Manipulatives

My Notes

Have you ever heard of the *Guinness Book of World Records*? Every year people across the world work to set records for everything you can imagine. If something can be measured (time, weight, height, length, speed, and so on), then a record can be set. There are records for the longest time standing on the handlebars of a moving bicycle and for holding the largest food fight in the world. Each year new records are set and old records are broken.

How quickly can you roll a coin around your fingers? According to a recent *Guinness Book of World Records*, the record holder can pass a half-dollar coin around the fingers of his right hand in just 1.33 seconds.

CONNECT TO **SOCIAL STUDIES**

Since 2005, November 9 has been named International Guinness World Records Day. People who want to set records are encouraged to do this on November 9th each year.

1. Try rolling a coin around your fingers while a partner uses a stopwatch to see how long it takes you. Try this three times, and record your times in this chart.

Trials	Times
1	
2	
3	

2. Using your fastest time, write *but do not evaluate* numerical expressions that could be used to answer each question.

   a. By how much did your time differ from the record?

   b. If the speed never changed, how long did it take the record holder to pass the coin 45 times? How long would it take you to pass the coin 45 times?

   c. How many times faster was the record holder than you, or were you than the record holder?

   d. Find your average time by calculating the mean of the three trials.

My Notes

To evaluate the expressions you wrote, you must be able to compute with rational numbers.

3. Explain why each number you wrote in the expressions for Question 2 is rational.

MATH TERMS

An **algorithm** is a set of steps or a procedure used to carry out a computation or solve a problem.

4. Represent the processes for operations on decimals with models, numbers, and words. Shade the grids to model each operation. Then show how to evaluate each expression with an algorithm, and use words to explain the algorithm.

Operation	With model	With algorithm	Explanation of algorithm
a. $1.4 + 0.37$			
b. $1.36 - 0.9$			
c. $0.6 \cdot 0.7$			
d. $1.5 \div 0.3$			

My Notes

Apply your explanations of the algorithm for each operation to evaluate these expressions. Then write a generalization telling how to compute with each operation.

Addition	**5.** **a.** $1.38 + 0.93$ **c.** $5.03 + 13.7 + 108$	**b.** $108.21 + 84.5$ **d.** $17.089 + 122.6$
	e. Generalization for adding decimals:	
Subtraction	**6.** **a.** $5.09 - 4.23$ **c.** $159 - 88.99$	**b.** $74.8 - 57.06$ **d.** $3.084 - 1.7$
	e. Generalization for subtracting decimals:	
Multiplication	**7.** **a.** $8.5 \cdot 2.3$ **c.** $1.08 \cdot 2.014$	**b.** $0.03 \cdot 14$ **d.** $0.015 \cdot 3.9$
	e. Generalization for multiplying decimals:	
Division	**8.** **a.** $300.6 \div 18$ **c.** $0.504 \div 6.3$	**b.** $9.552 \div 3.98$ **d.** $1.8 \div 0.45$
	e. Generalization for dividing decimals:	

9. Explain the similarities and differences of computing with whole numbers and decimals. How does understanding whole number computation help in decimal computation?

My Notes

Now consider how to work with negative decimals.

10. Solve each problem in Parts a–d. Then answer Part e.

   a. $-38.7 + 15.09$ **b.** $3.3 - (-19.42)$

   c. $2.3 \cdot (-1.55)$ **d.** $-13.266 \div 2.2$

   e. Can you use the generalizations found in Questions 5–8 to compute with decimals that include negatives? Explain.

You can use estimation to check the reasonableness of your answers to Questions 5–8. By now you have learned many different methods for estimating, so how do you know which to use? Explore this question by comparing different methods.

11. Look at the table below to see four different methods students used for checking Question 5a.

1.38 + 0.93			
Student 1	Student 2	Student 3	Student 4
$1 + 0 = 1$	$1 + 1 = 2$	$1.38 + 1 = 2.38$	$1.4 + 0.9 = 2.3$

   a. Explain the estimation strategy shown for each method.

   b. Which method gives the most accurate estimate for this expression? Justify your choice.

SUGGESTED LEARNING STRATEGIES: Think/Pair/Share, Create Representations, Think Aloud

My Notes

The four students decide they will each use the same estimation strategy to solve the next problem as they used for Question 11. They want to see whose estimate will be the closest to the actual value this time.

12. This time they are estimating the sum of 2.49 and 1.55.

   a. Show how each student determined the estimate.

2.49 + 1.55			
Student 1	Student 2	Student 3	Student 4

   b. Give the actual value and tell which student has the closest estimate. Is this the same method you found in Question 11b? Explain.

13. To estimate the sum of 0.79 + 14.55, one student reasoned that the whole numbers add to 14, and both decimal parts are more than half, so add another 1 to get 15.

   a. Predict whether this method, front end estimation, or rounding will give a better estimate.

   b. Use front end estimation and rounding to estimate the sum of 0.79 + 14.55. Which method gives a better estimate?

14. Look back at your answers to Questions 11–13. Explain what you can conclude about choosing estimation strategies.

My Notes

15. Use any estimation strategies that you like to check the reasonableness of your answers for each part of Questions 5–8. Then choose one part in each question and explain your estimation method for that part. (You may not choose Part a for Question 5.)

16. Now that you have reviewed decimal computation, evaluate each expression you wrote for Question 2 to determine how close you are to setting a new Guinness World Record. Show your work.

a. By how much did your time differ from the record?

b. About how long did it take the record holder to pass the coin 45 times? How long would it take you to pass the coin 45 times?

c. How many times faster was the record holder than you, or were you than the record holder?

d. Find your average time by calculating the mean of the three trials.

SUGGESTED LEARNING STRATEGIES: Marking the Text, Create Representations, Use Manipulatives, Think/Pair/ Share, Quickwrite, Self Revision/Peer Revision

My Notes

How far can you throw a paper airplane? According to a recent Guinness Book of World Records, the record holder can throw a paper airplane a distance of $207\frac{1}{3}$ feet.

17. Try to break the record by throwing a paper airplane. Record your results in the chart in the My Notes space. Mark a starting line, throw a paper airplane, then measure the distance to the nearest $\frac{1}{12}$ of a foot. Repeat two more times.

18. Write, but do not evaluate, numerical expressions that could be used to answer each question. Use your greatest distance from Question 17 for Parts a–c.

   a. What was the difference between the record and your best distance?

   b. If another student threw a paper airplane $1\frac{1}{4}$ times farther than you did, what would that distance be?

   c. How many times farther than you was the record holder able to throw the paper airplane?

   d. Find your average distance by calculating the mean of the three trials.

In order to evaluate the expressions, you wrote for Question 18 you must be able to compute with rational numbers.

19. Explain why each of the numbers in your expressions in Question 18 is rational.

Trial	Distances (ft)
1	
2	
3	

My Notes

20. Represent the processes for operations on fractions with models, numbers, and words. Shade the models to show each operation. Then show how to evaluate the expression with an algorithm, and use words to explain the algorithm.

Operation	With model	With algorithm	Explanation of algorithm
a. $2\frac{1}{8} + 1\frac{3}{8}$			
b. $1\frac{1}{4} - \frac{3}{4}$			
c. $\frac{1}{4} \cdot \frac{2}{3}$			
d. $1\frac{3}{5} \div \frac{2}{5}$			

SUGGESTED LEARNING STRATEGIES: Discussion Group, Quickwrite

Apply your explanations of the algorithm for each operation to evaluate these expressions. Then write a generalization telling how to compute with each operation.

Addition	21. **a.** $\frac{5}{6} + \frac{1}{3}$	**b.** $35\frac{3}{4} + 18\frac{3}{4}$
	c. $11\frac{1}{5} + \frac{7}{8}$	**d.** $4\frac{1}{2} + 1\frac{2}{7} + 3\frac{1}{3}$
	e. Generalization for adding fractions and mixed numbers:	

Subtraction	22. **a.** $\frac{13}{17} - \frac{5}{17}$	**b.** $132\frac{1}{6} - 99\frac{5}{6}$
	c. $41\frac{9}{11} - 27\frac{1}{3}$	**d.** $12\frac{2}{9} - \frac{4}{5}$
	e. Generalization for subtracting fractions and mixed numbers:	

Multiplication	23. **a.** $\frac{1}{8} \cdot 5$	**b.** $\frac{1}{10} \cdot \frac{3}{11}$
	c. $9\frac{2}{7} \cdot 2\frac{2}{13}$	**d.** $\frac{7}{10} \cdot 3\frac{3}{7}$
	e. Generalization for multiplying fractions and mixed numbers:	

Division	24. **a.** $\frac{3}{8} \div 2$	**b.** $\frac{2}{3} \div \frac{4}{7}$
	c. $21 \div 3\frac{1}{2}$	**d.** $1\frac{5}{6} \div 5\frac{2}{5}$
	e. Generalization for dividing fractions and mixed numbers:	

My Notes

My Notes

25. Use any estimation strategies to check the reasonableness of your answers for each part of Questions 21–24. Then choose one part in each question and explain your estimation method for that part.

26. Compare and contrast the four operations with fractions and mixed numbers.

Now consider how to work with negative fractions.

27. Solve each problem in Parts a–d. Then answer Part e.

a. $9\frac{1}{4} + \left(-\frac{4}{5}\right)$ b. $-4\frac{3}{10} - 2\frac{1}{3}$

c. $-\frac{2}{3} \cdot \left(-4\frac{1}{4}\right)$ d. $-\frac{2}{7} \div \frac{3}{8}$

e. Can you use the generalizations found in Questions 21–24 to compute with fractions that include negatives? Explain.

SUGGESTED LEARNING STRATEGIES: Think/Pair/Share, Self Revision/Peer Revision

My Notes

28. Now that you have reviewed fraction computation, evaluate each expression you wrote for Question 18 to determine how close you are to setting a new Guinness World Record for throwing a paper airplane. Show your work.

   a. What is the difference between the record and your best distance?

   b. If another student threw a paper airplane $1\frac{1}{4}$ times farther than you did, what would that distance be?

   c. How many times farther than you was the record holder able to throw the paper airplane?

   d. Find your average distance by calculating the mean of the three trials.

TRY THESE

Evaluate these expressions. Simplify your answers.

   a. $\frac{2}{3} - \left(-\frac{5}{8}\right)$

   b. $-2\frac{4}{5} \cdot \frac{5}{8}$

   c. $-2\frac{4}{9} \div 1\frac{3}{5}$

   d. $\frac{5}{8} + \frac{9}{20}$

CHECK YOUR UNDERSTANDING

Write your answers on notebook paper. Show your work.

1. At one time, the world record for running 100 yd backwards was 13.5 seconds. If the record is now 12.7 seconds, how many seconds faster is it?

2. Evaluate each expression.

   a. $0.34 + 495.5 + 99.008$

   b. $87.6 - 53.909$

   c. $-5.06 \cdot 11.4$

   d. $23.6 \div 0.015$

3. Two students were given the following difference to estimate: $9.1 - 2.6$

Student 1	Student 2
$9 - 3 = 6$	$9 - 2 = 7$

   Explain the method used by each student. Determine who has the better estimate and explain why.

4. One of the tallest men in the world is $7\frac{9}{12}$ ft tall. How much taller is he than you?

5. Evaluate each expression.

   a. $63\frac{4}{7} + 22\frac{4}{5}$

   b. $109\frac{1}{9} - 56\frac{1}{3}$

   c. $\frac{4}{13} \cdot 5\frac{2}{3}$

   d. $2\frac{2}{3} \div \left(-\frac{11}{17}\right)$

6. Estimate this sum using two different methods. Explain each.

   $$15\frac{4}{9} + 5\frac{3}{5}$$

7. Write and evaluate an expression for this model.

   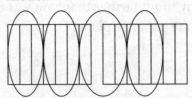

8. **MATHEMATICAL REFLECTION** Can you think of situations where it might be preferable to compute with decimals rather than fractions or to compute with fractions rather than decimals? Give examples of each situation and tell why you think that number form is preferable.

Percent Applications
We Mean Business

SUGGESTED LEARNING STRATEGIES: Marking the Text, Summarize/Paraphrase/Retell, Identify a Subtask, Vocabulary Organizer, Quickwrite

Eric and Marie are friends who have decided to start a summer business. In past summers they would often visit a nearby park where people play sports, have picnics, and swim. Every time Eric and Marie were there, they noticed that people became really thirsty but had nowhere to purchase drinks. So they have decided to sell cold bottled water at the park on weekends during the month of July. To do this, however, they have many decisions to make.

Eric and Marie decide that their goal is to sell at least one case of 24 bottles of water per day, for the four weekends in July.

1. If they buy two extra cases just in case they sell more than their goal, how many total cases of bottled water will they buy?

To get started, Eric and Marie need money to buy their supplies. Eric already has a large cooler, but they must purchase the cases of water as well as the ice to keep them cold. Marie's parents offer to loan them money for supplies, but say they must pay back the money with 2% interest at the end of the month.

They use information from a grocery store sales flyer to determine how much money they will need to borrow.

2. Explain what **discount** means, and how you can find the amount of a discount.

My Notes

> **CONNECT TO LANGUAGE ARTS**
>
> People who start their own businesses are called *entrepreneurs*.

Case of 24 Bottles Spring Water
Originally $7.99
Discount: 15% off

Ten Pound Bag of Ice
Originally $1.99
Now 20% off

3. Help Eric and Mary calculate their cost for water and ice.

a. Use the discounts to find the sale price of one case of water and one bag of ice. Show how you can estimate to check the reasonableness of your answers.

My Notes

> **MATH TERMS**
>
> A **sale price** is the reduced price of an item. **Sales tax** is a percentage of the cost of an item that is added by local or state governments.

b. What is the **sale price** for the total number of cases they plan to buy plus an equal number of bags of ice? Show your work.

c. Add a 4.9% **sales tax** to find the total cost.

4. At the end of July, they must repay Marie's parents the money they borrow plus an additional 2% in interest. How much money will they owe them?

Now Eric and Marie must decide how much they will charge for each bottle of water.

5. To determine this, first divide the amount they paid Marie's parents by the number of water bottles they have purchased. This will give their total cost per bottle.

6. If they sell each bottle for this amount of money, they will only break even. Since this is a business, their purpose is to make a **profit**. What does this mean?

7. Develop a formula that they can use for calculating profit.

8. To make a profit, they decide to **mark up** the cost of each bottle so that the selling price is $1.05.

a. How much of a **markup** is this from the price they found in Question 5? Explain what a markup is.

b. What percent of the original cost from Question 5 is this? In other words, what is the **percent of increase**?

My Notes

c. Explain your answer in Part b.

9. How are markup and percent of increase related?

10. How are finding markups and discounts similar and different?

11. Think about Eric and Marie's profit.

    a. How much money will they make as profit for each bottle using the sale price?

    b. What **percent of profit** is this? In other words, what percent of the sale price is this amount?

Just before Eric and Marie start selling the bottled water, they learn that the park put in a vending machine that sells bottled water for $1.00. So they decide to lower their price to $0.95.

12. By how much money are they **discounting** their original selling price of the bottled water?

13. What is the **percent of decrease** of their discount from the original sale price of $1.05?

14. What is the new percent of increase from their cost per bottle found in Question 5?

15. How are discount and percent of decrease related?

My Notes

Weekend	Day	Bottles Sold
1	Sat.	21
	Sun.	24
2	Sat.	1
	Sun.	37
3	Sat.	38
	Sun.	22
4	Sat.	61
	Sun.	29

SUGGESTED LEARNING STRATEGIES: Create Representations, Quickwrite

16. Eric and Marie made the table shown in the My Notes space for their water sales for the four weekends in July.

Did they meet their goal of selling one case of water each day? Explain.

17. One way to compare their sales for each day is to find the percent of their goal met each day.

a. On the first Saturday, they sold 21 out of the 24 bottles set as their goal. What percent is this? Write the answer in this table. Round to the nearest percent.

Weekend	Day	Bottles Sold	Percent of Goal Met
1	Sat.	21	
	Sun.	24	
2	Sat.	1	
	Sun.	37	
3	Sat.	38	
	Sun.	22	
4	Sat.	61	
	Sun.	29	

b. Complete the table in Part a by finding the percent of their goal met each of the other days. Round to the nearest percent.

18. Are the water sales on any of the days unusually high or low? What may have caused this?

My Notes

19. What does it mean for a percent to be over 100%?

20. Is it always possible for percents to be greater than 100%?
Give an example in your explanation.

21. What percent of the total water bottle sales occurred on each
Saturday and Sunday of the month? Complete this table.

Weekend	Day	Bottles Sold	Percent of Total Sales
1	Sat.	21	
	Sun.	24	
2	Sat.	1	
	Sun.	37	
3	Sat.	38	
	Sun.	22	
4	Sat.	61	
	Sun.	29	

22. What does it mean for a percent to be under 1%?

23. In the table to the right, for Weekends 2, 3, and 4, write
whether the total sales increased or decreased from the
previous weekend and find the percent of change.

Weekend	Increase or Decrease?	Percent Change
2		
3		
4		

My Notes

One of their friends helped Eric and Marie sell water in the park each weekend. Instead of paying a salary to their friend, they agreed to pay this friend a **commission** of $\frac{1}{4}$ of the total profit.

24. What do you think a commission is?

25. Calculate the total earnings for Eric and Marie from their business of selling bottled water.

26. Calculate the total profit.

27. How much money must they pay their friend for helping?

28. After paying their friend, what will be the remaining profit? How much profit will Eric and Marie each have?

Marie wants to open a savings account with the money she made selling bottled water and $47.32 she has from babysitting. She must decide which of four banks offers the best investment.

29. This table shows the differences in bank offerings.

Bank 1	Bank 2	Bank 3	Bank 4
Simple interest of 6%	6% compound interest: compounded annually	6% compound interest: compounded semi-annually	6% compound interest: compounded quarterly

a. How are the bank offerings similar and different?

b. Describe what you recall about **simple interest**.

SUGGESTED LEARNING STRATEGIES: Think/Pair/Share, Create Representations, Look for a Pattern, Vocabulary Organizer, Discussion Group, Quickwrite, Self Revision/Peer Revision

My Notes

30. Show what Marie's account balance would be after each year if she deposited her money in Bank 1 and never withdrew any.

Year	1	2	3
Interest Earned			
Account Balance			

31. Write a formula that can be used to find simple interest. Let $I =$ interest, $r =$ rate, $P =$ principal, and $t =$ time.

32. Suppose that at the end of the first year, the interest Marie earned is added to the principal, and the new amount is used to calculate the interest for the second year. How much money would she have after two years if she never makes any deposits or withdrawals?

33. When interest is calculated using this method, it is called **compound interest**. In your own words, write what you think compound interest means.

34. Show what Marie's account balance would be after each year if she deposited her money in Bank 2 without making any withdrawals.

Year	Interest Earned	Account Balance
1		
2		
3		

ACADEMIC VOCABULARY

The **principal** is the amount of money deposited into an account or the amount of money borrowed for a loan.

My Notes

35. What is the difference between simple and compound interest? Which type of interest is better for the customer, simple or compound? Explain.

36. If Marie plans to keep her money in the bank for only one year, and the bank will calculate interest only at the end of that year, which is the better choice, simple or compound interest? Explain.

37. Some interest is compounded semi-annually.

  a. What does semi-annually mean?

  b. Show what Marie's account balance would be after each year if she deposited her money in Bank 3 without making any deposits or withdrawals.

Year	Interest Earned	Account Balance
1		
2		
3		

CONNECT TO LANGUAGE ARTS

Semi is a prefix. Some other words with this prefix include:

- semicircle
- semifinal
- semicolon

My Notes

38. Some interest is compounded quarterly.

a. What does quarterly mean?

b. Show what Marie's account balance would be after each year if she deposited her money in Bank 4 without making any deposits or withdrawals.

Year	Interest Earned	Account Balance
1		
2		
3		

39. Compare the account balances after 3 years using Banks 2, 3, and 4. Write a generalization about compounding interest.

40. In which bank would you recommend that Marie deposit her money? Explain why.

CHECK YOUR UNDERSTANDING

Write your answers on notebook paper. Show your work.

1. It costs Tia $450 to purchase food to cater a picnic. She gets paid $725.

   a. How much money did she make as profit?

   b. What percent of profit is this?

2. Noah wants to buy a laptop that he sees for $799. By the time he goes to buy it, the price has increased to $1050.

   a. Find the percent of increase of the laptop.

   b. If the price increases by another 5%, what will be the additional markup and final sale price?

3. A video game originally priced at $65.50 is on sale at a 15% discount.

   a. What is the amount of the discount and the final sale price?

   b. Would it be a better or worse deal if the store had simply lowered the original price to $55.95? Use percent of decrease to explain.

4. Convert each number to the specified form.

   a. $\frac{107}{100}$ (percent)

   b. 345% (fraction)

   c. 225% (decimal)

   d. 1.42 (percent)

   e. 0.0047 (percent)

   f. 0.3% (decimal)

   g. 0.08% (fraction)

   h. $\frac{3}{1000}$ (percent)

5. A realtor sells a house for $460,000. If her commission is 3%, how much money does she make as commission?

6. Maria takes out a loan for $30,000 to buy a car. If her bank charges 5.4% simple interest, how much total interest will she pay in 3 years?

7. Gage must choose between two banks for investing his money that both offer compound interest. Bank 1 offers 3.9% interest compounded quarterly, and Bank 2 offers 4.3% interest compounded semi-annually.

   a. Show how much money Gage would have in his account after 2 years at each bank if he invests $1200.

Bank 1			Bank 2	
Year 1			Year 1	
Year 2			Year 2	

   b. Which bank should Gage use and why?

8. **MATHEMATICAL REFLECTION** Why is finding percent an important skill in the real world? Give two examples of how you would use percents in a real-world setting.

Scientific Notation
A Traveler's Tale

SUGGESTED LEARNING STRATEGIES: Summarize/Paraphrase/
Retell, Visualize, Vocabulary Organizer, Create Representations

My Notes

Jonathan Swift wrote the classic tale *Gulliver's Travels*. The story describes the adventures of Lemuel Gulliver, a ship's doctor who becomes stranded in many strange places. In one of those places, Lilliput, Gulliver finds that he is a giant compared to the people and the world around him. During another voyage, Gulliver is abandoned in another land, Brobdingnag, where he is as small to the inhabitants as the Lilliputians were to him.

The story never says how tall Gulliver is, but it does tell how the heights of the Lilliputian people and the heights of the people from Brobdingnag compare to Gulliver's height. The many descriptions of size in this tale provide ways to explore the magnitude of numbers. For this activity, assume that Gulliver is 6 feet tall.

1. What do you think the word *magnitude* means?

2. Since Gulliver is so much bigger than the Lilliputians, he consumes more food than 10^3 Lilliputians do. How many Lilliputians does this number represent?

3. If a person from Brobdingnag is 10 times taller than Gulliver, how tall is this person?

4. Write an expression using Gulliver's height and a power of 10 to represent the height of a person in Question 3.

5. If a person is 10 times taller than a person from Brobdingnag, how many times taller than Gulliver is this person?

6. Write an expression using Gulliver's height and a power of 10 to represent the height of the person in Question 5.

In Questions 4 and 6, each expression is the product of a factor and a power of 10 with an exponent that is a positive integer.

My Notes

7. Find the value of each expression. Each expression is the product of a factor and a power of 10 with an exponent that is a positive integer.

   a. 6×10^4

   b. 15×10^3

   c. 2×10^6

   d. 3.2×10^5

   e. 43.2×10^3

8. Describe any patterns you notice in evaluating expressions like those in Question 7.

9. After his boat capsizes in a violent storm, Gulliver swims ashore to Lilliput and falls asleep. When he wakes, Gulliver finds he has been tied to the ground and can only look up into the bright sun. The sun has a diameter of 1.39×10^9 m and a mass of 2.0×10^{30} kg. Use the patterns you described in Question 8 to rewrite the diameter and mass of the sun.

CONNECT TO LANGUAGE ARTS

A boat that *capsizes* has turned over or tipped over.

The measurements, 1.39×10^9 m and 2.0×10^{30} kg, are written in **scientific notation**, and the answers to Question 9 are written in **standard form**. A number is written in scientific notation when it is expressed in the form $a \times 10^n$, where $1 \le a < 10$ and n is an integer.

READING MATH

The expression $a \cdot 10^n$ is read "a times 10 raised to the nth power."

10. Explain why someone would want to write these numbers in scientific notation instead of standard form.

ACADEMIC VOCABULARY

scientific notation

My Notes

11. Tell whether each expression is written in scientific notation. If it is not written in scientific notation, explain why not and rewrite in scientific notation if possible.

   a. 6×10^4

   b. 15×10^3

   c. 2×10^6

   d. 3.2×10^5

   e. 43.2×10^3

   f. $5.9 \times 10^{0.5}$

12. Convert each number from standard form to scientific notation. Then work backward from your answer to check your work.

   a. 25,000,000,000   **b.** 6000

   c. 43,600,000   **d.** 16,000

13. Large numbers can also be named with words. For example, 9,000,000,000 in scientific notation is 9×10^9 and has the name 9 billion. This table shows names for some very large numbers.

Standard Form	Power of 10	Name
1,000	10^3	Thousand
1,000,000	10^6	Million
1,000,000,000	10^9	Billion
1,000,000,000,000	10^{12}	Trillion
1,000,000,000,000,000	10^{15}	Quadrillion
1,000,000,000,000,000,000	10^{18}	Quintillion
1,000,000,000,000,000,000,000	10^{21}	Sextillion
1,000,000,000,000,000,000,000,000	10^{24}	Septillion
1,000,000,000,000,000,000,000,000,000	10^{27}	Octillion
1,000,000,000,000,000,000,000,000,000,000	10^{30}	Nonillion
1,000,000,000,000,000,000,000,000,000,000,000	10^{33}	Decillion
There is not enough space to write this number.	10^{100}	Googol

SUGGESTED LEARNING STRATEGIES: Think Aloud, Create Representations, Look for a Pattern, Work Backward, Identify a Subtask, Quickwrite

Use what you have learned to complete this table.

Standard Form	Power of 10	Name
7,400,000,000,000,000	7.4×10^{15}	7.4 quadrillion
	3×10^3	
1,200,000,000		
		5 trillion
9,000,000		

14. The kingdom of Lilliput is said to have an area of 24 million square miles. Write this amount using scientific notation.

15. Convert each number from scientific notation to standard form. Check your work.

   a. 5.2×10^4 **b.** 4.23×10^6

   c. 2×10^3 **d.** 1.03×10^4

16. The fictional land of Brobdingnag had an area of 1.8×10^7 square miles. In its army were 32,000 cavalry and 2.07×10^5 soldiers. Order these numbers from greatest to least.

17. Explore the products of powers of 10.

   a. Write each product in expanded form. Then express the product as a power of 10. The first one has been done.

   $10^2 \cdot 10^4 = (10 \cdot 10) \cdot (10 \cdot 10 \cdot 10 \cdot 10) = 10^6$

   $10^3 \cdot 10^2 =$

   $10^5 \cdot 10^3 =$

   $10^4 \cdot 10 =$

   b. Describe a pattern that relates the exponents of the factors and the products for each entry in the list in Part a.

My Notes

c. Based on the pattern you described in Part b, write the missing exponent in this equation to show a rule for finding a product with exponents.

$$10^m \times 10^n = 10^{\underline{\quad}}$$

18. Suppose that a person from Brobdingnag consumes an average of 18,000 calories a day and that the land of Brobdingnag has a civilian population of 30,000.

   a. Express the number of calories consumed by one person in one day in scientific notation.

   b. Express the civilian population of Brobdingnag in scientific notation.

   c. Find the total number of calories consumed in one day in the land of Brobdingnag. Express the total number of calories in standard form and in scientific notation.

   d. Explain how to use the expressions from Parts a and b to find the answer for Part c.

19. Simplify each expression. Write the answer in scientific notation.

   a. $(9 \times 10^5)(3 \times 10^4)$

   b. $(1.6 \cdot 10^8)(3 \cdot 10^4)$

   c. $(4 \cdot 10^8)(6 \cdot 10^5)$

My Notes

20. Now you can compare the products of each expression from Question 19 with those found using a calculator.

    a. Write each output as shown on your calculator.

        a. $(9 \times 10^5)(3 \times 10^4)$

        b. $(1.6 \times 10^8)(3 \times 10^4)$

        c. $(4 \times 10^8)(6 \times 10^5)$

    b. Explain what the outputs on your calculator mean.

21. Find each product. Express the answers in decimal form.

    a. $2 \cdot \dfrac{1}{10}$ **b.** $15 \cdot \dfrac{1}{1000}$

    c. $6 \cdot \dfrac{1}{10,000}$ **d.** $3.2 \cdot \dfrac{1}{100}$

    e. $43.2 \cdot \dfrac{1}{1000}$

22. Describe any patterns you notice in evaluating expressions like those in Question 21.

23. Explore the quotients of powers of 10.

    a. Write each quotient in this list in expanded form, simplify, and then express the quotient as a single power of 10. The first entry of the list has been completed for you.

$$\frac{10^5}{10^2} = \frac{10 \cdot 10 \cdot 10 \cdot 10 \cdot 10}{10 \cdot 10} = 10 \cdot 10 \cdot 10 = 10^3$$

$$\frac{10^8}{10^6} =$$

$$\frac{10^7}{10^2} =$$

$$\frac{10^5}{10} =$$

My Notes

b. Describe a pattern relating the exponents in each row of the list on page 68.

c. Based on the pattern you described in Part b, write the missing exponent in this equation to show a rule for quotients with exponents.

$$\frac{10^m}{10^n} = 10$$

d. Complete this list as you did in Part a, but use the rule from Part c to express each quotient as a power of 10. The first entry in the list has been completed for you.

$$\frac{10^4}{10^6} = \frac{10 \cdot 10 \cdot 10 \cdot 10}{10 \cdot 10 \cdot 10 \cdot 10 \cdot 10 \cdot 10} = \frac{10}{10 \cdot 10 \cdot 10} = \frac{10^1}{10^3} = 10^{-2}$$

$$\frac{10^2}{10^5} =$$

$$\frac{10^3}{10^7} =$$

e. Based on your work in Part d, what fractional value do you think mathematicians give to 10^{-1}, 10^{-4}, and 10^{-n}?

f. Complete this list as you did in Part d. Remember to use the rule from Part c to express the quotient as a power of 10.

$$\frac{10^5}{10^5} =$$

$$\frac{10^3}{10^3} =$$

g. Based on your work in Part f, what meaning do you think mathematicians give to 10^0?

24. If the Lilliputians are 10 times shorter than Gulliver, how tall is a Lilliputian?

My Notes

25. In terms of Gulliver's height, express the height of a Lilliputian, using scientific notation.

26. In terms of Gulliver's height, use scientific notation to express the height of an insect if the insect is 10 times shorter than a person from Lilliput.

27. Convert each number from standard form to scientific notation. Check your work.

   a. 0.125

   b. 0.00006

   c. 7

   d. 0.000000000025

28. Explain why someone would want to write these numbers in scientific notation instead of standard form.

29. Convert each number from scientific notation to standard form. Check your work.

   a. 5.2×10^{-4}

   b. 4.23×10^{-6}

   c. 2.5×10^{0}

30. Order these numbers from least to greatest.

   $0.0051, 8 \times 10^{-4}, 1.89 \times 10^{-3}, 0.00079$

31. Suppose that all of the 500,000 Lilliputians consume a total of 15,000 gallons of water in one day.

   a. Express the total number of gallons of water consumed by all of the Lilliputians in one day in scientific notation.

My Notes

b. Express the population of Lilliput in scientific notation.

c. Find the average number of gallons of water consumed by one Lilliputian in one day. Express answer in both standard form and scientific notation.

d. Show how to use the expressions from Parts a and b to find the answer for Part c.

32. Simplify each expression. Write answers in scientific notation.

a. $\dfrac{6 \times 10^5}{3 \times 10^4}$

b. $(2 \times 10^{-5})(3 \times 10^4)$

c. $(4.2 \times 10^8)(3 \times 10^{-5})$

d. $\dfrac{3.2 \times 10^5}{4 \times 10^8}$

33. Think about the value of each expression.

4.3×10^3	3.8×10^{-5}	2.4×10^{12}	3.0×10^0
2.2×10^{-2}	7.8×10^{-4}	7.1×10^0	9.8×10^5
6.4×10^{-3}	3.8×10^{-14}	6.4×10^8	4.8×10^0

a. Place each expression in the appropriate column.

Between 0 and 1	From 1 to 10	10 and greater

My Notes

SUGGESTED LEARNING STRATEGIES: Quickwrite

b. Explain what you notice about the exponents in the scientific notation form of the numbers you sorted.

Numbers between 0 and 1:

Numbers from 1 to 10:

Numbers 10 and greater:

34. On a separate sheet of paper, explain how this activity about *Gulliver's Travels* involves magnitude of numbers and scientific notation.

CHECK YOUR UNDERSTANDING

Write your answers on notebook paper. Show your work.

1. Is 10.2×10^4 written in scientific notation? Explain.

2. Copy and complete.

Standard Form	Scientific Notation	Name
2,300,000,000		
	3.4×10^3	
		9 million

3. The following table shows the attendance for a year at four major league baseball stadiums.

Yankees	Mariners	Red Sox	Dodgers
3.8×10^6	2,000,000	2.5 million	3.2×10^6

Order the attendances from greatest to least.

4. Simplify each expression. Write the answers in scientific notation.

  a. $(2.2 \times 10^5)(4 \times 10^7)$

  b. $35,000 \cdot 9,000,000,000$

  c. $(8.1 \times 10^{12})(5.3 \times 10)$

5. Copy and complete.

Standard Form	Scientific Notation
0.00009	
	1.7×10^{-3}
	6.99×10^{-7}
0.00086	

6. Wire 1 has a diameter of 9×10^{-2} inches. Wire 2's diameter is 2.4×10^{-3} inches, and Wire 3 is 0.0023 inches in diameter. Order the wire diameters from smallest to largest.

7. Simplify each expression. Write the answers in scientific notation.

  a. $(6.5 \times 10^{-13})(2 \times 10^{-4})$

  b. $\dfrac{2.7 \times 10^4}{1.2 \times 10^9}$ **c.** $\dfrac{4.2 \times 10^{10}}{2.1 \times 10^3}$

8. MATHEMATICAL REFLECTION You used scientific notation to discuss size in Jonathan Swift's *Gulliver's Travels*. Describe how scientific notation aids the discussion of very small or very large numbers. Provide an example.

Computation with Rational Numbers
MUFFIN MADNESS

Write your answers on notebook paper. Show your work.

Muffin Madness is a bakery that sells all types of muffins, but only the tops. Everyone knows the top of the muffin is the best part. The bakery is best known for blueberry muffins. Tina is the owner of *Muffin Madness* and is also the best baker. Here is her secret recipe for the blueberry muffins.

Tina's Blueberry Muffins
Makes 12 muffins

$1\frac{1}{3}$ cups flour	1 Tbsp. baking powder
$\frac{1}{3}$ cup butter, melted	$\frac{3}{4}$ tsp. salt
1 cup milk	$1\frac{1}{2}$ tsp. grated orange peel
$\frac{1}{2}$ cup sugar	1 egg
	1 cup blueberries

Tina uses math to adjust recipes based on customer feedback, for special orders, and to help customers with their own baking problems. Look at the customer feedback and Tina's response to each.

Customer: "These muffins need a little more salt and they seem a little too thick and heavy."

Tina suggests adding $\frac{1}{2}$ tsp salt and reducing the flour by $\frac{3}{8}$ c.

1. How much salt will the recipe have? Show how you found the amount of salt Tina will now use.

2. How much flour will Tina now use in the recipe? Explain how you found this amount.

Customer: "I really need only about $\frac{3}{4}$ of a batch."

3. Tina plans to make $\frac{3}{4}$ of a batch for this customer.

   a. How much orange peel will she use?

   b. How much butter will she use?

   c. How many muffins will be in the batch?

4. **Customer:** "I lost my $\frac{1}{2}$-cup measuring cup. How can I measure out $1\frac{1}{2}$ cups of water for my recipe?"

Tina: suggests using $\frac{1}{4}$-cup measuring cup. How many times will the customer fill the measuring cup? Give an illustration to show how you arrived at your answer.

As the owner of the bakery, Tina also manages the finances.

Complete each statement. Show your work.

5. Twenty-pound bags of flour are on sale at two different suppliers:

   Supplier 1: $3.79, 15% off
   Supplier 2: $3.66 discounted to $3.20.

   From which supplier should Tina buy flour?

6. Tina's goal this month was to earn a total of $10,000. Her total earnings were $13,500. What percentage of her goal did she meet?

7. This month the bakery spent $9450 and earned a total of $13,500.

   a. What was the amount of profit for the bakery?

   b. What was the percentage of profit?

8. Last year Tina charged $0.79 per muffin, but this year she has decided to charge $0.99. What is the percent of increase in Tina's prices?

9. Next year Tina wants to mark up the price by 18% of this year's price. How much will Tina charge for muffins next year?

10. Tina keeps track of customer feedback using comment cards, and only 3 out of 346 comment cards were negative. What percentage of the feedback was negative?

Computation with Rational Numbers

MUFFIN MADNESS

Tina's town has two banks. First Town Bank offers compound interest at a rate of 5.1%, and it is compounded semi-annually. Second Town Bank offers compound interest at a rate of 5.3%, and it is compounded annually.

11. Use this month's earnings of $13,500 to decide which bank pays the best interest. Copy and complete the tables to show the earnings in interest from both banks.

First Town Bank		
Year	Interest Earned	Account Balance
1		
2		

Second Town Bank		
Year	Interest Earned	Account Balance
1		
2		

Which bank is paying the best interest?

12. Total sales over the last ten years were $1,610,000. The bakery had about 460,000 customers.

a. Write each number in scientific notation.

$1,610,000 =
460,000 =

b. Then write and evaluate an expression to find the average amount spent by each customer.

Computation with Rational Numbers

MUFFIN MADNESS

	Exemplary	Proficient	Emerging
Math Knowledge #1, 2, 6, 7, 8, 9, 10, 11	The student correctly: • Uses fraction operations to find the salt, the flour, orange peel, and butter amounts. (1, 2) • Determines percentages for the goal (6) and the negative feedback. (10) • Determines the percent profit (7) and percent increase in price. (8) • Determines the amount to charge for muffins next year. (9) • Completes the tables for both banks. (11)	The student attempts all twelve questions but is only able to give nine complete and correct answers.	The student gives only three complete and correct answers.
Problem Solving #3abc, #4, #12b	The student correctly: • Uses fraction operations to find the orange peel and butter amounts. (3a, 3b) • Finds how many muffins are in the batch. (3c) • Determines how to measure the water without the $\frac{1}{2}$-cup measure. (4) • Evaluates an expression written in scientific method. (12b)	The student gives complete and correct answers to only four of the five items.	The student gives only two complete and correct items out of five.
Representation # 5, 12a, 12b	The student correctly: • Determines from which flour supplier to buy. (5) • Represents numbers in scientific notation. (12a) • Writes expressions using numbers written in scientific notation. (12b)	The student gives only two complete and correct answers.	The student gives only one complete and correct answer.
Communication #3d, 4, 5	The student correctly: • Compares and contrasts methods used for multiplying fractions, mixed numbers and whole numbers. (3d) • Explains how to represent mixed numbers using smaller fractional parts. (4) • Explains with supporting work the choice of flour supplier. (5)	The student provides only two complete and correct responses.	The student provides only one complete and correct response.

ACTIVITY 1.1

Identify the set of numbers represented by the following symbols.

1. N
2. W
3. Q
4. Z

For each number, identify each set to which it belongs. Use the symbols N, W, Z, Q, and R to represent the sets of numbers.

5. -7
6. $\frac{4}{9}$
7. $\sqrt{15}$
8. 0
9. 0.45

Tell which property is illustrated by this problem.

10. $(2 + 3) + 3 = 2 + (3 + 3)$

11. Identify the most specific subset of real numbers to which all numbers in each given set belongs.

   a. $\{2, 0, 10\}$
   b. $\{-3, 7, 0.5\}$
   c. $\{0.2, \sqrt{3}, 5, -2\}$

ACTIVITY 1.2

12. Eyeglass prescriptions are written with $+$ values indicating farsightedness and $-$ values indicating nearsightedness. List the eyeglass prescriptions in order from least to greatest:

   Marley: $+2$ Brady: -1 Holly: 0

   Courtney: -3 Mariah: $+3$

13. Write the opposite of 4.

14. Evaluate $|-45|$.

15. Write two inequalities showing the relationship between the integers 23, and -23.

16. Graph the inequality $r \geq -8$ on a number line.

17. Can the sum of a negative integer and a positive integer be positive? Explain using a model.

18. Evaluate each expression. Use a number line if necessary.

   a. $-5 + -4$
   b. $-3 + 6$
   c. $2 + -4$
   d. $10 + 0$

19. Evaluate each expression. Use a number line if necessary.

   a. $-1 - (-9)$
   b. $-7 - 3$
   c. $4 - (-4)$
   d. $10 - 3$
   e. $9 + (-5) - 2$

ACTIVITY 1.3

20. Evaluate: $\dfrac{4 \times (-2) \times (-5)}{-4 \times 5}$

21. Find the mean of the following temperatures:
    $-5°$ F, $-10°$ F, $-20°$ F, and $-9°$ F.

22. The average low temperature in May at Telescope Peak is -6 F°. If the record low temperature recorded on Telescope Peak in Death Valley is three times the average low temperature for May what is the record low?

23. Dolphins dive at 3 feet per second. How far can a dolphin dive in one minute?

24. Evaluate each expression.
    a. $-8 \times 8 =$
    b. $-9 \times (-5) =$
    c. $4 \times (-3) =$
    d. $24 \div (-3) =$
    e. $-36 \div 12 =$

ACTIVITY 1.4

25. The area of a square is 288 m². A second square is half its area. What is the side length of the second square?

26. Dan bought 180 square feet of carpet to carpet a square room. When he finished, he had 11 square feet leftover. What is the area of the room he carpeted? What is the side length of the room?

27. What are two whole numbers that you can substitute for n to make this statement true?
    $$6 < \sqrt{n} < 7$$

28. Diane is putting the same carpet in her bedroom and walk-in closet. She says that the cost of carpeting the square floor of the closet will be $\frac{1}{3}$ the cost of carpeting the square floor of her bedroom. Do you agree or disagree? Use the diagram to help explain your answer.

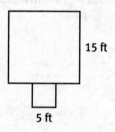

15 ft

5 ft

29. Evaluate this expression: $(3 \text{ m})^2$

30. If the side of a cube is 10 ft., what is the volume of the cube?

31. If the volume of a cube is 729 cm³, what is the length of one side?

32. Evaluate this expression: $\left(\dfrac{1}{8}\right)^2$

33. Evaluate this expression: 9^0

ACTIVITY 1.5

34. Domestic cats typically weigh between 5.5 and 16 pounds. The largest car ever weighed about 46.952 pounds! How many times heavier is this than the average weight of the typical cat? Round your answer to the nearest hundredth.

35. Draw a grid like the one below. Then use it to represent 0.7 • 0.9. Finally check your work with an algorithm.

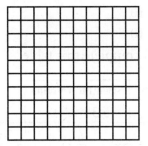

36. Compute.
   a. 105.95 + 6.6 + (−42.088)
   b. 55.09 − 37.175
   c. 3.7 × 12.502
   d. 9.47 ÷ 2.6 (Round to the nearest hundredth.)

37. How can you use estimation to determine whether the problem has the correct answer? 2.34 • 6.9 = 161.46. If there is an error, what is it?

38. The tallest dog in the world is a Great Dane named Gibson. The dog is about $3\frac{1}{2}$ ft tall. The average size of a Great Dane is about $2\frac{2}{3}$ ft tall. How much taller than the average is Gibson? Show your work.

39. Evaluate each expression.
   a. $5\frac{2}{9} + 2\frac{1}{5} + \frac{2}{3}$
   b. $18\frac{4}{11} - 17\frac{11}{12}$
   c. $3\frac{5}{6} \times (-4\frac{1}{3})$
   d. $7\frac{1}{4} \div 1\frac{7}{8}$

40. You decide to make cookies for a picnic, but must make $2\frac{1}{2}$ times the recipe in order to have enough for everyone. The recipe calls for $\frac{3}{4}$ c sugar. Is it reasonable to use front-end estimation in this situation to estimate the amount of sugar needed? Explain why or why not.

41. A person who held the record for having the longest hands had hands that measure about $12\frac{11}{16}$ in. long. Measure your hand to the nearest $\frac{1}{16}$ of an inch. Measure from the wrist to the end of the middle finger. Then, answer the questions below and show your work.

   a. What is the difference in length between your hand and that world record holder's hand?
   b. If your hand were $2\frac{1}{2}$ times longer, would you beat that world record? Explain.
   c. How many times longer is that world record holder's hand than yours?
   d. If you and a friend added your hand lengths together, would you beat that world record? If so, by how much? If not, how many more inches would be needed?

ACTIVITY 1.6

42. Cutting grass for neighbors, Casey made a total of $160. If her profit was 60%, how much money did Casey spend in costs such as gas, yard bags, and so on.

43. After a 30% discount, Kay's sneakers cost $36.

  a. What was the original price?

  b. If she had waited another week, the store would have sold them for $28. What percent of decrease would this be from the sale price of $36?

44. There was a 9% markup over last year's price on jet skiing. It now costs $125 per hour.

  a. What was last year's price?

  b. If next year the price goes up again to $140, what would be the percent of increase from $125?

45. The population of a school is 400 students. Next year it is expected to be about 120% of what it is now. What will be next year's student population?

46. A survey at Lake Middle School shows that only 0.8% of the student population walks to school each day. If 1200 students attend the school, about how many walk?

47. Kirk makes $4.25 an hour working at a clothing store, and earns an additional 7% commission on his daily sales total.

  a. If he sells a total of $375 in clothing, how much money will he make in commission?

  b. If he works 8 hours that day, what is his total earnings per hour?

48. Mia takes out a loan for $2000. She must pay simple interest at 6.1%. How much money will she owe in interest after 4 years?

49. You put $700 in a bank earning 7.5% compound interest, and the interest is compounded annually. How much money will you have in your account after 3 years?

ACTIVITY 1.7

50. Tell which of the following numbers has been correctly written using scientific notation?

  a. 0.9×10^6

  b. 11×10^{-5}

  c. $2.5 \times 10^{0.9}$

  d. 3.4×10^{-7}

51. Copy and complete this table.

Standard Form	Scientific Notation	Name
	5.35×10^5	
		76 thousand
	4.1×10^7	
1,800,000,000		
		8 million
3,400		

52. Which amount is the greatest? Explain your thinking.

  a. 9×10^5

  b. 8×10^6

  c. 6×10^5

  d. 6×10^6

53. The population of a city started at 3×10^3 and grew 2.1×10^4 times larger. What is the population of the city now?

54. Only 27 out of 35,000 species of spiders have been known to have caused human fatalities. When this ratio is written as a decimal by dividing 35,000 by 27, the calculator shows: 7.714285714E-4. Explain what this means.

55. Copy and complete this table.

Standard Form	Scientific Notation
	8×10^{-4}
0.0029	
6	
	4.6×10^{-9}

56. Ty's computer downloads a picture at a speed of 0.009 seconds. Emma's computer can do it in 1×10^{-2} seconds, and Scott's computer takes 89 thousandths of a second. Whose computer is the fastest? Justify your answer.

57. The mass of Pluto is 13,000,000,000,000,000,000,000 kg and the mass of Earth is 5,973,700,000,000,000,000,000,000 kg.

   a. Write each mass using scientific notation.

   b. Write and solve an expression showing how many times larger the mass of Earth is than the mass of Pluto. Round your answer to the nearest tenth.

Reflection

An important aspect of growing as a learner is to take the time to reflect on your learning. It is important to think about where you started, what you have accomplished, what helped you learn, and how you will apply your new knowledge in the future. Use notebook paper to record your thinking on the following topics and to identify evidence of your learning.

Essential Questions

1. Review the mathematical concepts and your work in this unit before you write thoughtful responses to the questions below. Support your responses with specific examples from concepts and activities in the unit.

   ● Why is it important to understand properties and operations involving integers and negative rational numbers?

   ● How can number lines and diagrams be used to interpret solutions of real-world problems?

Academic Vocabulary

2. Look at the following academic vocabulary words:

   ● exponential form   ● set of real numbers

   ● principal   ● set notation

   ● scientific notation

Choose three words and explain your understanding of each word and why each is important in your study of math.

Self-Evaluation

3. Look through the activities and Embedded Assessments in this unit. Use a table similar to the one below to list three major concepts in this unit and to rate your understanding of each.

Unit Concepts	Is Your Understanding Strong (S) or Weak (W)?
Concept 1	
Concept 2	
Concept 3	

   a. What will you do to address each weakness?

   b. What strategies or class activities were particularly helpful in learning the concepts you identified as strengths? Give examples to explain.

4. How do the concepts you learned in this unit relate to other math concepts and to the use of mathematics in the real world?

1. What is the value of the expression $8 + (-7) - 5$?

   A. 20   **C.** -4

   B. 4   **D.** -6

   1. Ⓐ Ⓑ Ⓒ Ⓓ

2. Jerry went scuba diving in North Carolina where he dove a depth of -35 feet. Last week he went diving in caves off the coast of Florida at 3 times the depth of his dive in North Carolina. What was the depth of his cave dive?

   2.

3. A youth group clears trash from an area of 7 square miles in a state park. The area that the group clears is a square. About how long is each side of the area?

   Read
   Solve
   Explain

   Part A: Use the number line to find the approximate length of the side of the square.

   Part B: Give the answer to the nearest tenth of mile. Explain how to check whether your answer is correct.

   Answer and Explain

   _____

   _____

   _____

   _____

   _____

   _____

   _____

   _____

   _____

Read
Solve
Explain

4. This chart shows the statistics for a team quarterback during a recent season as reported by the National Football League.

Team	NATIONAL FOOTBALL LEAGUE			
	Passing Statistics			
	Attempted	**Completed**	**Decimal**	**Fraction**
Tampa Bay Buccaneers	343	227		
Arizona Cardinals	394	232		
Miami Dolphins	446	299		
Indianapolis Colts	548	364		

Part A: Complete the chart by finding the decimal equivalent (to at least four places) of the ratio of the number of passes completed to the number of passes attempted. Then express that ratio as a percent (to the **nearest whole percent**).

Part B: Tell whether the decimals you listed in Part A are terminating or non-terminating. Then describe the difference between terminating and non-terminating decimals.

Answer and Explain

_____

_____

_____

_____

_____

_____

Part C: Which form of the ratio gives more information about the passing success of each quarterback? Explain your answer with an example.

Answer and Explain

_____

_____

_____

_____

_____

_____

Equations, Inequalities, and Linear Relationships

Unit Overview

In this unit you will create and solve linear equations and inequalities using tables and graphs, verbal representations, and algebraic approaches. You will develop and apply the connections between rate of change and linear relationships. You will explore some of the various ways that equations describe change.

Academic Vocabulary

As you work through this unit, add these words to your vocabulary notebook.

- direct variation
- function
- inequality
- like terms
- open sentence

Essential Questions

? Why is it important to understand how to solve linear equations and inequalities?

? How can graphs be used to interpret solutions of real world problems?

EMBEDDED ASSESSMENTS

This unit has three Embedded Assessments, the first following Activity 2.2, the second after Activity 2.4, and the third after Activity 2.6. These embedded assessments allow you to demonstrate your understanding of linear relations and linear equations, your ability to solve linear equations and inequalities, and ways to use and recognize direct variation.

Write your answers on notebook paper.
Show your work.

1. A car travels 50 miles per hour.
   a. Complete the table below to show the total distance traveled for each time given.

Number of hours that have passed	Total distance traveled
1	
2	
3	

   b. Plot the data from the table.
   c. If the car has traveled n hours, write an expression for the total distance traveled.
   d. How far has the car traveled after 10 hours? Explain how you determined your answer.

2. Solve each equation below.
   a. $3x = 12$
   b. $x + 5 = -4$
   c. $2x - 5 = 7$

3. Convert each of the following.
   a. 2 cm = _____ m
   b. 3 inches = _____ cm

4. Graph each inequality on a number line.
   a. $x < 3$
   b. $x \geq -1$

5. Two measures of two angles in a triangle are 68° and 70°. What is the measure of the third angle?

Linear Equations
The Adventures of Grace and Bernoulli

SUGGESTED LEARNING STRATEGIES: Marking the Text, Create Representations, Look for a Pattern

Bernoulli Bug and Grace Grasshopper are best friends. Bernoulli lives near the creek and Grace lives 92 feet away in the garden. They often visit each other. One afternoon, Grace left Bernoulli's place and started toward her home.

Shortly after Grace leaves, Bernoulli sees that Grace forgot to take her knapsack. He decides to try to catch up with Grace so he can give it to her. Bernoulli crawls at 5 feet per minute and Grace hops at only 3 feet per minute, but Grace has a four-minute head start.

1. Use the diagram below to show where each critter is as Bernoulli starts after Grace. Place the letter *B* at Bernoulli's location and the letter *G* at Grace's location.

2. Use the diagram below to show where each critter is two minutes after Bernoulli starts after Grace. Place the letter *B* at Bernoulli's location and the letter *G* at Grace's location.

3. Complete this table to show how far Bernoulli and Grace are from the creek for each time value.

Time (minutes) Since Bernoulli Left the Creek	0	1	2	3	4	5
Bernoulli's Distance (feet) from the Creek						
Grace's Distance (feet) from the Creek						

4. Use words to describe a pattern you see in the distance values of Grace's row of the table.

My Notes

Let t represent the number of minutes from the time that Bernoulli started after Grace.

5. Write an expression in terms of t for Bernoulli's distance from the creek.

6. Write an expression in terms of t for Grace's distance from the creek.

7. What does the **coefficient** of t in your answer to Question 6 mean? Include appropriate units in your explanation.

8. What meaning does the **constant** term in your answer to Question 6 have in this problem? Include appropriate units in your explanation.

9. Write an equation that can be used to find the value of t at which Bernoulli catches up with Grace. Explain why the equation works and tell what each side of the equation means.

10. If Bernoulli left his place near the creek at 1:00 P.M., at what time would he catch up with Grace?

11. How long will it take Grace to reach her home from the spot where Bernoulli catches up with her? Explain your answer.

> **MATH TERMS**
>
> A **coefficient** is the number by which a variable is multiplied.
>
> - The coefficient of $2a$ is the number 2.
>
> A **constant** term does not change.
>
> - The constant term in $3b + 6$ is 6.

SUGGESTED LEARNING STRATEGIES: Think/Pair/Share, Marking the Text, Debriefing

12. Write a description of a situation involving Bernoulli and Grace that could be described by each equation:

   a. $3t + 12 = 2(5t)$

   b. $92 - 5t = 42$

Bernoulli and Grace have a turtle friend, Hypatia, who sometimes plays in the field with them. Hypatia arrived at Bernoulli's place shortly after he left to catch up with Grace. She tried to overtake them to tell them that tomorrow there would be a Critter Race between a tortoise and hare!

   The equation $H = 6.4t - 7.2$ describes Hypatia's attempt to catch up with Bernoulli and Grace. In this equation, H represents Hypatia's distance from the creek and t represents the number of minutes from the time Bernoulli left the creek.

13. Tell in words what this equation tells you about Hypatia's attempt to catch up with them.

> **CONNECT TO AP**
>
> In Algebra and AP courses you will work with equations in a variety of ways: graphical, numerical, analytical, and verbal.

14. The graph to the right shows the distance each critter is from the creek during the first four and one-half minutes after Bernoulli left the creek to catch up with Grace. Label each line to show which critter's travel is represented by that line. Explain clearly why you made each association.

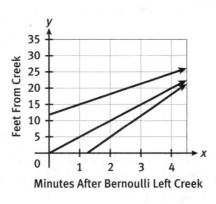

My Notes

This is a larger version of the graph on page 89. The larger graph helps you find a more accurate answer to Item 15.

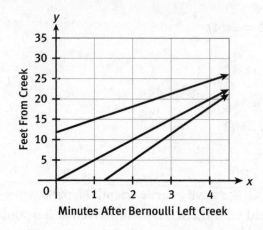

15. Remember that the graph shows the distance each critter is from the creek during the first four and one-half minutes after Bernoulli left the creek to catch up with Grace.

   a. Use the graph to estimate how far from each other the critters are three minutes after Bernoulli left the creek.

   b. Check your estimates by using appropriate algebraic expressions.

Hypatia wants to tell Bernoulli and Grace that the race tomorrow between a tortoise and a hare is part of a celebration of fables. In one of Aesop's fables, a hare challenges a tortoise to a race.

SUGGESTED LEARNING STRATEGIES: Look for a Pattern

16. This graph gives information about part of that race. Use the graph to answer each question.

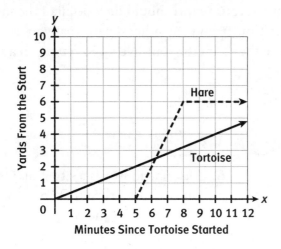

a. Who got a head start? How many minutes was it?

b. How far did the racer with the head start go before the second racer started?

c. What is the speed of the tortoise? Of the hare?

d. How far ahead of the tortoise was the hare eight minutes after the tortoise started the race?

e. Give a possible explanation for the change in the hare's line, eight minutes after the tortoise started the race.

f. If the patterns in the graph of the race continue to be the same after 12 minutes as they are for 8 to 12 minutes, and the tortoise finishes the race in 16 minutes, who wins the race? Explain how you determined your answer.

MATH TiP

Remember to include units in your answers.

My Notes

SUGGESTED LEARNING STRATEGIES: RAFT

My Notes

17. Suppose you were hired by a local radio station to give a live report of the race of the tortoise and the hare described in Question 16. Your report should include all of the information from Question 16 and any other details that you feel are important. Write the script for your live radio report on a sheet of paper.

CHECK YOUR UNDERSTANDING

Write your answers on notebook paper. Show your work.

Janice and Patricia each want to buy a new DVD player. They go to Hot Electronics and find a DVD player for $75.00. Hot Electronics offers different payment plans. Janice is going to pay $15 now, and then $7.50 per month. Patricia is going to pay $12.50 per month.

1. How much will Janice and Patricia pay for each month?

Time in Months	0	1	2
Janice's Payment			
Patricia's Payment			

2. Write expressions for the amounts that Janice and Patricia will have paid on the DVD player at the end of any month, m.

3. What is the meaning of the coefficient of m in the expressions that you wrote?

4. What is the significance of any constant term in the expressions that you wrote?

5. Write and solve an equation that shows when Janice and Patricia would have paid off the same amount on their DVD players.

6. Describe in words a situation involving Janice and Patricia that could be represented by the equation
$$5m + 13.50 = 3m + 18.$$

Marcy was offered two jobs during the summer. With both jobs, she earns a certain amount plus an hourly rate. The graph below gives information about her pay for each job.

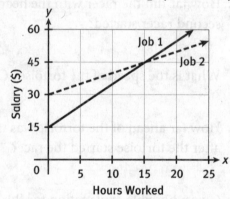

7. Which job starts her off with more pay? How do you know?

8. How many hours will she have to work before both jobs pay the same?

9. Which job would you recommend that Marcy take? Explain why.

10. **MATHEMATICAL REFLECTION** You have used tables, equations, and graphs to study patterns in this activity. When would you use each representation? Explain why.

Solving Two-Step Equations
Melody's Music Solution

SUGGESTED LEARNING STRATEGIES: Close Reading, Marking the Text, Look for a Pattern, Quickwrite, Think/Pair/Share, Create Representations

My Notes

Melody is a singer for the Green Guppy Records label. She is paid a monthly base salary plus a commission for every CD sold. Chuck, her producer, earns money only if a CD is sold. Melody is paid a monthly base salary of $4250 plus $2 per CD sold each month. Chuck makes $8 per CD.

1. Complete this table below to show the income for Melody and Chuck with the given number of CDs sold.

Number of CDs Sold	Melody's Income	Chuck's Income
0		
1		
2		
3		
4		
5		
n		

2. Describe any patterns you notice in the columns of the table.

3. Let n represent the number of CDs sold.

   a. Write an expression for Melody's income.

   b. Fill in this flowchart to show how to find Melody's income if she sells 100 CDs.

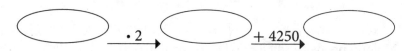

My Notes

c. Write an expression for Chuck's income.

d. Create a flowchart to represent the expression you wrote for Chuck's income.

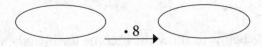

4. Chuck needs to earn $6000 this month to cover his expenses. How many CDs must be sold? Explain how you found your answer.

5. Melody needs to earn $6000 this month to cover her expenses. How many CDs must be sold? Explain how you found your answer.

You could have answered Questions 4 and 5 by writing and solving equations.

To find the number of CDs that Melody needs to sell to earn $6,000, let x stand for the number of CDs and use the equation $2x + 4250 = 6000$.

To solve this equation you can make a flowchart to show the equation and then work backwards to find the value for x that makes this equation true. Show what operations were used at the bottom of the flowchart.

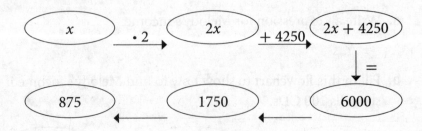

Melody needs to sell 875 CDs to earn $6,000.

My Notes

6. Explain the flowchart at the bottom of page 94.

7. How is order of operations used in the flowchart?

8. Write and solve an equation to show how many CDs need to be sold for Chuck to earn $6,000.

9. How does this answer compare to your answer for Question 4?

Melody has hired a new accountant. He has gathered her pay stubs and is trying to figure out how many CDs were sold during each month. Her pay stub for June was $4890. Melody tells him that she makes $4250 plus $2 per CD sale.

10. Use the expression you wrote for Question 3.

   a. Write an equation to answer the question, "How many CDs were sold for Melody to have an income of $4890 for the month of June?"

   b. Complete this flowchart to solve the equation you wrote in Part a.

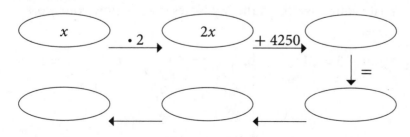

My Notes

Green Guppy Records pays Timely Trucking to ship the CDs to retail stores. They are paid $1650 per shipment minus $25 per hour for each hour the delivery arrives past the promised time. Because the truck broke down and was late with the last delivery, Green Guppy paid Timely Trucking only $1325.

11. Write an equation that will answer the question, "How late was the delivery made?" Use the flowchart to solve your equation.

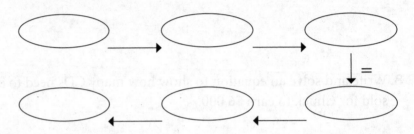

You can also solve equations without the flowchart, by *undoing* operations.

> **MATH TIP**
>
> An operation is *undone* by using the opposite operation. Opposite operations are called *inverse operations*.

EXAMPLE 1

Use inverse operations to solve the equation $3c - 5 = 5.5$.

Step 1:	*Write the equation.*	$3c - 5 = 5.5$
Step 2:	*Since addition is the inverse of subtraction, add 5 to both sides of the equation.*	$3c - 5 + 5 = 5.5 + 5$
Step 3:	*Simplify.*	$3c = 10.5$
Step 4:	*Since division is the inverse of multiplication, divide both sides of the equation by 3.*	$3c \div 3 = 10.5 \div 3$
Step 5:	*Simplify.*	$c = 3.5$

Solution: The solution to $3c - 5 = 5.5$ is $c = 3.5$.

TRY THESE A

Write your answers in the My Notes space. Show your work. Solve.

a. $6m - 3 = 21$ **b.** $\dfrac{g}{4} + 7 = 10$ **c.** $3 + 2x = 17$

Solving Two-Step Equations
Melody's Music Solution

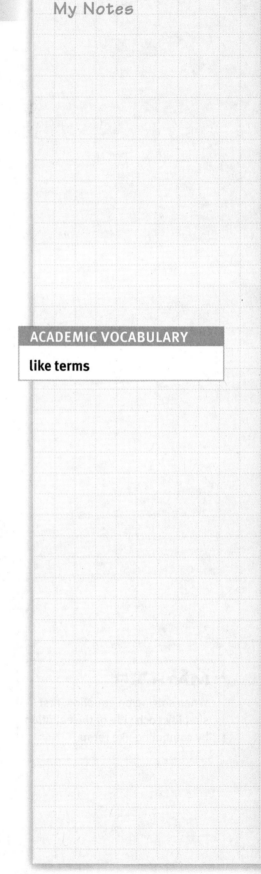

My Notes

Green Guppy Records sells to three retail stores, Musical Numbers, Triangle Tunes, and Century Songs.

12. Let *n* represent the number of CDs shipped to Musical Numbers.

  a. Green Guppy Records ships twice as many CDs to Triangle Tunes as to Musical Numbers. Write an expression to represent the number of CDs shipped to Triangle Tunes.

  b. Green Guppy Records ships three times as many CDs to Century Songs as to Musical Numbers. Write an expression to represent the number of CDs shipped to Century Songs.

The expressions that you wrote in Questions 12a and 12b are called **like terms**. Like terms have the same variable with the same exponent.

13. The terms $7c$ and $4c$ are like terms. The terms $4c$ and $8d$ are unlike terms. The terms $5c$ and $5c^2$ are unlike terms.

  a. Explain why x and $2x$ are like terms.

  b. Explain why 3 and 4 are like terms.

  c. Explain why $5a$ and 7 are not like terms.

  d. Explain why $6a$ and $7a^2$ are not like terms.

14. Name any like terms in the expression.
$4x + 3y - 3y^2 + 8x^3 + 2y^2 + 5x$

You can use the distributive property to simplify a variable expression containing like terms. The process is called **combining like terms**. Unlike terms cannot be combined.

$4a + 7a - 3a$ can be rewritten as $(4 + 7 - 3)a = 8a$

My Notes

15. You know that Green Guppy Records ships twice as many CDs to Triangle Tunes as to Musical Numbers and three times as many CDs to Century Songs as to Musical Numbers. Let n represent the number of CDs shipped to Musical Numbers.

   a. Write an expression to represent the total number of CDs that Green Guppy Records shipped.

   b. Simplify the expression you wrote in Part a by combining like terms.

16. Harmony and Rocky are two other singers for the Green Guppy Record label.
   - Harmony recorded twice the number of CDs as Melody.
   - Rocky recorded 5 more CDs than Melody.

   Let n represent the number of CDs recorded by Melody.

   a. Write an expression to represent the number of CDs recorded by Harmony.

   b. Write an expression to represent the number of CDs recorded by Rocky.

17. Harmony and Rocky together recorded 11 CDs.

   a. Write an equation to answer the question, "How many CDs did Melody record?"

   b. Solve the equation you found in Part a and tell the meaning of your answer.

   c. How many CDs did Harmony record? How many CDs did Rocky record? Explain how you got you answer.

MATH TIP

When solving an equation, first simplify each side of the equation by combining like terms.

Solving Two-Step Equations
Melody's Music Solution

SUGGESTED LEARNING STRATEGIES: Think/Pair/Share, Create Representations, Quickwrite, Group Presentation

My Notes

Angel and Keith went to Triangle Tunes to buy copies of Melody's latest CD to give as gifts. Angel bought 4 more CDs than Keith. Together they purchased 14 CDs.

18. One way to figure out how many CDs they each purchased is to let k represent the number of CDs that Keith purchased.

   a. Write an expression for the number of CDs that Angel purchased.

   b. Write and solve an equation to answer the question, "How many CDs did Keith purchase?"

   c. How many CDs did Angel purchase? Explain how you got your answer.

19. Another way to find how many CDs each of them purchased is to let a represent the number of CDs that Angel purchased.

   a. Write an expression for the number of CDs that Keith purchased.

   b. Write and solve an equation to answer the question, "How many CDs did Angel purchase?"

   c. Did you get the same answer as your answer in question 18? Explain.

   d. Which method did you like better? Explain.

MATH TIP

Identifying what each variable represents in an equation is *defining the variable*.

My Notes

20. Chuck now produces CDs for Melody, Harmony, and Rocky. He earns $8 for each of their CDs that is sold. To calculate his monthly income he uses the following formula: $8(M + H + R) = T$ where:
   - M represents the number of Melody's CDs sold.
   - H represents the number of Harmony's CDs sold.
   - R represents the number of Rocky's CDs sold.
   - T represents the total amount of income Chuck earned from the sale of the CDs.

To meet his budget for July, Chuck needs to earn $4256. In July, 225 of Harmony's CDs and 115 of Rocky's CDs were sold.

a. Use Chuck's formula to write an equation to answer the question, "How many of Melody's CDs must have been sold for Chuck to earn $4256?"

b. Solve the equation you found in Part a by using the distributive property.

c. Solve the equation you found in Part a without using the distributive property.

SUGGESTED LEARNING STRATEGIES: Quickwrite, Close Reading, Marking the Text, Question the Text, Shared Reading, Group Presentation, Create Representations

My Notes

d. Compare the methods you used to solve the equation in Parts b and c. Which method did you like better? Explain.

Harmony just negotiated a new deal with Purple Parrot Records. She will be paid a monthly base salary of $3900 plus a commission of $5 per CD sold. Melody is trying to decide if this is a better deal than her monthly base salary of $4250 plus a commission of $2 per CD sold.

21. Let n represent the number of CDs sold.

    a. Write an expression for Melody's income.

    b. Write an expression for Harmony's income.

22. Complete the table below to show the income for Melody and Harmony with the given number of CDs sold.

Number of CDs Sold	Melody's Income	Harmony's Income
0		
50		
100		
150		
200		
250		

23. Who do you think has a better deal, Melody or Harmony? Explain.

My Notes

Some equations have variables on both sides. You can use algebra tiles to solve these equations.

- Each rectangle (or *x*-tile) represents *x*: ▭
- Each small square (or unit tile) represents 1: □

Work with this visual model of the equation $4x + 2 = 1x + 8$.

$4x + 2$ $=$ $1x + 8$

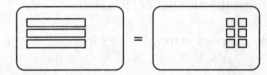

To solve the equation, remove 2 unit tiles and 1 *x*-tile from each side. Be sure to take away the same amount from both sides of the equation to maintain a balance.

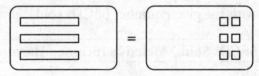

When no more *x*-tiles and unit tiles can be removed, group the remaining unit tiles so each *x*-tile is assigned an equal number. The number of unit tiles assigned to each *x*-tile is the **solution** to the original equation.

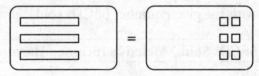

24. Check the solution by substituting $x = 2$ into the original equation. Show your work below.

Algebra tiles can be used to represent and explain each step of the solution to an equation.

Solving Two-Step Equations
Melody's Music Solution

SUGGESTED LEARNING STRATEGIES: Create Representations, Quickwrite

EXAMPLE 2

$4x + 2 = 1x + 8$

	Algebra Tiles	Equations
Step 1:	Use 5 x-tiles and 10 unit tiles to represent the equation.	$4x + 2 = 1x + 8$
Step 2:	Remove 2 unit tiles on each side.	$4x + 2 - 2 = 1x + 8 - 2$
Step 3:	New equation.	$4x = 1x + 6$
Step 4:	Remove 1 x-tile from each side.	$4x - 1x = 1x - 1x + 6$
Step 5:	New equation.	$3x = 6$
Step 6:	Divide the 6 unit tiles evenly into 3 groups—1 group for each x-tile.	$\dfrac{3x}{3} = \dfrac{6}{3}$

Solution: The solution to $4x + 2 = 1x + 8$ is $x = 2$.

TRY THESE B

a. Use algebra tiles to solve the equation $5x + 2 = 3x + 8$. Show your work by drawing pictures in the My Notes space. Cross out the tiles that you remove and draw lines to show how you evenly divide the remaining unit tiles among each x-tile.

b. Explain each step of your work for Question a and write the equation that represents each step.

Step	Explanation	Equation

My Notes

25. Solve the following equations using the method of your choice. Show all your work.

   a. $3x + 1 = 2x + 7$

Step	Explanation	Equation

   b. $7x + 25 = 3x - 11$

26. When solving an equation step-by-step using algebra, the equation at each step is *equivalent* to the equations in the other steps. **Equivalent equations** are equations that have the same solution.

   a. Show that the following equations are equivalent equations.

   $2x + 7 = x - 3$ and $2x - 30 = 6x + 10$

   b. Which of the following pairs of equations are equivalent?

   i. $5x + 7 = 3x + 13$ and $2x + 7 = 13$

   ii. $3x = x + 2$ and $2x + 4 = x + 6$

   iii. $x + 3 = 5x - 5$ and $4x - 5 = 3$

SUGGESTED LEARNING STRATEGIES: Create Representations, Quickwrite, Close Reading, Marking the Text, Group Presentation

27. Think back to the situation with Melody and Harmony. Use the expressions you wrote for Question 21 to write and solve an equation that will answer the question, "How many CDs must be sold for Melody to have the same income as Harmony in a given month?"

28. Who do you think has a better deal, Melody or Harmony? How does this compare to your thinking in Question 23?

Based on sales over the past few months Melody feels that at most 150 of her CDs will be sold in a given month. She decides to negotiate a new deal with Green Guppy Records. She wants to decrease her base salary to $3960 and increase her commission to $4 per CD sold.

29. Write and solve an equation that will answer the question, "How many CDs must be sold for Melody to have the same income in a given month under her present contract as she would have under her newly proposed contract?"

30. Is Melody's proposed new contract a good deal? Explain.

CHECK YOUR UNDERSTANDING

Write your answers on notebook paper. Show your work.

1. Solve and check each equation.

   a. $12n = 36$ **b.** $n - 5 = 8$

   c. $-8 = 2x + 4$ **d.** $2w - 3 = -9$

2. Jim gets $12 for each lawn that he mows. Write and solve an equation that will answer how many lawns he mowed to earn $276.

3. Brenda gets paid $50 per week plus a commission of $0.50 for each book she sells. Write and solve an equation to find the number of books she sold to earn $125.

4. Simplify each expression, if possible, by combining like terms. If not possible, write *simplified*.

   a. $2x + 9x$

   b. $4c - 8c$

   c. $7d^2 - 5d$

   d. $6n^3 + 2n^3$

   e. $3y^2 + 7y^2 + 2y^3$

   f. $4a + 5 + 6a - 3$

   g. $z + 8z - 3$

5. Solve and check each equation.

   a. $3x + 7x - 2 = 8$

   b. $32 = 9w - 3w + 2$

   c. $6y - 4y + 11 = 7$

   d. $81 = 3a - 8a - 4a$

   e. $6(x + 2) = 18$

   f. $-25 = 5(b - 3)$

   g. $7z + 12 = 3z$

6. What is an equivalent equation for $4x + 14 = 2x + 30$?

7. Kay and Simon bought mugs at the gift shop. Simon bought 6 more mugs than Kay. Together they bought 32 mugs. Use an equation to find the number of mugs Kay bought and the number of mugs Simon bought.

8. Bart, Sandy, and Julia went shopping at the market. Bart spent twice as much as Sandy. Julia spent $15 more than Sandy. If all together they spent $119, how much did each one spend shopping?

9. Tracy has a choice at her new job of getting paid $300 per week plus $5 for each magazine subscription that she sells or $450 per week plus $2 for each magazine subscription that she sells. She feels that she can sell an average of 48 subscriptions each week.

   a. Write and solve an equation to find the number of subscriptions she must sell for the two options to pay the same salary.

   b. Which option should she take? Explain.

10. **MATHEMATICAL REFLECTION** Summarize the different methods you learned for solving equations. Are there times when one method might be more effective than another? Give an example.

Expressions and Equations

FUNDRAISING FUN

Write your answers on notebook paper. Show your work.

1. Talia, Lacey, and Chris decide to raise money for a homeless shelter by selling calendars. Lacey sold three times as many calendars as Chris. Talia sold five more calendars than Chris.

   a. Write an expression for the number of calendars that each student sold.

   b. If they made a profit of $8 per calendar, write an expression for the total profit the students made selling the calendars.

   c. Write and solve an equation to answer the question, "How many calendars did Chris sell if the students made a total profit of $1000?"

   d. Write a summary report that details the results of the calendar sale.

2. After getting approval to do additional fundraising, Chris and Lacey decided to participate in a walkathon to raise money for the shelter. Chris walked 5 miles less than twice the number of miles that Lacey walked. The students will collect $18 in pledges for every mile that they walk.

   Let *n* represent the number of miles that Lacey walked.

   a. Write an expression for the number of miles that Chris walked and an expression for the amount of money that Chris collected in pledges.

   b. Write and solve an equation to answer the question, "How many miles did Lacey walk if Chris collected $450 in pledges?"

   c. How many miles did Chris walk?

   d. Create a report for the director of the shelter. Include the following:

   • How each student included the amount collected

   • How much Chris and Lacey are donating to the shelter and how they determined that amount

Expressions and Equations

FUNDRAISING FUN

3. Owen also participated in the walkathon. He will collect \$10 in pledges for each mile he walks and his Aunt Judy gave him a \$72 donation. The graph to the right shows the funds collected by Owen and Lacey

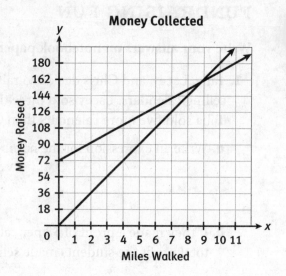

Money Collected

a. Label each line to show which line is the money collected by Lacey and which line is the money collected by Owen.

b. After how many miles will Owen and Lacey have raised the same amount of money?

c. Explain how to use the graph to determine when each student will have raised \$162.

	Exemplary	Proficient	Emerging
Math Knowledge #1a, 1b, 2a	Correct expressions for: • Number of calendars sold (1a) • Total profit from selling calendars (1b) • Number of miles walked (2a) • Amount of pledges collected. (2a)	Creates correct and complete expressions for three of the four items	Creates only one correct and complete expression
Problem Solving #1c, 2c, 3b	Correctly: • Solves the equation from calendar situation. (1c) • Solves the equation from walkathon situation using two different methods. (2c) • Finds the number of miles Chris walked. (2c) • Finds the number of miles when Owen and Lacey will raise the same amount of money. (3b)	Completes three of the four items correctly	Completes only one of the four items correctly
Representation #1c, 2b, 3a	Correctly: • Writes equations for the calendar and walkathon situations. (1c, 2b) • Labels the lines for Owen and Lacey. (3a)	Creates only one equation that is correct and complete	• Creates equations that are incorrect • Labels the lines incorrectly
Communication #1d, 2d, 3c	Writes: • A proposal for approval of calendar fundraising. (1d) • A report explaining how money was raised from the walkathon. (2d) • Explains how to use the graph to find when each student will have raised \$126. (3c)	Responses for two of the three items are correct and complete.	Response for only one of the three items is correct and complete.

My Notes

It takes four identical toothpicks to build a square.

1. How many identical toothpicks does it take to build a line of two adjacent squares, as in this drawing?

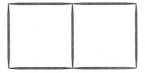

2. Use toothpicks to build lines of three, four, and five adjacent squares. Write the number of toothpicks needed and make drawings of your work in the My Notes space.

   a. 3 squares

   b. 4 squares

   c. 5 squares

3. The number of toothpicks needed, y, depends on the number of squares, x. Use your results from Items 1–2 to complete this table.

Squares (x)	Toothpicks (y)
1	
2	
3	
4	
5	

4. Describe any patterns you see in the table in Item 3.

My Notes

5. Use numbers to complete this statement: Each time the number
of squares in the line increases by _____, the number of
toothpicks increases by _____.

6. Use this grid to make a scatter plot of the data from Question 3.
Label the axes and title the graph.

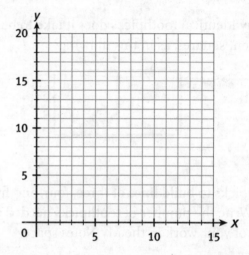

7. Label the leftmost point on the graph point *A*. Label the other
points, from left to right, points *B*, *C*, *D*, and *E*. Explain what
you notice about the points in your scatter plot.

8. Describe how to move along the grid between each pair of points.

   a. From *A* to *B*: Go Up _____ and Go Right _____.

   b. From *B* to *C*: Go Up _____ and Go Right _____.

9. Each movement you described in Question 8 can be written
as a ratio in the form $\frac{\text{units up}}{\text{units right}}$. Describe each movement
by writing a ratio in the form $\frac{\text{units up}}{\text{units right}}$.

   a. *A* to *B*

   b. *B* to *C*

You can think of *units up* as a change in the *y* direction and of *units
right* as a change in the *x* direction. A movement up or to the right
is positive.

MATH TIP

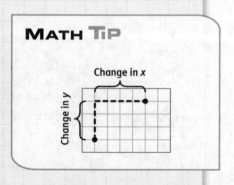

SUGGESTED LEARNING STRATEGIES: Debriefing,
Look for a Pattern, Think/Pair/Share, Visualize,
Create Representations

My Notes

10. Describe moves along the grid between each pair of points.

   a. From *A* to *C*: units up = _____ and units right = _____

   Ratio form: _____

   b. From *B* to *E*: units up = _____ and units right = _____

   Ratio form: _____

   c. From *A* to *E*: units up = _____ and units right = _____

   Ratio form: _____

11. What do you notice about these ratios?

12. How do the ratios relate to the number of squares and toothpicks?

13. When points on a scatter plot lie on a line, a ratio such as $\dfrac{\text{units up}}{\text{units right}}$ or $\dfrac{\text{change in } y}{\text{change in } x}$ is the **slope** of that line.

   a. What is the slope of the line in the scatter plot you made for Question 6?

   b. What do you think is true about the slope ratios between any two points on a line?

14. Use the grid to move from *B* to *A* and from *E* to *B*.

   a. Describe the movement from *B* to *A* and express the movement from *B* to *A* as a ratio.

   b. Describe the movement from *E* to *B* and express the movement from *E* to *B* as a ratio.

> **MATH TERMS**
> The **slope** of a line is the ratio $\dfrac{\text{change in } y}{\text{change in } x}$ between any two points that lie on the line.

> **WRITING MATH**
> Some mathematicians call the change in *y* the *rise* and the change in *x* the *run*. You may see the ratio for **slope** written as $\dfrac{\text{rise}}{\text{run}}$.

My Notes

c. What kind of numbers did you use when you wrote the ratios in Parts a and b?

d. How do the slope ratios compare to the slope ratios you wrote in question 10?

e. Use this slope ratio to add another point to the graph and explain what the point represents.

15. Suppose that you wanted to find the number of toothpicks needed to build 50 squares.

   a. Would your graph be helpful for finding that number? Explain your answer.

   b. Recall that the variable x represents the number of squares in a line and the variable y represents the number of toothpicks used to build the squares.

   Complete this table that was made by adding more rows for more squares to the table from Question 3.

Squares (x)	Toothpicks (y)
1	
2	
3	
4	
5	
6	
7	
8	
10	
20	

   c. Explain how you found the number of toothpicks needed for 10 squares and for 20 squares.

16. Use the information from the graph and the table to write an equation that represents this situation.

My Notes

17. Use your equation from Item 16 to help answer each part. Show your work or explain how you arrived at your answers.

   a. How many toothpicks are needed to build 50 squares?

   b. How many squares can be built from a total of 94 toothpicks?

   c. How many squares can be built from a total of 62 toothpicks?

Now examine how slope is a part of other linear relationships. Recall that the coordinate plane is divided into four quadrants.

18. Label the quadrants I, II, III, and IV on the coordinate grid.

   a. Then plot and label each ordered pair.

   $A(3, -5)$ $B(5, 0)$ $C(-2, 4)$ $D(-3, -4)$ $E(0, 5)$

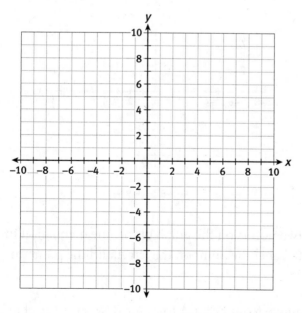

MATH TIP

Thinking about how you would write the letter "c" might help you to remember how to label the quadrants correctly.

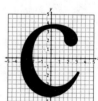

   b. What ordered pair represents the origin? Plot the origin on the grid.

My Notes

ACADEMIC VOCABULARY

function

CONNECT TO AP

Functions allow you to study how things change, which is a fundamental concept in the branch of mathematics known as calculus.

19. Linear functions can be graphed in the coordinate plane. A **function** pairs each input value with *exactly one* output value and can be represented by a table, a graph, or an equation.

a. Complete this input/output table for the equation $y = \frac{1}{2}x - 2$.

Input, x	Output, y	Ordered pair (x, y)
−2		
−1		
0		
2		
3		

b. Then plot each ordered pair on the coordinate plane. Finally, connect the points with a line.

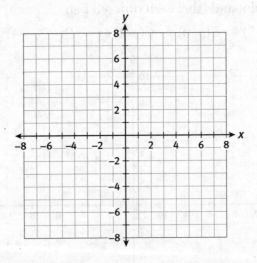

20. Select two points on the graph of the linear equation in Item 20. Label the point on the left A and the point on the right B.

a. To move from point A to point B, what is the change in y?

b. To move from point A to point B, what is the change in x?

c. What is the slope between point A and point B?

SUGGESTED LEARNING STRATEGIES: Create Representations, Think/Pair/Share, Debriefing, Quickwrite

My Notes

21. Make an input/output table for the linear equation $y = 3x + 1$. Choose your own values for x. Include some positive values, negative values, and zero. Then calculate the values of y and graph the equation.

x	y

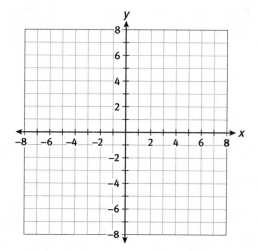

> **MATH TIP**
>
> When you choose input values, it is a good idea to choose a negative number that is close to (0, 0) and a small positive number so that you can see what is happening around the origin.

22. Find the slope of the linear equation in Item 21.

23. Look back at the previous two equations, tables, and graphs. How do the slopes in these problems relate to the original equations?

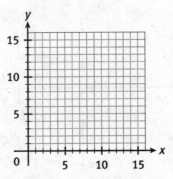

My Notes

SUGGESTED LEARNING STRATEGIES: Shared Reading, Marking the Text, Create Representations, Debriefing, Quickwrite

Before the invention of clocks, candles were sometimes used to measure time. The height of a burning candle depends on the amount of time that has elapsed since the candle was lighted. In this table, t represents the time in hours that a candle has been burning and h represents the height of the candle in inches.

t	h
3	7.5
4	6
5	4.5
6	3

24. Use this grid to make a scatter plot of the data for the rate at which the candle burns. Label the axes and title the graph.

25. From left to right, label the points on your scatter plot A, B, C, and D. Describe moves along the grid between each pair of points and express the moves as a sloop ratio in lowest terms.

   a. From B to D: change in $y =$ _____ and change in $x =$ _____

   Slope ratio form: _____

   b. From C to D: change in $y =$ _____ and change in $x =$ _____

   Slope ratio form: _____

   c. From C to A: change in $y =$ _____ and change in $x =$ _____

   Slope ratio form: _____

My Notes

26. What do you notice about the slope ratios in Item 25?

27. Interpret the slope for this graph. What does it tell you about the rate at which the candle burns?

28. Use your scatter plot from Item 25 and the slope to answer these questions. Explain how you arrived at your answers.

   a. How tall was the candle before it was lighted?

   b. How much time elapses from the time the candle is lighted until it is completely melted?

29. Recall that t represents the time in hours that a candle has been burning and h represents the height of the candle in inches. Write an equation for h in terms of t.

> 📱 **TECHNOLOGY TiP**
>
> These equations can be graphed using a graphing calculator.

30. Use the equation you wrote in Item 29 to answer these questions. Show your work.

   a. How tall was the candle after it had been burning for 3.5 hours?

   b. After how many hours was the burning candle 4 inches tall?

CHECK YOUR UNDERSTANDING

Write your answers on notebook paper or grid paper. Show your work.

1. Make an input/output table for $y = 2x$. Use 1, 2, 3, 4, and 5 as the input, or x, values. Then plot the ordered pairs on a coordinate grid.

2. Plot (1, 2) and (4, 3) on a coordinate grid. Then determine the change in y, change in x, and slope of the line between the two points.

3. Find the change in y, change in x, and slope of this graph.

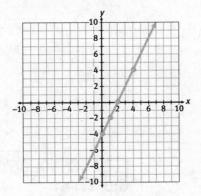

4. Copy and complete the input/output table for the equation $y = \frac{2}{3}x + 1$. Then graph the equation.

Input, x	Output, y
−3	
0	
3	
6	

5. Graph $y = -3x - 6$. Use this input/output table.

Input, x	Output, y
−2	0
−1	−3
0	−6
1	−9

6. **MATHEMATICAL REFLECTION** Give some examples of how slope might be used in real-world applications.

Writing and Solving Equations
Racing Along

SUGGESTED LEARNING STRATEGIES: Close Reading, Activating Prior Knowledge, Group Presentation, Create Representations, Quickwrite

My Notes

Rob has a pet rabbit and Tim has a pet turtle. Rob challenged Tim to a pet race. Rob gave Tim's turtle a head start of 1194 feet. The racecourse was 1200 feet long.

1. Rob's rabbit can run 24 feet per second. Tim's turtle can run 0.12 feet per second.

   a. Write an expression to represent the rabbit's distance from the start of the race after n seconds of running.

   b. Write an expression to represent the turtle's distance from the start of the race after n seconds of running.

   c. Write and solve an equation to answer the question, "When will the animals' distance from the start of the race be the same?"

   d. When will Rob's rabbit reach the finish line?

   e. Who won the race? Explain.

After the pet race Rob and Tim agreed that they should race each other in a few months. Tim wanted to improve his running time. He made this table and tracked his progress for four weeks.

Training Time (weeks)	0	1	2	3	4
Running Speed (mi/min)	0.105	0.120	0.135	0.150	0.165

2. If the pattern of progress shown in the table continues, what will Tim's speed in miles per minute be after 10 weeks of training? Explain your reasoning.

> **CONNECT TO AP**
>
> Distance, speed, and time as well as geometric models for measurements like area, perimeter, and volume are used in many application problems you will encounter in advanced math courses.

My Notes

3. Tim noticed that his speed was increasing at an average rate of 0.015 miles/min each week of training. Let *n* represent the number of weeks that Tim has been training.

   a. If Tim's initial speed is 0.105 miles per minute, write an expression that represents Tim's speed after *n* weeks of training.

   b. Tim's goal is to be able to run at a rate of 0.25 mi/min. Write and solve an equation which will answer the question, "When will Tim reach his goal?"

Rob and Tim decide to bike to Freedom Lake. They want to estimate how long it will take to bike there. They know that they can bike at a rate of 24 km/h but they don't know the distance to Freedom Lake. They use a map to estimate the distance.

4. On their map the distance from Tim's house to Freedom Lake is 1.8 centimeters. The map scale shows that 2 cm = 40 km.

   a. What is the distance from Tim's house to Freedom Lake? Explain your reasoning.

   b. How long will it take the boys to bike to Freedom Lake?

Rob and Tim know that regular exercise strengthens your heart. They learned in health class that a person's pulse rate should not exceed a certain limit during exercise. The maximum rate, *R*, is represented by the equation $R = 0.8(220 - y)$ where *y* is the person's age in years.

5. Find the age of a person whose maximum pulse rate during exercise is 164.

SUGGESTED LEARNING STRATEGIES: Create Representations, Quickwrite, Activating Prior Knowledge

My Notes

Rob and Tim feel that it is just as important to exercise their brains as to exercise their bodies. To help them do this, they often do their math homework together. They used Questions 6–13 as practice for an upcoming math test and they want you to try them too.

Solve each problem. Be sure to check your answers.

6. One half of a number increased by 16 is four less than two-thirds of the number. Find the number.

7. This figure is a square.

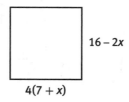

16 − 2x

4(7 + x)

   a. Find the value of x.

   b. Does your answer make sense? Explain.

8. Find the value of x and the measures of angles A, B, and C.

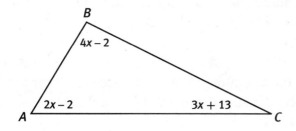

MATH TIP

Remember that the sum of the measures of the angles of a triangle equals 180 degrees.

9. Jan is y years old. In 30 years she will be 3 times as old as she is now. How old is Jan now?

My Notes

10. This drawing shows the frame and screen of a television set. The perimeter around the outside of the frame is 92 inches. Find the length and width of the television screen.

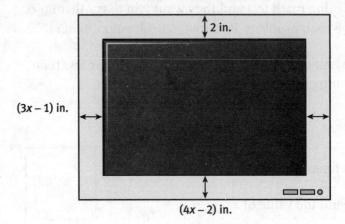

2 in.

(3x – 1) in.

(4x – 2) in.

11. The formula $A = p + prt$ gives the amount of money A in an account where the initial deposit is p and the money grows at a simple annual interest rate of r for t years. For all parts of this problem, no other deposits or withdrawals are made.

   a. How much money is in the account after 5 years, if $20 is deposited and the annual interest rate is 5%?

   b. How much was deposited in the account, if the amount in the account after 6 years is $17.70 and the interest rate is 3%?

   c. What would the annual interest rate have to be for $50 to grow to $70 in 10 years?

   d. How long would it take $25 to grow to $35, if the annual interest rate is 2%?

MATH TIP

Use the decimal form of a percent in a formula where r is the annual interest rate. For 3%, you would use 0.03.

12. Isolate the w in the formula $P = 2l + 2w$.

    a. What is the first step?

    b. What is the second step?

    c. Write the new formula with w isolated.

13. Isolate the variable t in the formula: $A = p + prt$.

_____

    Use the new formula to complete the table at the right.

14. Rob and Tim volunteer to run a lemonade stand at the school's annual health fair. They estimate it will cost them $10 for the materials to build their stand and buy pitchers. They calculate the cost per cup to make the lemonade is $1.

A	p	r	t
92	80	0.015	
72	45	0.03	
130	100	0.06	
207	75	0.055	

    a. Let n be the number of cups of lemonade that they sell and C be the amount of money it cost to make n cups of lemonade. Write an equation for the cost to make n cups of lemonade.

    b. Rob and Tim are going to sell their lemonade for $2 per cup. Let n be the number of cups of lemonade that they sell and R be the amount of money they bring in selling the lemonade. Write an equation for the amount of money they bring in selling n cups of lemonade.

15. Write and solve an equation to answer the question, "How many cups of lemonade do Tim and Rob have to sell for the cost to equal the amount of money they bring in?"

CHECK YOUR UNDERSTANDING

Write your answers on notebook paper. Show your work.

1. The local train is 25 miles down the track from Central Station when the express leaves the station. The local train travels at a rate of 50 mi/hr and the express train travels at a rate of 80 mi/hr. Let n represent the number of hours since the express train left Central Station.

   a. Write an expression that represents the express train's distance from Central Station in n hours.

   b. When will the express train catch up with the local train?

2. Steve's doctor put him on a diet. He is losing weight according to the following chart.

Week	0	1	2	3
Weight	128	125	122	119

   a. If the pattern in the table continues, what will Steve weigh after 8 weeks of dieting?

   b. Let n represent the number of weeks that Steve has been dieting. Write and solve an equation to answer the question, "When will Steve reach his goal of weighing 95 pounds?"

3. On a map the distance between Summerville and Springtown is 1.2 inches. If 1 inch = 30 miles, what is the distance from Summerville to Springtown?

4. Find x so that the triangle is equilateral.

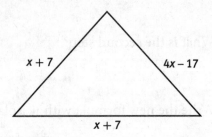

5. Solve each formula for the indicated variable.

   a. $I = prt$, for t **b.** $y = mx + b$, for x

6. Today, the Lincoln School has 400 packages of paper and the Washington School has 300 packages.

   a. Each week 12 packages of paper are used at the Lincoln School. Let n equal the number of weeks that have passed since today. Write an equation to represent the number of packages, y, left in the school after n weeks.

   b. Each week 8 packages of paper are used at the Washington School. Let n equal the number of weeks that have passed since today. Write an equation to represent the number of packages, y, left in the school after n weeks.

   c. Graph your equations from Parts a and b.

   d. Use the graph to predict when the schools will have the same number of packages. Check your prediction by writing and solving an equation.

7. **MATHEMATICAL REFLECTION** Create a poster showing how to solve word problems involving equations.

Equations and Graphs

NEGOTIATING AN ALLOWANCE

Write your answers on notebook paper. Show your work.

Brad and Brenda each had to negotiate their weekly allowance with their parents.

1. Brad made a deal to get a weekly allowance of $10 plus $2 for each household chore performed during the previous week.

 a. Write an equation that represents Brad's total allowance, y, if he did x household chores during the previous week. Create a graph of possible amounts for Brad's allowance.

 b. Explain what the slope tells you about Brad's allowance.

 c. Write and solve an equation to answer the question, "If Brad's allowance is $24, how many household chores did he do the week before?" Explain the steps that you used to solve the equation.

2. Brenda made a deal to get a weekly allowance of $5 plus $3 for each household chore performed during the previous week.

 a. Write an equation that represents Brenda's total allowance, y, if she did x household chores during the previous week. Create a graph of possible amounts for Brenda's allowance.

 b. Write and solve an equation that will answer the question, "If Brenda's allowance is $23, how many household chores did she do the week before?"

 c. For what number of household chores do Brad and Brenda receive the same allowance? Explain your method for finding this number.

3. Who negotiated the better allowance? Use your work to justify your answer.

Equations and Graphs

NEGOTIATING AN ALLOWANCE

	Exemplary	Proficient	Emerging
Math Knowledge #1b	The student correctly explains what the slope indicates about Brad's allowance (1b).		The student's explanation of the slope is incorrect or incomplete.
Problem Solving #1c, 2b, 2c	The student correctly solves equations to determine: • The number of chores Brad did the week before. (1c) • The number of chores Brenda did the week before. (2b) • The number of chores for Brad and Brenda to receive the same allowance. (2c)	The student correctly solves two of the equations.	The student correctly solves only one of the equations.
Representation #1a, 2a	The student correctly: • Writes equations to represent Brad's and Brenda's allowance. (1a, 2a) • Creates a graph (1a) and a representation (2a) to visualize the equations for Brad's and Brenda's allowance.	The student: • Creates incorrect equations and graphs that correctly represent them, OR • Correctly creates the two equations but is able to represent only one of the equations correctly.	The student: • Creates correct equations but is unable to represent them visually, OR • Creates a correct equation and visual representation for only one of the situations.
Communication #1c, 2c, 3	The student correctly: • Explains the steps used when solving Brad's equation. (1c) • Explains the method for finding number of chores that will give Brad and Brenda the same allowance. (2c) • Explains and justifies whether Brad's or Brenda's allowance is better. (3)	The student response correctly and completely explains two of the situations.	The student response correctly and completely explains only one of the situations.

Solving and Graphing Inequalities
Up and Away

SUGGESTED LEARNING STRATEGIES: Marking the Text, Shared Reading, Create Representations, Think/Pair/Share

Geri wants to become a commercial airline pilot someday. She found this information while doing research on this career.

- The airplane's captain must be at least 23 years old.
- The captain must have a minimum of 1,500 hours of flying experience.
- By law pilots can fly a maximum of 100 hours in a month.
- By law pilots may not fly more than 32 hours during any 7 consecutive days.

Each piece of information that Geri found can be modeled best by using an **inequality**. Phrases like *at least, no less than,* and *a minimum of* are used to indicate that one quantity is greater than or equal to another. Phrases like *at most, no more than,* and *a maximum of* are used to indicate that one quantity is less than or equal to another.

Equations and inequalities that contain variables are **open sentences**. Use these open sentences to answer Item 1.

$$x > 20 \qquad x < 20 \qquad x \leq 20 \qquad x \geq 20$$

1. For each situation below, write the open sentence that represents it. Some of the open sentences will be used more than once. Then tell what x represents—this is called defining the variable.

   a. She finished the license test in no more than 20 minutes.
   _____, x represents _____

   b. The temperature was less than 20°F the day of the test.
   _____, x represents _____

   c. More than 20 students were in her flight school class.
   _____, x represents _____

   d. No one under 20 is admitted to the flight school.
   _____, x represents _____

   e. No more than 20 students will get a job with the airline.
   _____, x represents _____

   f. Training uniforms cost at least $20.
   _____, x represents _____

My Notes

ACADEMIC VOCABULARY

An **inequality** is a mathematical statement showing that one quantity is greater than or less than another.
Inequalities use these symbols:

> is greater than

< is less than

≥ is greater than or equal to

≤ is less than or equal to

ACADEMIC VOCABULARY

An **open sentence** is an equation or inequality with variables. An open sentence can be true or false, depending on what values are substituted for the variables.

My Notes

> **MATH TIP**
>
> In a correctly stated inequality the symbol points toward the smaller number.
>
> $2 < 5$; 2 is smaller
>
> $2 > 0$; 0 is smaller

2. Write an inequality to describe each situation. Define your variable by explaining what it represents.

   a. An airplane's captain must be at least 23 years old.

   b. An airplane's captain must have a minimum of 1,500 hours of flying experience.

   c. A pilot may not fly more than 32 hours during any 7 consecutive days.

   d. A pilot can fly a maximum of 100 hours in a month.

   e. Geri's age is less than 23.

A **solution of an inequality** is any number that produces a true statement when it is substituted for the variable in the inequality. One possible solution to the equation $p < 25$ is 18 because $18 < 25$ is a true statement.

3. Commercial airplanes are required to fly at least 1500 feet above the highest fixed object in a residential area. The highest building in Geri's town is 240 feet.

   a. Write an inequality to describe this situation. Define your variable.

   b. Find three possible solutions to the inequality you wrote in part a.

   c. List one value that is not a solution.

My Notes

Consider the inequalities $x > 2$ and $x < 8$. These two inequalities can be combined like this: $2 < x < 8$. Combining inequalities in this way forms a **compound inequality**.

4. Use words to describe $2 < x < 8$. Then list six values of x that satisfy the inequality: $2 < x < 8$.

Inequalities that are open sentences usually have many solutions. The solutions are often easier to graph than to list. Inequalities with one variable are graphed on a number line.

5. Graph all solutions to $a > 3$.

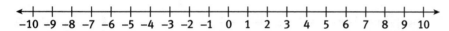

6. Graph all solutions to $y \leq -1$

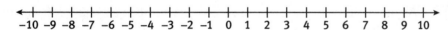

7. Consider the compound inequality $-3 \leq w < 2$. This inequality can be expressed as $w \geq -3$ and $w < 2$.

a. Graph $w \geq -3$ on the number line below.

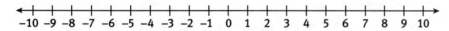

b. Graph $w < 2$ on the same number line but in a different color.

c. What do you notice about the intersection of these two graphs?

d. Graph the solution to $-3 \leq w < 2$ on the number line below.

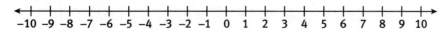

e. Describe the graph of the solution.

My Notes

8. Consider $w < -3$ or $w \geq 2$.

  a. Graph $w < -3$ on the number line below.

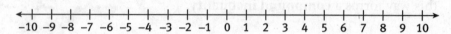

  b. Graph $w \geq 2$ in a different color on the same number line.

  c. When you graph a compound inequality with the word *or*, what will the graph be?

  d. Graph the solution of $w < -3$ or $w \geq 2$ on the number line below.

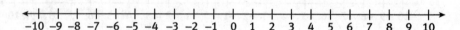

EXAMPLE 1

As inequalities become more complex, you need a systematic way to solve them just as with equations. Use the rules for solving equations to solve the inequality $w + 3 \leq 8$. Check your answer.

Step 1:   *Write the inequality.*
$$w + 3 \leq 8$$

Step 2:   *Subtract 3 from both sides.*
$$w + 3 - 3 \leq 8 - 3$$
$$w \leq 5$$

Solution: $w \leq 5$, so any number ≤ 5 is a solution.

Check: Choose a value for w that satisfies the solution.
Use 2.
Substitute the chosen value for w in the original inequality.
$$2 + 3 \leq 8$$
$$5 \leq 8 ✔$$

TRY THESE A

Write your answers in the My Notes space. Show your work.

Solve each inequality.

  a. $z - 7 \leq -2$ **b.** $3m > 15$ **c.** $\dfrac{y}{5} < 4$

My Notes

In some cases the rules for solving equations will not work for solving inequalities.

EXAMPLE 2

Solve the inequality $-2a \leq 6$.

Step 1: *Write the inequality.*

$$-2a \leq 6$$

Step 2: *Divide both sides by −2.*

$$\frac{-2a}{-2} \leq \frac{6}{-2}$$

Solution: $a \leq -3$

Check: Choose a value for a that satisfies the solution. Use −5.

Substitute the chosen value for a in the original inequality.

$$-2(-5) \leq 6$$
$$10 \leq 6$$

Since the chosen value does not make the inequality true, the solution is not correct.

The rules for solving an equation do not work for solving an inequality when you must multiply or divide by a negative number. In these situations, you must reverse the inequality symbol in the solution. In the example above, the solution should be $a \geq -3$. Choosing a value that satisfies this solution will make the original inequality true.

Check: Choose a value for a that satisfies $a \geq -3$. Use 5.

Substitute 5 for a in the original inequality.

$$-2(5) \leq 6$$

$$-10 \leq 6$$

TRY THESE B

Write your answers in the My Notes space. Show your work.

Solve. $\frac{x}{-3} > 4$ $\qquad\qquad -4x \geq -12$

My Notes

9. Do the rules for solving equations work for solving inequalities? Explain why or why not.

10. Solve each inequality. Graph the solution.

a. $\frac{1}{3}x + 2 \geq -1$

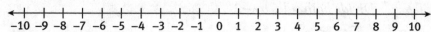

b. $-5x - 3 \leq 7$

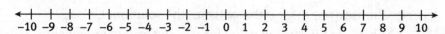

c. $-3x > 15$

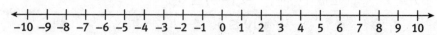

11. The pilot of a small plane wanted to stay at least 1600 feet beneath some storm clouds at 11,200 feet. After takeoff, for how long could the pilot ascend at a rate of 640 ft/min?

> **MATH TIP**
>
> Question 11 can be modeled with the inequality $640t + 1600 \leq 11{,}200$ where t is the number of minutes that the pilot ascends at 640 ft/min. Solve $640t + 1600 \leq 11{,}200$. Be sure to check your solution.

CHECK YOUR UNDERSTANDING

Write your answers on notebook paper. Show your work.

1. Write an inequality to describe each situation. Define your variable.

   a. You must be at least 4.4 feet tall to ride the kiddie roller coaster.

   b. You must drive between 45 mph and 65 mph inclusive on the highway.

   c. You may have no more than one C on your report card to be eligible to play sports.

2. Graph all solutions to each inequality.

   a. $x > 6$ b. $y \leq -4$

   c. $2 < w < 7$ d. $x < 4$ or $x \geq 6$

3. Solve each inequality

   a. $x + 5 \geq 11$ b. $y - 2.2 < 1.7$

   c. $-8 + 3x > 1$ d. $-2x - 1 \geq 5$

4. Karen has a $150 e-gift card. She wants to buy sweaters. Each sweater costs $27 and there is a $10.95 shipping charge per order. Write and solve an inequality to find the number of sweaters that Karen can purchase. Define your variable.

5. **MATHEMATICAL REFLECTION** Think about something in your own life that might be represented as an inequality. Describe the situation and write an inequality for that situation.

Equations and Change
Vary Interesting

SUGGESTED LEARNING STRATEGIES: Close Reading, Summarize/
Paraphrase/Retell, Quickwrite, Debriefing, Look for a Pattern,
Create Representations

Equations help you analyze, understand, and solve problems about change. Because change occurs in many different ways, you need to know how different kinds of equations represent change.

As you studied linear equations in Activities 2.3 and 2.4, you wrote and solved equations such as $y = 2x$ and $y = 2x + 1$. These may seem like similar equations, but they have important differences.

You can explore these differences by analyzing the ways that Janice is paid for two different babysitting jobs. Her first babysitting job is for Mr. and Mrs. Irwin. They pay her $4.00 for each hour worked. Her second babysitting job is at the local community center. Every time she works there, the center pays her $10.00 plus $2.00 per hour.

1. Which job do you think is better? Explain your reasoning.

2. Janice wants to compare her income for each of her jobs.

    a. If Janice works 2 hours for the Irwins, how much money would she earn? Show how you found your answer.

    b. If she works 2 hours at the community center, how much money would she earn? Show how you found your answer.

To determine how much money she would make at each job for working various amounts of time, she organizes her information in input/output tables.

3. Make an input/output table for Janice's job with the Irwins. Then use the grid in the My Notes to graph the data. Be sure to label the axes.

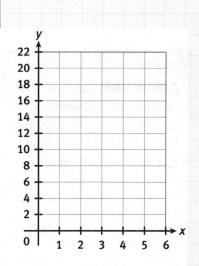

Time (h)	x	1	2	3	4	5
Earnings	y					

The equation for the money earned, y, for x hours worked is $y = 4x$.

My Notes

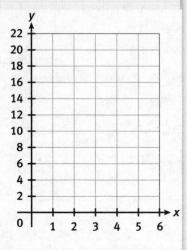

4. Make an input/output table for Janice's job at the community center. Then use the grid in the My Notes to graph the data. Be sure to label the axes.

Time (h)	x	1	2	3	4	5
Earnings	y					

5. Write an equation to represent the amount of money that Janice would earn, y, for x hours worked at the community center.

6. If Janice doubled the amount of time that she worked for the Irwins, would she double the amount of money that she made? Explain using examples.

7. If Janice doubled the amount of time that she worked at the community center, would she double the amount of money that she made? Explain using examples.

ACADEMIC VOCABULARY

A **direct variation** is a relationship between two variables, x and y, with the form $y = kx$, where k is any constant other than zero.

If changing one variable in an equation by a factor causes the other variable to change by the same factor, the equation is a **direct variation** equation. Direct variation relationships describe many real-life situations. For example, to relate time and distance for a car traveling at 55 mi/h, you can use the equation $d = 55t$. If you drive one hour, you travel 55 miles. If you double the time and drive 2 hours, you travel 110 miles or twice as far.

8. Consider the equations for the number of hours that Janice works and the amount that she earns at each of her jobs. Which of these is a direct variation equation? Explain.

SUGGESTED LEARNING STRATEGIES: Create Representations, Look for a Pattern, Quickwrite

My Notes

You can recognize direct variation relationships in tables, graphs, and equations.

9. Create three representations for each situation: a table, a graph, and an equation. Do these in any order you choose.

   A. The number of middle schools is two times the number of high schools.

   B. The number of dogs is one more than two times the number of cats.

   C. The number of erasers is half the number of pencils.

Situation A		Situation B		Situation C	
x	*y*	*x*	*y*	*x*	*y*

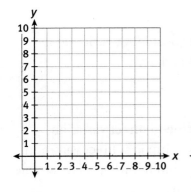 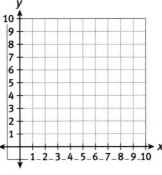 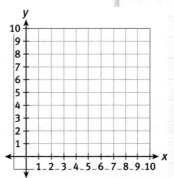

_____   _____   _____

10. Situations A and C are examples of direct variation.

   a. How do the tables for Situations A and C differ from the table for Situation B?

   b. How do the graphs for Situations A and C differ from the graph for Situation B?

My Notes

c. How do the equations for Situations A and C differ from the equation for Situation B?

Direct variation equations are written in the form $y = kx$.

11. The value k in the equation $y = kx$ is the **constant of variation**. This is also known as the rate of change. Solve for k in the equation $y = kx$.

MATH TERMS

In a direct variation equation, y varies directly as x. The ratio of y to x is the **constant of variation**.

12. Look back at the equations you wrote for Situations A and C in Item 9. Find the value of k for each equation.

13. Look back at the graphs you made for Situations A and C in Item 9. Find the slope for each line.

14. For Situations A and C, how are the constant of variation in the equation and the slope of the line related?

15. Decide whether each situation describes a direct variation. Explain your reasoning. If the relationship is a direct variation, write an equation in the form $y = kx$ and tell what each variable and the constant of variation represent.

    a. At a carnival Michael pays a $5.00 entrance fee and $1.50 for each ride.

    b. Janice eats 3 pieces of fruit each day.

    c. Janice pays $0.50 for each arcade game she plays.

SUGGESTED LEARNING STRATEGIES: Close Reading, Summarize/Paraphrase/Retell, Create Representations

Now explore some additional situations that are not direct variations.

Not all equations with two variables and a constant are direct variation equations. Two variables can vary inversely. Think again about driving a car. The distance equation $d = rt$ is a direct variation equation, but if you make the distance the constant, then when the rate increases, the time has to decrease. A driver who has to drive 500 miles could drive 20 hours at 25 mi/h or 10 hours at 50 mi/h. This kind of change is known as **inverse variation**.

The graphs of inverse variation equations are not straight lines, but are curves. You will learn more about inverse variation when you take an algebra course.

16. Here are two equations that represent inverse variation. Complete the following tables and graph each. What do you notice about the equations and the graphs?

A. $y = \dfrac{15}{x}$

B. $xy = 24$

Equation A	
x	**y**
3	
7.5	
10	

Equation B	
x	**y**
3	
4	
6	

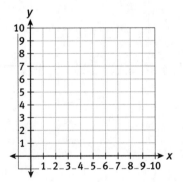

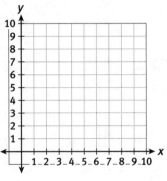

My Notes

MATH TERMS
An **inverse variation** is a relationship between two variables, *x* and *y*, with the form $xy = k$ or $y = \dfrac{k}{x}$, where *k* is any constant other than zero. Inverse variation is sometimes called indirect variation.

MATH TIP
If you cannot connect the three points with a straight line, try drawing a smooth curved line.

CONNECT TO AP
In later math courses, you will study nonlinear functions, such as the ones in Item 16, in more depth. Nonlinear functions do not have a constant rate of change.

My Notes

17. The table for an inverse variation will not contain the ordered pair (0, 0). Explain why this is so by using the form $y = \frac{k}{x}$.

Equations, such as $y = x^2$ and $y = x^3$, describe change and are curves. For equations like these, you can make tables and graphs to examine how they differ from linear equations.

18. Complete the input/output tables for each equation. Then graph the equation on the coordinate grid.

📱 **TECHNOLOGY TIP**

If a graphing calculator is available, use it to verify that the graphs you create are correct.

$y = 3x$	
x	y
−2	
−1	
0	
1	
2	
3	

$y = x^2$	
x	y
−3	
−2	
0	
1	
2	
3	

$y = x^3$	
x	y
−2	
−1	
0	
1	
1.5	
2	

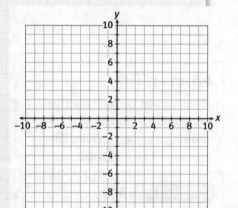
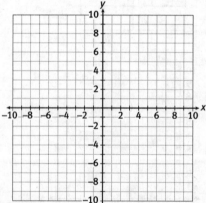
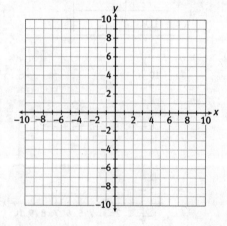

SUGGESTED LEARNING STRATEGIES: Look for a Pattern, Think/Pair/Share, Create Representations

19. Compare and contrast the equations, tables, and graphs in Item 18.

20. An architect is designing a new fitness center. The center will have eight equipment closets each with a square floor. To calculate the total floor area of the eight closets, the architect can use the equation $y = 8x^2$, where x is the side length in feet and y is the floor area in square feet.

a. Complete the input/output table for the architect.

$y = 8x^2$	x	2	4	6	8	10
	y					

b. Explain why you need only Quadrant 1 to graph the ordered pairs from the input/output table in Part a.

c. Graph the ordered pairs from Part a.

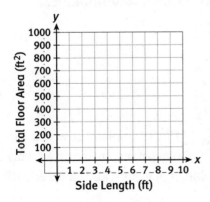

CONNECT TO AP

The operation of division by zero is called *undefined* because the operation does not make sense. In calculus, you will consider what happens when you divide something by smaller and smaller amounts without actually dividing by the number zero.

My Notes

d. Describe the graph in Part c. Tell whether it is linear, whether it has direct variation, inverse variation, or neither. Explain why the ordered pair (0, 0) would be on the graph.

e. The fitness center will have a total floor area of 50,000 square feet. The architect wants the eight equipment closets to take up less than 1% of the total area. To the nearest half foot, what can the side length of the closets be?

CHECK YOUR UNDERSTANDING

Write your answers on notebook paper or grid paper. Show your work.

Rickey is training to compete in a half marathon. He currently runs at a rate of 4.5 miles per hour.

1. Complete an input/output table that represents Rickey's distance for the amount of time he runs. Graph the data.

2. Write an equation that represents the relationship between time and distance.

3. Is the relationship in questions 1 and 2 an example of direct variation? Explain your answer.

4. Which of these graphs represent direct variation?

a.

b.

c.

5. Find the constant of variation for the function represented by the data in the table. Then write the equation that describes the relationship.

x	y
1	0.2
4	0.8
8	1.6
12	2.4

Determine what kind of change each equation represents. Explain your thinking.

6. $y = \dfrac{3}{x}$

7. $y = 3x - 3$

8. $y = 3x$

9. $y = 2x^2$

10. **MATHEMATICAL REFLECTION** Explain how you can recognize direct variation in a table, in a graph, and in an equation.

Inequalities and Direct Variation

PARKSIDE AMUSEMENTS

Write your answers on notebook paper. Show your work.

Betty, Tammy, and Shawn are spending the day at Parkside Amusements with their parents. As they arrive, they see that some of the rides have height restrictions. At the ticket counter, they get a brochure that lists the minimum heights for riding some rides and the maximum heights for other rides.

Ride	Minimum Height	Ride	Maximum Height
Roller Skater	36"	Rockin' Coaster	45"
Pin Ball Machine	48"	Mini-Ferris	36"
Bumper Cars	44"	Choo-Choo	42"
Sport Zoom	59"		
Slippery Slide	52"		
Bumper Boats	44"		
Astro Blazer	51"		

- Betty is 6 years old and is 3 feet, 7 inches tall.
- Tammy is 10 years old and is 4 feet tall.
- Shawn is 13 years old and is 4 feet, 8 inches tall.

1. On which rides can each sister go? Justify your selections.

2. Are there any rides on which none of the girls can go? Explain.

3. Betty, Tammy, and Shawn have been saving their allowances and together have no more than $51.00 to spend on ride tickets. Shawn saved three times as much as Betty and Tammy saved $5.00 more than Betty.

   a. Write and solve an inequality to determine how much money Betty has to spend on ride tickets.

   b. Graph the solution to the inequality.

4. An exhibit at the amusement park contains ice sculptures. The temperature of the exhibit hall must be kept between (−7)°C and 0°C. Write a compound inequality to show the required temperatures and then graph the inequality.

5. One section of the park was devoted to games of skill. It cost $3.00 for the first game, and then $2.00 for each game after that. Is this an example of direct variation? Explain.

	Exemplary	Proficient	Emerging
Math Knowledge #1, #2, #5	The student correctly: • Converts the heights to inches or the ride heights to feet and inches. (1) • Finds the rides that the sisters can ride. (1) • Finds the rides that the sisters cannot ride. (2) • Determines if a situation represents direct variation. (5).	The student accomplishes three of the four items correctly and completely.	The student is able to correctly and completely answer fewer than two items.
Problem Solving #3a	Student correctly: • Writes an inequality to determine the amount of money Betty can spend on rides. (3a) • Solves the inequality to determine the amount of money Betty can spend on rides. (3a)	The student either: • Writes a correct inequality and is unable to solve it, OR • Is able to solve an incorrectly formulated inequality that in some way reflects the situation.	The student is unable to correctly and completely accomplish either item.
Representation #3b, 4	The student correctly: • Graphs the solution to the inequality. (3b) • Graphs the compound inequality showing the required temperatures. (4)	The student is able to graph only one of the inequalities correctly and completely.	The student's graphs of the inequalities are neither correct nor complete.
Communication #1, 2, 5	The student correctly: • Justifies on which rides the sisters can go. (1) • Explains on which rides the sisters cannot go. (2) • Explains whether the "games of skill" price structure represents direct variation. (5)	The student's response is complete and correct for two of the items.	The student's response is complete and correct for only one of the items.

ACTIVITY 2.1

Mark and Sandy are participating in a Bike-a-Thon for charity. Mark oversleeps, so Sandy gets a one-hour head start and bikes at a speed of 12 miles per hour. To catch up to Sandy, Mark decides that he needs to bike at a speed of 15 miles per hour.

1. Make a chart that shows how far Mark and Sandy ride their bikes during the first three hours of the Bike-a-Thon.

2. Write an expression that represents Sandy's journey. Be sure to define your variables.

3. An expression that represents Mark's journey is $15(t - 1)$.

    a. What does the coefficient 15 describe?

    b. What does $(t - 1)$ represent?

4. Write and solve an equation to determine when Mark catches up to Sandy.

5. Describe in words, a situation involving Mark and Sandy that could be represented by the equation $4t + 8 = 3(3.5t)$.

The graph below gives information about Sam and Hannah, two participants in a Walk-a-Thon.

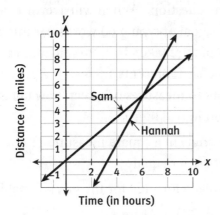

6. Which walker got a head start? How much of a head start did he (she) get?

7. Approximately how long did it take before Sam and Hannah had traveled the same distance? How far had they traveled?

8. Which walker was traveling at a faster rate? Explain how you know.

ACTIVITY 2.2

9. Solve and check each equation.

    a. $15n = 60$

    b. $n + 6 = 14$

    c. $3w - 2 = 10$

    d. $11 = 3 + 4x$

10. Sharon's club is selling greeting cards for a fundraiser. They will profit $3 for each box of cards that they sell. They are trying to raise $825. Write and solve an equation to answer how many boxes of greeting cards they sold to make a profit of $825.

11. Sam makes $400 per week plus a $20 commission on each insurance policy he sells. Write and solve an equation to determine how many policies he sold to earn $680.

12. Simplify each expression, if possible, by combining like terms. If not possible, write *simplified*.

    a. $24x + 2y + 7x$

    b. $5a - 2a$

    c. $8z - 3z^3 + 12z$

    d. $n^3 + 5n^3$

    e. $6b - 7b^2 - 13b^2$

    f. $8 + 4y - 3y^2 - 14$

    g. $9z - z - 3$

13. Solve and check each equation.

    a. $7x - 4x + 3 = -15$

    b. $12n - 8n - 6 = 62$

    c. $y - 3y + 5 = 17$

    d. $27 = 15a - 6a - 6a$

    e. $-4(x - 5) = 36$

    f. $18 = 6(b + 7)$

    g. $-3x + 5 = -2x$

14. Henry sold 8 more plants than Diane. Together they sold 56 plants. Write and solve an equation to answer these questions: How many plants did Diane sell? How many plants did Henry sell?

15. Ralph bought 5 times as many raffle tickets as Darlene. Lou bought 15 more raffle tickets that Darlene. Together they bought 120 raffle tickets. How many raffle tickets did each buy?

16. Bob sells DVD's by phone. He can have a base salary of $375 per week and $5 for each set of DVD's sold or $225 per week and $12 for each set of DVD's sold. Bob feels that he can sell an average of 25 sets of DVD's per week. Which option should Bob take? Explain.

ACTIVITY 2.3

17. Make an input/output table for this pattern and then graph the ordered pairs.

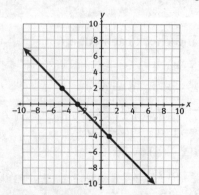

Figure 1   **Figure 2**   **Figure 3**

18. Plot the ordered pairs $(-4, 7)$, $(3, -7)$ on a coordinate grid and connect them. Find the change in y, the change in x, and the slope.

19. How does the slope of a line through the points $(9, 8)$ and $(2, 7)$ compare to the slope of a line through $(5, 9)$ and $(1, 5)$?

20. Find the change in y, the change in x, and the slope of the line shown on this graph.

21. Graph the function $y = -2x + 6$.

ACTIVITY 2.4

22. Jenna was late meeting Dan and Bruce at the start of the walkathon. When she arrived and called them, they were already at the 3-mile point in the 25-mile walk. She told them to continue walking and she would catch up.

    a. If they are walking at a rate of 0.05 miles/min and she jogs at a rate of 0.2 miles per minute, how long will it take her to catch up to them?

    b. How far from the start of the walkathon will they be when Jenna catches up?

23. To get a job as a receptionist you have to be able to type 60 words per minute. Trevor wanted to work as a receptionist for the summer so he was working on building up his typing speed. He made the following table to track his progress.

Week	0	1	2	3
Words/min	20	26	32	38

    a. If the pattern of progress shown in the table continues, how many words per minute will Trevor be able to type in 6 weeks?

    b. Write and solve an equation to answer the question, "When will Trevor reach his goal of typing 60 words per minute?"

24. On a picture taken by a surveillance camera 0.2 inches represents 1.5 feet. If a person in the photo measures 0.75 feet, how tall is the person in real life?

25. Each angle in a square measures $(124 - x)°$. What does x equal?

26. Solve each formula for the given variable.

    a. $K = 273 + C$, for C

    b. $E = mc^2$, for m

    c. $A = \frac{1}{2}bh$, for h

    d. $A = \frac{1}{2}h(b_1 + b_2)$, for b_1

27. Dana is 60 inches tall today and is growing at a rate of 0.7 inches each year. Her grandmother is 72 inches tall today and is shrinking at a rate of 0.1 inches each year. Let n equal the number of years from today.

   a. Write an equation that represents Dana's height, y, after n years.

   b. Write an equation that represents her grandmother's height, y, after n years.

   c. Graph the equations you found in parts a and b.

   d. Use the graph to predict when Dana and her grandmother will be the same height. Check your prediction by writing and solving an equation.

ACTIVITY 2.5

28. Write an inequality to describe each situation. Be sure to define your variable.

   a. You must be able to reach at least 6'10" to be a fight attendant.

   b. No one under 17 is admitted to see certain movies.

   c. There are at most 20 tickets left for the play.

   d. The maximum speed on the highway ranges from 55 mph through 75 mph.

29. Graph all solutions to each inequality.

   a. $x \geq 4$

   b. $-9 \leq y \leq -2$

   c. $x < 1$

   d. $x \leq -1$ or $x \geq 3$

30. Solve each inequality.

   a. $x - 5 \geq 3$

   b. $y + 1.4 > 3.8$

   c. $8 - \frac{1}{2}x > 5$

   d. $-0.2x + 1 \leq 5$

   e. $\frac{x}{-3} < \frac{2}{3}$

31. On an ocean dive Ricky wants to stay at least 5 m above his deepest previous depth of 40 m. Write and solve an inequality to find how long he can descend at a rate of 2 m/min. Be sure to define the variable.

ACTIVITY 2.6

Kwame can type 25 words per minute. Complete an input/output table that represents the speed at which Kwame can type and then graph the data.

32. Write an equation that represents the relationship between the number of words Kwame can type and his typing speed.

33. Does the relationship in question 32 represent direct variation? Explain your answer.

34. Sketch a graph that represents direct variation.

35. Sketch a graph that does not represent a direct variation.

36. Does this input/output table represent a direct variation? Show your work.

x	y
4	7
6	8
9	11
12	14

Reflection

An important aspect of growing as a learner is to take the time to reflect on your learning. It is important to think about where you started, what you have accomplished, what helped you learn, and how you will apply your new knowledge in the future. Use notebook paper to record your thinking on the following topics and to identify evidence of your learning.

Essential Questions

1. Review the mathematical concepts and your work in this unit before you write thoughtful responses to the questions below. Support your responses with specific examples from concepts and activities in the unit.

   - Why is it important to understand how to solve linear equations and inequalities?

   - How can graphs be used to interpret solutions of real world problems?

Academic Vocabulary

2. Look at the following academic vocabulary words:

   - direct variation
   - like terms
   - function
   - open sentence
   - inequality

   Choose three words and explain your understanding of each word and why each is important in your study of math.

Self-Evaluation

3. Look through the activities and Embedded Assessments in this unit. Use a table similar to the one below to list three major concepts in this unit and to rate your understanding of each.

Unit Concepts	Is Your Understanding Strong (S) or Weak (W)?
Concept 1	
Concept 2	
Concept 3	

   a. What will you do to address each weakness?

   b. What strategies or class activities were particularly helpful in learning the concepts you identified as strengths? Give examples to explain.

4. How do the concepts you learned in this unit relate to other math concepts and to the use of mathematics in the real world?

1. Which words best describe the kind of change represented by this equation?

   $$y = \frac{k}{x}$$

   F. direct variation   **H.** inverse variation

   G. exponential change   **I.** linear relationship

1. Ⓕ Ⓖ Ⓗ Ⓘ

2. What is the solution to the equation $-10x + 8 = 7x + 12$?

2.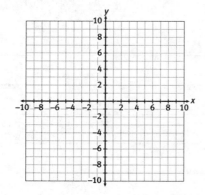

Read
Solve
Explain

3. Given the equation $y = -\frac{x}{2} + 5$.

   Part A: Make an input/output table. Explain why you chose the x values.

x	y

   Answer and Explain

   _____

   _____

   _____

   Part B: Graph the equation.

Read

Solve

Explain

4. Four friends went out together for dinner. They always share the bill equally when they go out. The total dinner bill was $78.00. They were happy with the service and decided to give a 20% tip to the waiter.

Part A: Write and solve an equation to find what each friend will pay for dinner and tip. Give your answer to the nearest half dollar and to the nearest whole dollar.

Answer and Explain

_____

_____

Part B: The next time the friends went to that restaurant, they all ordered the same meals as the time before, but there had been a 10% increase in prices. Their service was very slow and the waiter was surly, so they decided to leave only a 10% tip. What was the total cost of the dinner bill including the tip and **how much more** will each person pay then they paid the first time? (**needed to the nearest cent**). Show your work or explain in words how you found your answer. (rounded to the nearest cent).

Answer and Explain

_____

_____

_____

_____

Part C: One of the friends, Wonlce, thought the total bill for the second visit would be exactly the same as the total bill for the first visit. He used the formula: Total Bill: 1.2(78) to determine the total bill plus the tip. Explain whether his reasoning was correct and justify your thinking.

Answer and Explain

_____

_____

_____

_____

_____

Two-Dimensional Geometry and Similarity

Unit Overview

In this unit you will write general statements that define and relate two-dimensional figures. You will extend your knowledge of relationships between angles and two-dimensional figures. You will develop and apply similarity relationships, use the Pythagorean theorem, and explore other indirect measurement methods to solve problems.

Academic Vocabulary

As you work through this unit, add these terms and others you think are important to your vocabulary notebook.

- angle
- coordinate plane
- polygon
- Pythagorean Theorem
- ratio

Essential Questions

? Why is it important to understand properties of angles and figures to solve problems?

? How can diagrams be used to interpret solutions to real world problems?

EMBEDDED ASSESSMENTS

These assessments, following activities 3.3, 3.5, and 3.10, will give you an opportunity to demonstrate your understanding of area and perimeter of figures, measures of angles, transformations, ratios and rates, measurement conversions, similar figures, and the Pythagorean Theorem and apply this knowledge to real word problems.

Write your answers on notebook paper or grid paper. Show your work.

1. Compare and contrast the terms *complementary* and *supplementary* when referring to angles.

2. Think about triangles.
   a. List three ways to classify triangles by side length.
   b. List four ways to classify triangles by angle measure.

3. Polygons are named by the number of sides they have. Give the names of four different polygons.

4. Evaluate each expression.
   a. $\frac{1}{2}(9)(6.5)$
   b. $\sqrt{81}$
   c. $\sqrt{45}$ (Round to the nearest tenth.)

5. Use the Property of One to name a fraction that is equivalent to $\frac{3}{4}$.

6. Use a ruler to draw a segment that is 3 centimeters long.

7. Write an expression that can be used to determine the area of each figure.
   a. Circle
   b. Trapezoid
   c. Parallelogram
   d. Triangle

8. Use a protractor to determine the measure of the angle below.

9. Copy the grid below.
   a. Give the coordinates of point A.
   b. Plot the points $B(-2, 3)$ and $C(4, -1)$.

   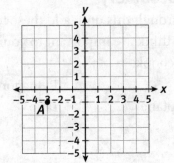

Angle Pairs
What's Your Angle?

SUGGESTED LEARNING STRATEGIES: Think/Pair/Share, Use Manipulatives

Two rays with a common endpoint form an **angle**. The common endpoint is called the vertex. You can use a protractor to draw and measure angles in degrees.

1. Angles can be classified by their measures. Name the three classifications and then draw an example of each.

2. Measure each angle and classify it according to its measure.

a.

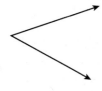

b.

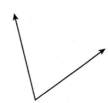

c.

d.

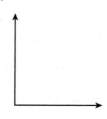

e.

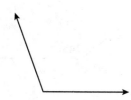

My Notes

ACADEMIC VOCABULARY

angle

> **READING MATH**
>
>
>
> To read this angle, say "angle *ABC*," "angle *CBA*," or "angle *B*."

My Notes

Angles can be paired in many ways.

3. Compare and contrast complementary and supplementary
angles.

4. Name pairs of angles that form complementary or
supplementary angles. Justify you choices.

a.

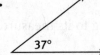

b.

c.

d.

e.

f.

g.

h.

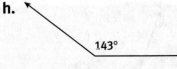

SUGGESTED LEARNING STRATEGIES: Think/Pair/Share, Group Presentation, Quickwrite, Work Backward, Create Representations

My Notes

5. Why are angles 1 and 2 in this diagram complementary?

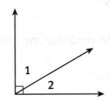

> **MATH TERMS**
>
> In Items 5 and 6, angles 1 and 2 are examples of adjacent angles. **Adjacent angles** have a common side but no common interior.

6. Why are angles 1 and 2 in this diagram supplementary?

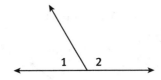

7. Can two obtuse angles be supplementary? Explain your reasoning.

8. Give the complement and supplement, if possible, of an angle that measures 32°.

9. Give the complement and supplement, if possible, of an angle that measures 98°.

10. Two angles are complementary. One measures $(2x)°$ and the other measures 48°.

   a. Write an equation to find the measure of the missing angle.

   b. Solve the equation for x.

   c. What is the value of the other angle? Show your work.

SUGGESTED LEARNING STRATEGIES: Create
Representations, Use Manipulatives, Think/Pair/Share,
Quickwrite

11. Two angles are supplementary. One angle measures $(3x)°$ and
the other measures $123°$.

   a. Write an equation to find the measure of the missing angle.

   b. Solve the equation for x.

   c. What is the measure of the other angle? Show your work.

MATH TERMS
Vertical angles share a vertex
but have no common rays.

Vertical angles are formed when two lines intersect.

12. $\angle 1$ and $\angle 3$ are vertical angles. Find the measure of each angle
using your protractor.

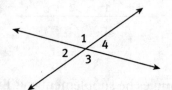

MATH TIP
It may be easier to measure the
angles if you extend the rays.

13. Name another pair of vertical angles and find the measure
of each angle.

14. What conjectures can you make about the measures of a pair
of vertical angles?

When two parallel lines are cut by a transversal, eight angles
are formed.

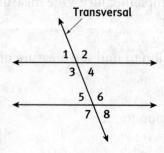

SUGGESTED LEARNING STRATEGIES: Quickwrite, Group Presentation, Think/Pair/Share

My Notes

Use the drawing of parallel lines cut by a transversal on page 154.

15. ∠4 and ∠8 are **corresponding angles**.

  a. Why do you think that they are called corresponding angles?

  b. Measure angles 4 and 8. $m\angle 4 =$ $m\angle 8 =$

  c. Name three more pairs of corresponding angles and give their measures.

  d. What conjectures can you make about pairs of corresponding angles formed when parallel lines are cut by a transversal?

16. ∠3 and ∠6 are **alternate interior angles**.

  a. Why are they called alternate interior angles?

  b. Measure angles 3 and 6. $m\angle 3 =$ $m\angle 6 =$

  c. Name another pair of alternate interior angles and give their measures.

  d. What conjectures can you make about pairs of alternate interior angles formed when parallel lines are cut by a transversal?

17. ∠2 and ∠7 are **alternate exterior angles**.

  a. Why are they called alternate exterior angles?

  b. Measure angles 2 and 7. $m\angle 2 =$ $m\angle 7 =$

  c. Name another pair of alternate exterior angles and give their measures.

  d. What can you conclude about pairs of alternate exterior angles formed when parallel lines are cut by a transversal?

My Notes

18. In Figure A, two parallel lines are cut by a transversal. The measure of ∠1 = 42°. Find $m∠2$ and describe the relationship that helped you determine the measure.

Figure A

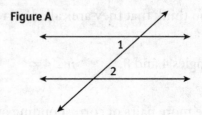

19. In Figure B, two parallel lines are cut by a transversal. The measure of ∠1 = 138°. Find $m∠2$ and describe the relationship that helped you determine the measure.

Figure B

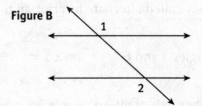

20. In Figure C, two parallel lines are cut by a transversal. The measure of ∠1 = 57°. Find $m∠2$ and describe the relationship that helped you determine the measure.

Figure C

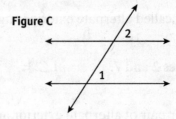

SUGGESTED LEARNING STRATEGIES: Group Presentation

My Notes

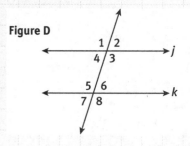

Figure D

Use the work you did and the conjectures you made in Questions 14–17 to help answer Questions 21 and 22.

21. In Figure D, lines *j* and *k* are parallel and are cut by a transversal. The measure of ∠4 = 72°. Give the measures of the remaining seven angles. Justify your answers.

Angle	Measure	Explanation
1		
2		
3		
4	72°	Given.
5		
6		
7		
8		

22. Find an angle pair that supports your conjecture about each type of angle pair.

   a. Vertical angles

   b. Corresponding angles

   c. Alternate interior angles

   d. Alternate exterior angles

23. Think about things, such as buildings, bridges, billboards, and bicycles, which you see all around you. Describe examples of angle pairs and angle relationships that you can observe in such everyday objects.

CHECK YOUR UNDERSTANDING

Write your answers on notebook paper.
Show your work.

1. Find the complement and/or supplement of each angle.

   a. 32°

   b. 113°

2. Find the measure of angle 1. Explain how you found your answer.

   a.

   b.

3. ∠TUV and ∠MNO are supplementary. $m\angle TUV = 75°$ and $m\angle MNO = (5x)°$. Find the measure of ∠MNO. Show your work.

4. Find the measure of ∠1, ∠2, and ∠3. Explain how you found each measure.

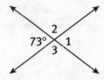

Two parallel lines are cut by a transversal as shown below.

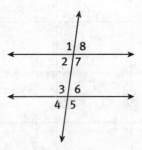

5. Find each measure if $m\angle 8 = 82°$.

   a. Find $m\angle 3$. Explain your answer.

   b. Find $m\angle 7$. Explain your answer.

   c. Find $m\angle 5$. Explain your answer.

6. **MATHEMATICAL REFLECTION** Suppose that a transversal intersects two lines that are **not** parallel. Do you think that the angle pairs that you studied in this activity would still be congruent? Justify your answer.

Two-Dimensional Figures
Plane Shapes

SUGGESTED LEARNING STRATEGIES: Activating Prior Knowledge

Each year the students in Mr. Klein's classes create a stained glass project when they finish the geometry unit. They create designs for their stained glass with **two-dimensional** figures. This drawing shows the design for one of the projects done last year.

1. Name the figures that you see in the design. Describe one attribute for each shape.

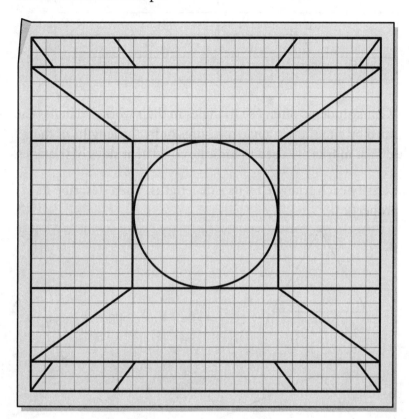

My Notes

READING MATH

A **two-dimensional** figure lies in a plane, which can be thought of as a flat surface.

My Notes

ACADEMIC VOCABULARY

A polygon is a closed figure formed by three or more line segments that intersect only at their endpoints. The word polygon comes from the Greek *polus* which means "many" and *gonia* which means "angle."

MATH TERMS

Tick marks indicate when line segments are congruent.

2. The name of a **polygon** tells the number of sides it has. Complete this table with the names of some polygons.

Number of Sides	Name of Polygon
3	
4	
5	
6	
7	
8	

Mr. Klein's students often use triangles in their work. Triangles can be classified by either their angle measures or by the lengths of their sides. **Tick marks** are used to indicate congruent sides of triangles.

3. Classify each triangle by its side lengths. Then describe its properties.

a.

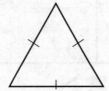

b.

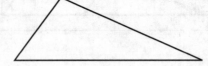

c.

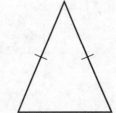

SUGGESTED LEARNING STRATEGIES: Use Manipulatives, Discussion Group

My Notes

4. Classify each triangle by its angle measures. Then describe its properties. You may measure the angles with your protractor.

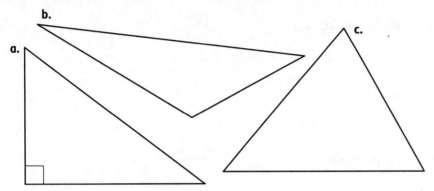

5. Use a ruler and protractor. Draw an isosceles triangle that has two equal sides with measures of 6 centimeters and an angle with a measure of 30°. Is there only one triangle that meets these conditions? Explain.

6. Another shape that students use in the stained glass designs is a quadrilateral.

a. Parallelogram   b. Trapezoid

c. Rectangle   d. Rhombus   e. Square

For each attribute, write the letter of the quadrilateral to which it applies. More than one letter may be listed for each attribute.

Attribute	Quadrilateral
Both pairs of opposite sides are parallel.	
Both pairs of opposite sides are congruent.	
All sides are congruent.	
Exactly one pair of parallel sides.	
Four right angles.	

SUGGESTED LEARNING STRATEGIES: Group Presentation, Quickwrite, Create Representations

My Notes

7. Use your work from Question 6 to write the best definition of each quadrilateral.

    a. Parallelogram

    b. Trapezoid

    c. Rectangle

    d. Rhombus

    e. Square

8. Compare and contrast the circumference of a circle to the perimeter of a polygon.

MATH TIP

The base and height of a figure are perpendicular to each other. Perpendicular lines meet to form right angles.

Find the distance around and area of each two-dimensional figure. Choose the appropriate formula. Show your work.

$$A = bh \quad A = \pi r^2 \quad A = lw \quad A = \frac{1}{2}h(b_1 + b_2) \quad A = s^2 \quad A = \frac{1}{2}bh$$
$$P = 2l + 2w \quad C = \pi d \quad C = 2\pi r \quad P = 4s$$

MATH TIP

The value of π is approximately 3.14. When reporting the area or circumference of a circle, use the "approximately equal to" symbol: $\sim$.

9.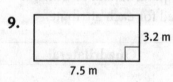
3.2 m
7.5 m

10.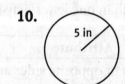
5 in

Two-Dimensional Figures
Plane Shapes

SUGGESTED LEARNING STRATEGIES: Create Representations, Simplify the Problem, Think/Pair/Share

My Notes

11.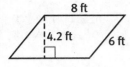

12.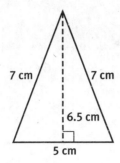

13.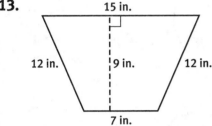

14.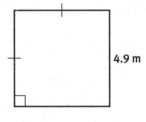

Some shapes that students used in their stained glass designs do not have their own formulas for area and perimeter. To find their areas and perimeters, the students divided these figures into simpler geometric shapes for which they knew the formulas.

Find the area and perimeter of each **composite figure**. Show your work. Label your answers with the appropriate unit of measure.

MATH TERMS

A **composite figure** is made up of two or more geometric figures.

15.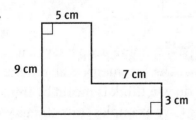

16.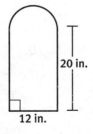

17. A student dropped a piece of stained glass. One fragment had the shape shown to the right. Estimate the area of the fragment if each square on the grid represents 2 cm².

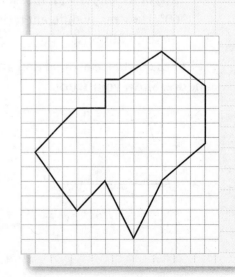

CHECK YOUR UNDERSTANDING

Write your answers on notebook paper.
Show your work.

1. Classify each triangle by its angle measures.

   a. 32°, 58°, 90°

   b. 15°, 45°, 120°

   c. 30°, 75°, 75°

2. Classify each triangle by the lengths of its sides.

   a. 12, 15, 24

   b. 5, 8, 8

   c. 12, 12, 12

3. Give the most accurate name for a figure with the given attributes. Then draw an example of each figure.

   a. A parallelogram with four congruent sides.

   b. A quadrilateral with exactly one pair of parallel sides.

   c. A polygon with eight sides.

4. Use a ruler and protractor to draw a triangle with one side measuring 5 cm and two of its angles with measures of 30° and 60°. How many different triangles meet these conditions?

Find the distance around and area of each figure. Show your work.

5.

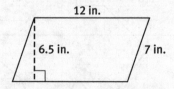

6.

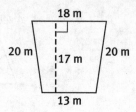

7.

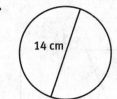

8.

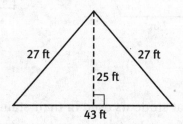

9.

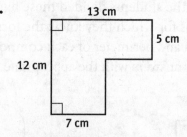

10. MATHEMATICAL REFLECTION Some people say that "geometry is all around us." What do you think is meant by this statement? Give examples from things you see every day to support your answer.

Angles of Polygons
Some Sums

ACTIVITY
3.3

SUGGESTED LEARNING STRATEGIES: Think/Pair/Share

My Notes

Some polygons are **convex** polygons and some are **concave** polygons.

1. Quadrilateral A is convex, and Quadrilateral B is not convex.

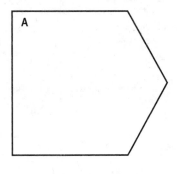
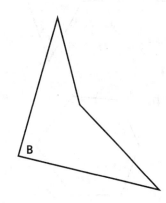

a. Use a colored pencil and ruler to extend each side of Quadrilaterals A and B.

b. Compare and contrast the lines that you drew in Part a.

c. Explain how to tell the difference between a convex polygon and a concave polygon.

My Notes

2. Determine whether each polygon is convex or concave. Justify your answers.

a.

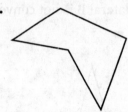

b.

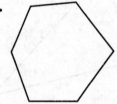

c.

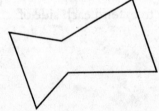

Now you will explore some relationships of the interior angles of convex polygons.

3. Begin with triangles. Of all convex polygons, triangles have the least number of sides.

a. Find the sum of the measures of the angles in each triangle.

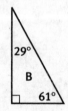
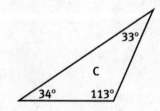

b. What do the sums have in common?

My Notes

4. Now consider quadrilaterals.

   a. Draw a *diagonal* from one vertex in each quadrilateral.

> **MATH TERMS**
> A *diagonal* of a polygon is a line segment connecting two vertices that are not adjacent to each other.

5. Look at the quadrilaterals with their diagonals in Question 4.

   a. Complete this sentence:

   If the sum of the measures of the interior angles in *one* triangle is ____, then the sum of the measures of the interior angles in *two* triangles is ____.

   b. What is the sum of the measures of the interior angles in any quadrilateral?

6. Find the measure of the unknown angle in Quadrilateral Q.

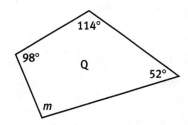

7. Now look at pentagons.

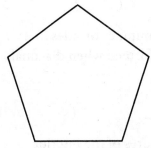 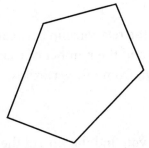

   a. Draw all possible diagonals from one vertex in each pentagon.

   b. How many triangles are formed by drawing all possible diagonals from one vertex in each pentagon?

My Notes

7. *(continued)*

c. Complete this sentence:

If the sum of the measures of the interior angles in one triangle is _____ then the sum of the measures of the interior angles in _____ triangles is _____.

d. What is the sum of the measures of the interior angles of any pentagon?

8. Find the measure of the unknown angle in Pentagon P.

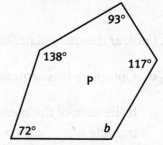

9. Draw a convex hexagon and use diagonals to determine the sum of the measures of its interior angles. Show your work.

10. What is the relationship between the number of sides in a polygon and the number of triangles formed when diagonals are drawn from one vertex?

11. How do you find the sum of the measures of the interior angles of any convex polygon?

Angles of Polygons
Some Sums

SUGGESTED LEARNING STRATEGIES: Create Representations, Group Presentation

Find the measure of the unknown interior angle in each polygon. Show your work.

12.

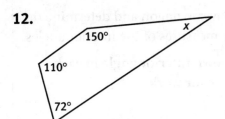

13.

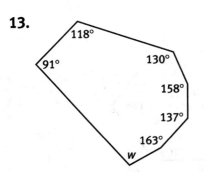

14. The home plate for a baseball and a softball diamond is in the shape of a pentagon. It has three right angles and two other congruent angles. Find the measure of each of the congruent angles.

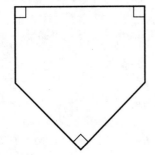

CHECK YOUR UNDERSTANDING

Write your answers on notebook paper.
Show your work.

Determine whether each polygon is convex.
Justify your answers.

1.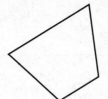

2.

3. Draw a convex heptagon. Then draw all
possible diagonals from one vertex.

   a. How many triangles are formed?

   b. What is the sum of the measures of the
interior angles of a heptagon? Explain
your answer.

4. Find the unknown angle. Show your work.

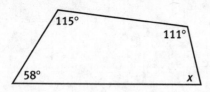

5. Draw a convex octagon and determine the
sum of the measures of the interior angles.

Find the unknown interior angle in each
polygon. Show your work.

6.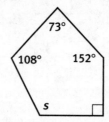

7.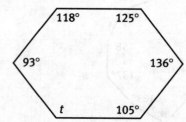

8. **MATHEMATICAL REFLECTION** Look around to find
examples of convex and
concave polygons. Describe each example
and determine the type of polygon.

Polygons

STAINED GLASS DESIGNS

1. Caleb, a graphic artist, sketched the design to the right on a piece of grid paper. Each square on his grid is 1 cm by 1 cm. Use his design to answer Question 1. Show your work and include appropriate units in your answers.

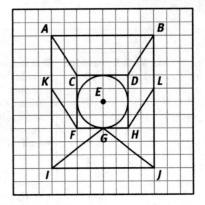

    a. Find the area of parallelogram *ACFK*.

    b. Find the area of triangle *IGJ*.

    c. Find the area and circumference of circle *E*.

    d. Find the area of trapezoid *ABDC*.

    e. Find the area and perimeter of square *CDHF*.

2. Two parallel lines, *MN* and *OP*, are cut by a transversal, *QT*, and $m\angle QSO = 39°$. Find each angle measure, and explain how you found the measure.

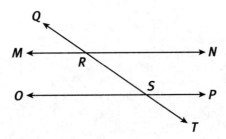

    a. $m\angle NRT$ **b.** $m\angle OST$ **c.** $m\angle PST$

3. Find the measure of the unknown angle in this polygon. Show your work.

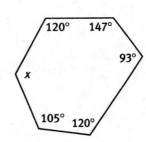

	Exemplary	Proficient	Emerging
Math Knowledge 1a–e, 2a–c, 3	The student: • Finds the correct areas of parallelogram *ACFK*, triangle *IGJ*, circle *E*, trapezoid *ABDC*, and square *CDHF*. (1a–e) • Finds the correct circumference of circle *E* and the perimeter of square *CDHF*. (1c, e) • Finds the correct measure of angles *NRT*, *OST*, and *PST*. (2a–c) • Finds the correct measure of angle *x*. (3)	The student: • Finds the correct areas of three or four of the figures. • Finds only one of the correct measurements. • Finds the correct measure of only two of the angles. • Uses a correct method to find the measure but makes a computational error.	The student: • Finds the correct areas for fewer than three of the figures. • Finds neither of the correct measurements. • Finds the correct measure of fewer than two of the angles. • Shows evidence of a misconception when trying to find the angle measure.
Communication 2a–c, 3	The student: • Gives an explanation of a correct method of finding the angle measures. (2a–c) • Shows correct work for finding the measure of angle *x*. (3)	The student: • Gives an explanation of a correct method of finding some but not all of the angle measures. • Shows some correct work and no incorrect work for finding the angle measure.	The student: • Gives incorrect explanations for finding the angles. • Shows incorrect work for finding the angle measure.

Exploring Transformations
Movin' On

SUGGESTED LEARNING STRATEGIES: Quickwrite, Create
Representations

Transformations—rotations, reflections, and translations—allow
you to change the position of a figure.

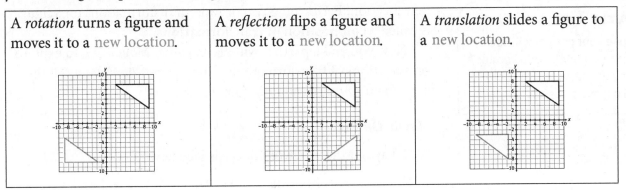

| A *rotation* turns a figure and moves it to a new location. | A *reflection* flips a figure and moves it to a new location. | A *translation* slides a figure to a new location. |

1. Draw each triangle on the **coordinate plane**. Then follow
   the instructions in the table to transform it. Record its new
   coordinates, plot them on the grid, and draw the new triangle.
   Identify and record the transformation.

Triangle ABC	A(1, 4)	B(3, 4)	C(3, 7)	**Transformation**
Switch x- and y-coordinates.				
Triangle DEF	D(−3, 1)	E(−1, 1)	F(−3, −3)	**Transformation**
Add 4 to the y-coordinate.				
Triangle GHI	G(1, 2)	H(3, 2)	I(1, 0)	**Transformation**
Take the opposite of the y-coordinate.				
Triangle JKL	J(−1, 6)	K(−6, 6)	L(−6, 5)	**Transformation**
Take the opposite of the y-coordinate and switch the x- and y-coordinates.				
Add 5 to the x-coordinate.				

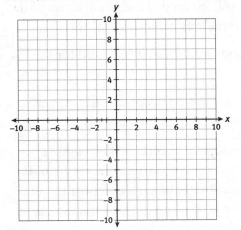

ACADEMIC VOCABULARY

A **coordinate plane** is a
two-dimensional system
for graphing ordered pairs
formed by two perpendicular
number lines intersecting
at their zero points creating
four quadrants.

My Notes

> **MATH TIP**
>
> You and your partner will use only one set of *Movin' On* cards to play the game but you both need a game piece.

You performed two transformations on triangle *JKL*. You moved it from its original position and then you moved it again from the new location. Performing two or more transformations on a figure is called a **composition of transformations**.

Now you and a partner will play a game, *Movin' On*, to explore compositions of transformations. Go to page 179 and cut out the five *Movin' On* cards and one game piece.

Movin' On Rules

1. Lay out the 5 *Movin' On* cards face down.

2. Take turns choosing a *Movin' On* card. You will each take 2 cards. The extra card may be used later as a tiebreaker.

3. Working independently, each of you will use your *Movin' On* cards to complete the two game sheets on page 175.

4. To complete the first game sheet, follow these steps:

   - Record the number of one of your *Movin' On* cards on your game sheet. You may use either one first.

   - Plot and label the points for Position 0 on the grid. Then use those points as the vertices to draw a triangle.

   - Follow the directions on the *Movin' On* card to find the coordinates of the vertices for Position 1.

   - Record the new coordinates on your game sheet, plot the new points on the grid, and draw a triangle.

   - Use your game piece to identify the transformation you made and record its name on your game sheet.

   - Continue until you have moved the figure to all 5 positions on the *Movin' On* card. Then record the coordinates of the *composition of transformations*, which is Position 5.

5. Repeat the process with your other *Movin' On* card for the second game sheet.

6. When you and your partner have completed your two cards, exchange game sheets and check each other's work.

7. Your teacher will score your game sheets. You will get 2 points for each transformation you correctly identify and 5 points for the correct coordinates of each composition of transformations. The player with more points wins the game.

Movin' On **Game Sheets**   **Player:** _____

Movin' On **Card:** _____

Position 0: A( ), B( ), C( )	Type of Transformation
Position 1: A( ), B( ), C( )	
Position 2: A( ), B( ), C( )	
Position 3: A( ), B( ), C( )	
Position 4: A( ), B( ), C ( )	
Position 5: A( ), B( ), C( )	

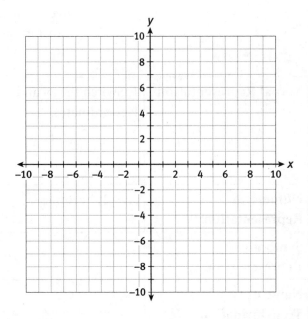

Composition of Transformations:
A(   ), *B*(   ), *C*(   )

Points Earned for *Movin' On* Card: _____

Movin' On **Card:** _____

Position 0: A( ), B( ), C( )	Type of Transformation
Position 1: A( ), B( ), C( )	
Position 2: A( ), B( ), C( )	
Position 3: A( ), B( ), C( )	
Position 4: A( ), B( ), C( )	
Position 5: A( ), B( ), C( )	

Composition of Transformations:
A(   ), *B*(   ), *C*(   )

Points Earned for *Movin' On* Card: _____
Total Points for Game: _____

Transformations, such as translations, rotations, and reflections,

My Notes

SUGGESTED LEARNING STRATEGIES: Create
Representations

can be represented verbally, numerically, and symbolically.

EXAMPLE 1

Use (1, −2) as the starting point and show the representations for
two transformations.

Transformation 1

Verbal representation: Subtract the *x*-coordinate from 4.
Numerical representation: (1, −2) becomes (3, −2)
Symbolic representation: (*x*, *y*) → (4 − *x*, *y*).
Transformation: This move results in a reflection.

Transformation 2

Verbal representation: Take the opposite of the *x*-coordinate and
then switch the *x*- and *y*-coordinates.
Numerical representation: (1, −2) becomes (−2, −1)
Symbolic representation: (*x*, *y*) → (*y*, −*x*).
Transformation: This move results in a rotation.

TRY THESE A

For each verbal representation, use the point (1, −2) as the starting
point and write a numerical representation of the move. Then
give the symbolic representation of the move and identify the
transformation that took place.

Verbal Representation	1. Switch the *x*- and *y*-coordinates.	2. Add 5 to the *x*-coordinate.	3. Take the opposite of the *x*- and the *y*-coordinates and switch the *x*- and the *y*-coordinates.
Numerical Representation	(1,−2) becomes	(1, −2) becomes	(1, −2) becomes
Symbolic Representation			
Name of Transformation			

SUGGESTED LEARNING STRATEGIES: Quickwrite, Think/Pair/Share, Look for a Pattern, Debriefing

My Notes

2. Work with your partner to discover a composition of transformations that has the same result as one from the *Movin' On* game but takes fewer transformations.

   a. Choose any *Movin' On* game card.

   b. Follow the instructions on the card and use the grid to draw the locations of Position 0 and Position 5.

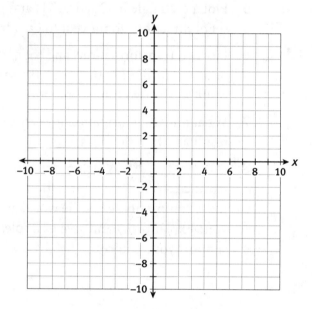

   c. Use what you know about reflections, translations, and rotations to move the game piece from Position 0 to Position 5 in 4 or fewer steps.

   d. Write the directions for the moves you found in Part c on a sheet of paper. Then trade directions with your partner and follow each other's directions to see whether the new transformation is correct.

3. What were some of the patterns you noticed about the verbal representations and the transformations they produced?

CHECK YOUR UNDERSTANDING

Write your answers on notebook paper or grid paper. Show your work.

Write the composition of transformations to move Shape A to the location of Shape B.

1.

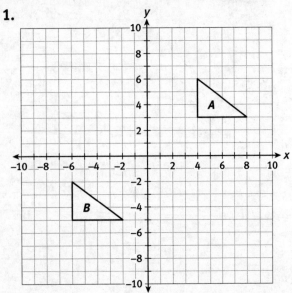

2.

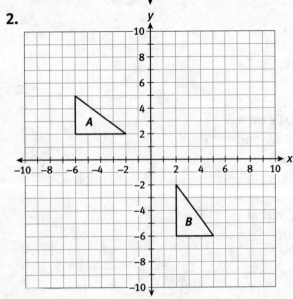

3. Plot a triangle in Quadrant III and give directions to move it to Quadrant I.

4. Plot a square in Quadrant I and give directions to move it to Quadrant IV.

5. Plot a rectangle in Quadrant II and give a set of directions to move it to Quadrant I.

6. List two transformations and then name one transformation that gives the same result as the two transformations.

7. What one transformation gives the same result as two reflections?

8. **MATHEMATICAL REFLECTION** Which of the three transformations do you most commonly see in the world around you? Explain why and give examples to support your choice.

Movin' On Game Cards

Movin' On Card 1	*Movin' On* Card 2	*Movin' On* Card 3
Position 0: $A(3, 4)$, $B(3, 1)$, $C(7, 1)$	**Position 0:** $A(1, 1)$ $B(1, -2)$ $C(5, -2)$	**Position 0:** $A(-5, 0)$ $B(-5, -3)$ $C(-1, -3)$
Position 1: Multiply x-coordinates by -1.	**Position 1:** Add 2 to each x-coordinate.	**Position 1:** Multiply y-coordinates by -1; switch x- and y-coordinates.
Position 2: Add 3 to each x-coordinate and 4 to each y-coordinate.	**Position 2:** Multiply x-coordinates by -1.	**Position 2:** Multiply x-coordinates by -1.
Position 3: Multiply y-coordinates by -1.	**Position 3:** Subtract each y-coordinate from 4.	**Position 3:** Subtract each x-coordinate from -6.
Position 4: Add -1 to each x-coordinate.	**Position 4:** Multiply y-coordinates by -1; switch x- and y-coordinates.	**Position 4:** Add 3 to each x-coordinate and 4 to each y-coordinate.
Position 5: Multiply y-coordinates by -1; switch x- and y- coordinates.	**Position 5:** Add -1 to each x-coordinate.	**Position 5:** Multiply y-coordinates by -1; switch x- and y-coordinates.

Movin' On Card 4	*Movin' On* Card 5	**Game Pieces**
Position 0: $A(-3, -4)$ $B(-3, --7)$ $C(1, -7)$	**Position 0:** $A(0, -1)$ $B(0, -4)$ $C(4, -4)$	Cut out one game piece. Use another one if you lose it.
Position 1: Multiply x-coordinates by -1.	**Position 1:** Multiply x-coordinates by -1; switch x- and y-coordinates.	
Position 2: Add 5 to each x-coordinate.	**Position 2:** Subtract each y-coordinate from 2.	
Position 3: Add 2 to each x-coordinate and -1 to each y-coordinate.	**Position 3:** Multiply y-coordinates by -1.	
Position 4: Subtract each x-coordinate from 4.	**Position 4:** Add 2 to each x-coordinate.	
Position 5: Add 2 to each x-coordinate and 3 to each y-coordinate.	**Position 5:** Multiply y-coordinates by -1.	

My Notes

Transformations
Changing Evergreen Park

SUGGESTED LEARNING STRATEGIES: KWL, Activating
Prior Knowledge, Create Representations

My Notes

The Westfield Public Works Department is going to build a social center, a children's center, a greenhouse, and an office with a cafeteria in Evergreen Park. The staff is deciding where to lay out these new buildings in the park. Kent Reed, the city civil engineer, had some ideas about where to place the buildings. He decided to model his layout on a coordinate grid.

Kent placed the center of the park at the origin with coordinates of (0, 0). The *x*-axis runs east west through the park and the *y*-axis runs north south through the park. Kent sketched three buildings on the grid. These sketches are a bird's-eye view of the buildings.

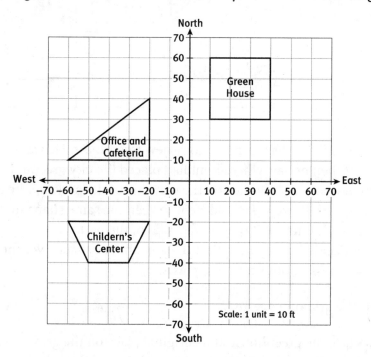

1. Kent needs to place the social center in his layout.

  a. Plot the points $J(10, -10)$, $P(10, -50)$, $T(40, -50)$, and $Z(40, -10)$.

  b. Then connect the points in order with line segments to form a bird's-eye view of the social center. Be sure to label it.

My Notes

Kent knew that he could use his layout on the coordinate grid to determine the area of each figure and its dimensions.

2. Use the grid on Kent's layout to complete this table of dimensions for the new buildings. Give your answers in units.

Building	Base	Height	Area
Greenhouse			
Office and Cafeteria			
Children's Center	Base 1: Base 2:		
Social Center			

Kent's boss, Tom Silver, came in to review the project. He was unhappy when he saw where Kent had placed the city greenhouse because it was near his office on the east side of the park and he is very allergic to flowers. He told Kent to keep the same shape for the greenhouse, but to put it on the west side of the park.

Kent decided he would reflect the greenhouse shape over the north-south line of the park, the *y*-axis.

3. Use the grid on page 183.

   a. Place the greenhouse at its original place on the grid: *F*(40, 30), *L*(40, 60), *W*(10, 30), and *R*(10, 60).

   b. Reflect the shape of the building across the *y*-axis.

   c. Which point is the **image** of point *F*? Label it *F′*.

   d. What are the coordinates of the remaining vertices of the image? Label them as *L′*, *W′* and *R′*.

MATH TERMS

The **image** of a figure is its position after a transformation. A prime symbol (′) is placed after the letter for the original point to show that the new point is its image.

Example: point *A′* is the image of point *A*.

My Notes

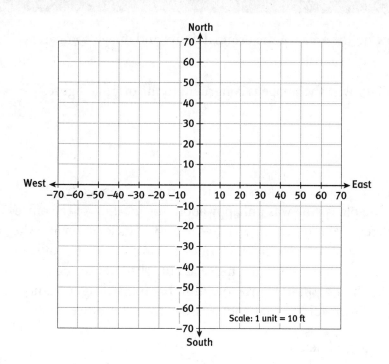

4. Explain why F', L', W' and R' represent the vertices in the image.

5. Is the y-axis the only line a shape can be reflected across? Explain.

Mr. Silver came back in to check on Kent's work. He was quite happy about where the building was now placed, but told Kent the building had to be the same size, or congruent, to the original building. Kent assured Mr. Silver that the new building, or image, was indeed congruent to the original. Mr. Silver was not convinced.

6. What are the dimensions of the original figure?

7. What are the dimensions of the image?

My Notes

8. How do the areas of the original figure and image compare?

9. Explain why the image is congruent to the original figure.

Another of Kent's coworkers, Laurie Martinez, dropped by to review the plans. She was unhappy about the location of the office and cafeteria. Her office was just to the west of its location and she did not want to have the smell of food cooking outside her office.

Kent told Laurie he would move it, but asked her to suggest where he should put it. Laurie told him that translating it 7 units (70 feet) down would be far enough away from her office.

10. Use the grid below.

  a. Place the office and cafeteria building on the grid by plotting the points $A(-20, 40)$, $C(-60, 10)$, and $B(-20, 10)$.

  b. Transform this shape as Laurie suggested and label the vertices of the image A', C', and B'.

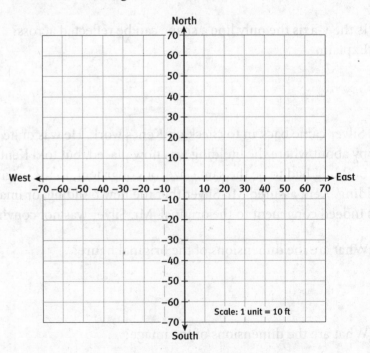

SUGGESTED LEARNING STRATEGIES: Quickwrite, Think/Pair/Share, Debriefing, Self/Peer Revision, KWL, Visualize, Group Presentation

My Notes

11. Is the image of the office and cafeteria congruent to the original? Explain.

Another worker, Art Littlefeather, came to see Kent about the project. Art noticed that his office was just south of the children's center. He said he could not work with the noise from children playing outside his window all day.

   Kent was willing to move the building, but asked for help deciding where it should go. Art suggested that he rotate the building counterclockwise 90° around the center of the park, the origin. Kent agreed but hoped no one else would want to see his plans.

12. Turning 90° counterclockwise is not the only way to rotate a shape. How else can a shape be rotated?

13. Use the grid below.

   a. Place the children's center on the grid by plotting the points $K(-20, -20)$, $I(-60, -20)$, $D(-50, -40)$, and $S(-30, -40)$.

   b. Transform the shape as Art suggested and label the vertices of the image K', I', D', and S'.

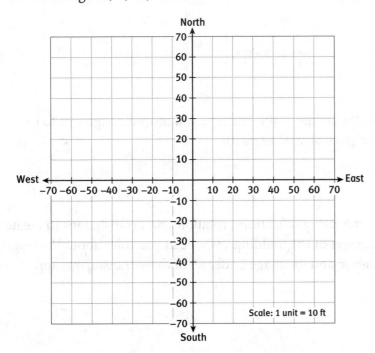

My Notes

MATH TERMS

The *x*-axis and the *y*-axis divide the coordinate plane into four separate areas called *quadrants*.

14. Are the original children's center and its image congruent? Tell how you know this.

One new building has not yet been moved. It needs to move so that is not in the same quadrant as any of the other new buildings.

15. Use this grid. Choose a transformation to move the social center to a new location. Be sure to label the vertices of the image. Name the transformation you used.

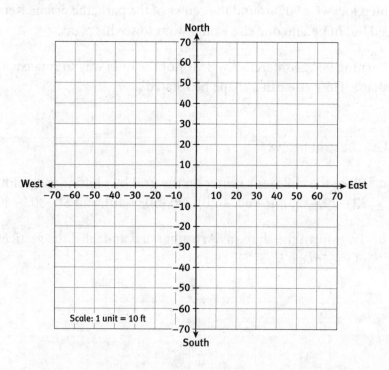

16. Is the image of the building you moved congruent to its original shape? Explain.

17. After using reflections, rotations, and translations to create images of the buildings, what can you infer about the original figure and its image under all of these transformations?

SUGGESTED LEARNING STRATEGIES: Visualize, Think/Pair/Share, Quickwrite

Ben Olinski, contractor for the project, came in to discuss the changes with Kent. He was very upset because he already had made some windows for the new buildings. Now he was not sure about which sides of the buildings he would install the windows. Kent told Ben he could use congruency and corresponding parts to locate where to install the windows.

Kent explained that when figures are congruent, they have corresponding parts and told Ben he would show him how to find some corresponding parts of the city greenhouse.

18. Kent told Ben to start with the drawing of the greenhouse in its original location on the grid on page 187. This is how they made another drawing to find the corresponding walls.

   a. Draw the reflection of *RLFW* across the *y*-axis. It may be helpful to look back at Question 5.

   b. Find line segment *FL*. Draw a tick mark on it.

   c. Find the line segment in the image of this shape that corresponds to line segment *FL*. Draw a tick mark on it too.

> **MATH TERMS**
>
> **Corresponding parts** of congruent figures are elements (sides and angles) in the figures that match exactly. In similar figures, the corresponding angles are congruent and the corresponding sides are in proportion.

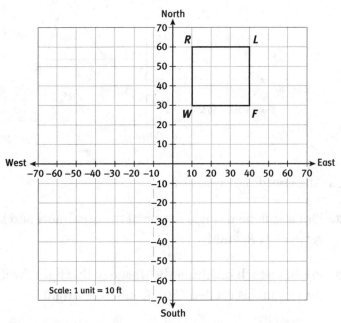

   d. What is the name of this line segment?

   e. Why do you think this line segment has this name?

SUGGESTED LEARNING STRATEGIES: Visualize, Create
Representations, Quickwrite, Think/Pair/Share

My Notes

19. Choose another side in the city greenhouse and find its corresponding side.

   a. Put double tick marks on each of these sides.

   b. Name these two line segments.

20. Why do you think corresponding shapes need to be labeled in a specific order?

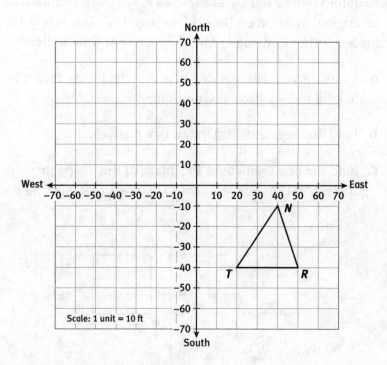

21. Use the coordinate grid above.

   a. Plot a scalene triangle in one of the quadrants and label the vertices *T*, *R*, and *N*.

   b. Predict which quadrant the image of this figure will be in if the original is rotated 180° around the origin.

   c. Why was the rotation's direction not needed in the directions for this transformation?

My Notes

d. Confirm your predication by rotating the figure and labeling the vertices T', R' and N'.

e. Give the dimensions of the original figure and its image.

f. Give the areas of your original figure and its image.

g. Give the names of the pairs of corresponding sides in your figure and its image.

22. Congruent figures have corresponding angles as well as corresponding sides. List the pairs of corresponding angles in triangle NRT and triangle $N'R'T'$.

23. How did understanding congruency under transformations make Kent's job easier?

CHECK YOUR UNDERSTANDING

Write your answers on notebook paper or grid paper. Show your work.

1. Make a coordinate plane on grid paper. Draw and label a figure having the vertices $C(2, 2)$, $A(2, 6)$, and $T(5, 2)$.

Perform each transformation on the coordinate plane you made for Question 1. Label each image with the problem number.

2. Reflection of *CAT* across the *y*-axis.

3. Rotation of *CAT* 90° clockwise.

4. Translate *CAT* left 9 units.

5. In the figure below, name the side that corresponds to side *CD*.

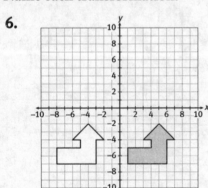

For questions 6–8, the shaded figure is the original figure. The other figure is the image. Name each transformation.

6.

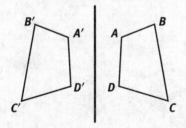

7.

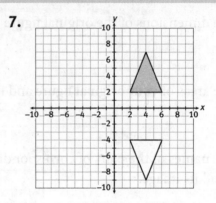

8.

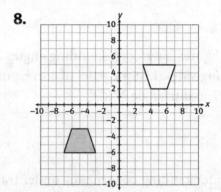

9. **MATHEMATICAL REFLECTION** Write a note to Tom Silver (Kent's boss) explaining why all the transformations resulted in images that are congruent to the original shapes. Help him see that the moves will not affect the space needed for the buildings. Justify your reasoning.

Transformations

A GEOMETRIC ARTWORK

Write your answers on grid paper and notebook paper. Show your work.

Leonardo da Vinci lived from 1452 to 1519 and invented many devices that we still use today. Among his books of sketches are plans for a helicopter. He had the idea for one hundreds of years before someone finally made one.

He used reflections, one of the transformations you have learned about, to code his work so that others would not see his work and have him punished for ideas that were considered by some authorities to be contrary to established principles.

What does this reflected code say?

Transform yourself with math.

Leonardo da Vinci was also a great artist. You may have heard of his famous work, the *Mona Lisa*. Now it is your turn to be an artist with transformations. You will use transformations to create a geometric artwork. Follow the steps below.

1. Draw a scalene triangle on a coordinate grid so that each vertex can be named with an ordered pair. List the ordered pairs that form the vertices of your triangle.

2. Now choose a transformation that will place a congruent triangle in another position on the grid. Draw the image on the grid.

3. Give the name of the transformation and the ordered pairs that form the vertices of the image after this transformation. Explain what operation(s) were made on the coordinates to perform this transformation and write the symbolic representation for the move.

4. Repeat steps 2 and 3 to make at least two more transformations, each starting with the last image you drew. Be sure that you use each type of transformation at least once.

5. Color the triangles and the coordinate grid in any way that you choose to finish the geometric artwork.

Transformations

A GEOMETRIC ARTWORK

	Exemplary	Proficient	Emerging
Math Knowledge #1, 3, 4	The student: • Lists the three ordered pairs that form the vertices of the triangle. (1) • Lists the ordered pairs that form the vertices of the three transformed triangles. (3, 4)	The student: • Lists only two correct ordered pairs. • Lists the ordered pairs for only two of the triangles.	The student: • Lists fewer than two correct ordered pairs. • Lists the ordered pairs for fewer than two of the triangles.
Problem Solving #3, 4	The student gives the correct names for the three transformations. (3, 4)	The student gives the correct names for only two of the transformations.	The student gives the correct names for fewer than two of the transformations.
Representations #1, 2, 3, 4, 5	The student: • Draws a scalene triangle. (1) • Draws three transformed triangles. (2, 4) • Writes the correct symbolic representations for the moves. (3, 4) • Completes the geometric artwork. (5)	The student: • Draws a triangle that is not scalene. • Draws only two transformed triangles. • Writes the correct symbolic representations for some, but not all of the moves. • Colors some, but not all, of the triangles.	The student: • Draws a figure that is not a triangle. • Draws fewer than two transformed triangles. • Writes the correct symbolic representation for none of the moves. • Does not complete the geometric artwork.
Communication #3, 4	The student explains what operation(s) were made on the coordinates to perform the three transformations. (3, 4)	The student explains some, but not all, of the correct operations that were made on the coordinates.	The student explains none of the operations correctly.

Proportional Reasoning
Outdoor Concert

SUGGESTED LEARNING STRATEGIES: Visualize, Identify a Subtask, Quickwrite, Use Manipulatives, Create Representations, Think/Pair/Share, Group Presentation

My Notes

Your school is holding an outdoor concert. The principal has asked your class to help in the event planning by answering some questions that involve math.

The concert will be held on the recreational field, so the principal has asked you to determine how many people can fit on the field with standing room only. The field measures 100 feet long by 75 feet wide. The concert stage will cover 200 square feet.

1. How many square feet are available for people to stand and watch the concert?

2. Would it be reasonable to fill the field with people in order to determine the number that will fit? Explain why or why not.

You can use a sampling method and proportional reasoning to determine the amount of standing room in the field. Your teacher will put you into different size groups to create samples.

Once in your group, stand comfortably together as you would at a concert. Use tape to create a rectangle on the floor around your group. Then measure the dimensions of the rectangle.

3. Draw and label your rectangle, then find its area.

4. Write a **ratio** of the number of people in your group to the area of your rectangle.

5. Use your sample and proportional reasoning to determine the number of people that could fit on the field. Explain your strategy.

ACADEMIC VOCABULARY

A **ratio** compares two values or quantities.

MATH TERMS

When comparing two different units, such as people and square feet, a ratio is called a *rate*.

WRITING MATH

Ratios can be written as fractions, with a colon, or using the word "to." Example $\frac{3}{5}$, 3:5, 3 to 5. Each is read the same way: 3 to 5.

My Notes

6. Post your data in the class table. Once everyone has posted, recreate the class table in the space below. Then discuss the similarities and differences in the data.

7. Graphs allow us to represent data more visually.

   a. Create a scatter plot of the class data. Let the x-axis represent the number of students and the y-axis represent the area needed.

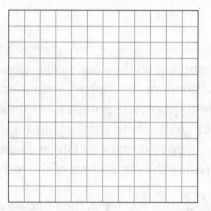

   b. What do you notice about the graphed data?

8. Find the class mean for the number of students that can fit on the field.

My Notes

9. Use the class mean from Question 8 to estimate how much space is needed for just one person.

   a. Write your answer as a ratio.

   b. What kind of ratio is this? Explain.

   c. Explain why this answer is reasonable.

10. The principal wants to know how many square inches of the recreation field are needed for one person. To explore this, first find the number of square inches in one square foot.

    a. Draw a model to represent 1 square foot. Divide each side of your square foot into inches. Draw horizontal and vertical lines to divide your square foot into square inches.

    b. Determine the number of square inches in 1 square foot.

    c. Write a ratio relating the number of square inches to 1 square foot. What you have written is called a **conversion factor**.

SUGGESTED LEARNING STRATEGIES: Think/Pair/Share, Quickwrite, Vocabulary Organizer, Create Representations, Self/Peer Revision, Identify a Subtask, Group Presentation

11. How many square inches of the field are needed for one person? Multiply the conversion factor you found in Question 10 by the number of square feet for one person you found in Question 9 to determine the total number of square inches.

12. The science teachers suggested to the principal that the metric system be used for measuring. To start working with the metric system, first convert square inches to square centimeters.

$$1 \text{ in.}^2 = \underline{\hspace{2cm}} \text{ cm}^2$$

13. How many square centimeters are in 1 square foot?

$$1 \text{ ft}^2 = \underline{\hspace{2cm}} \text{ cm}^2$$

14. Judy says the conversion factor between square millimeters and square centimeters is $\frac{100 \text{ mm}^2}{1 \text{ cm}^2}$, but Andy says it is $\frac{10 \text{ mm}^2}{1 \text{ cm}^2}$. Who is correct and why?

15. How many square millimeters are in a square foot?

16. Use these conversion factors to find the number of square millimeters of the field that are needed for one person. Show your work and explain your method. (Start with your answer to Question 9.)

17. Is the number of people that can fit on the field an exact answer or an estimate? Explain.

> **MATH TIP**
>
> 1 in. = 2.54 cm

SUGGESTED LEARNING STRATEGIES: Discussion Group, Quickwrite, Self/Peer Revision, Group Presentation, Think/Pair/Share, Identify a Subtask

My Notes

18. How is converting among measures similar to using the Property of One to find equivalent fractions?

Now that the principal knows how many people will fit on the recreation field, you can explore some other questions about the concert with your group. Work with your group and create samples if needed. Your teacher will give you stopwatches and tape. Show the ratios and conversion factors used to answer each question.

19. The average blink lasts 0.3 second. How much of the concert will you miss due to blinking if the concert lasts for two hours?

> **MATH TIP**
> Create a sample by timing how many times you blink in a minute.

20. You have to be at least 378,432,000 seconds old to attend the concert. Can you go?

21. Parking at the concert will be limited, so your family decides to consider walking. You live 2 miles from the school. How many minutes will it take to walk to the concert? Explain how you determined your answer.

> **MATH TIP**
> 1 mi = 5280 ft

My Notes

22. Applications of proportional reasoning may involve either exact answers or estimates, depending on the situation. Determine which of the questions you explored in Questions 19–21 involved estimates and which involved exact answers. Explain your reasoning for each.

CHECK YOUR UNDERSTANDING

Write your answers on notebook paper. Show your work.

1. Density is the ratio of mass to volume. A 3-liter jug of honey has a mass of 4.5 kg.

   a. Write the density of honey using a ratio, in 3 different ways.

   b. Write the density of honey as a unit rate.

2. A store sells 3 rolls of wrapping paper for $5.55, or 2 rolls for $3.80. Which is the better buy? Explain your answer.

3. If 1° C equals 33.8° F, and 2° C = 35.6° F, are Celsius and Fahrenheit proportional measurements? Explain.

4. Troy is going to Spain and needs to convert his dollars to euros. He knows that $5.00 in the United States is equivalent to about 3.47 euros.

   a. How many euros will he get for $125?

   b. Find the unit rate comparing dollars to euros.

5. The average elephant weighs about 5.5 tons. How many ounces is this?

6. Throughout a week, Charlotte drinks about 2.5 gallons of water. How many cups of water does she drink on average per day?

7. **MATHEMATICAL REFLECTION** What does proportional reasoning mean? Give an example of how it relates to conversions.

SUGGESTED LEARNING STRATEGIES: Summarize/Paraphrase/
Retell, Vocabulary Organizer

Mrs. Fickle likes to rearrange her classroom often, even though her students complain about how often she moves them. She is running out of ideas, so she has asked the students to work in groups to create new classroom arrangements. She has decided to change the arrangement of the classroom once each week using a different group's plan.

Mrs. Fickle tells the class that the most efficient way to create a floor plan is to make a **scale drawing**.

1. What do you know about scale drawings?

Mrs. Fickle showed her class the scale drawing she made for this week's arrangement.

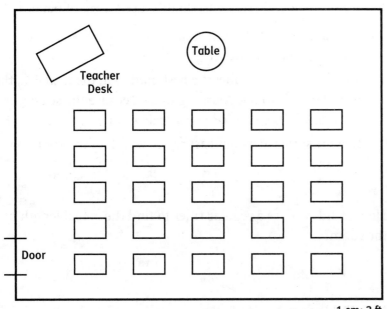

1 cm: 3 ft

2. A **scale** shows the relationship between the dimensions of the objects in the drawing to the dimensions of the actual objects. This relationship is written as a **scale factor**.

  a. What is the **scale factor** on the drawing, and what does it indicate?

  b. In what form is the scale factor written?

MATH TIP

When writing scale factors, the scale model is usually listed first, and the actual object listed second.

My Notes

Sometimes scales are written without units. This means that the units are the same, and are given in the context of the problem or by using the grid on the drawing.

The scale factor 1 in.:4 ft may be written as 1:48 if 4 feet is converted to 48 inches. Then the unit *inches* is not needed and is dropped from the scale factor.

3. Write the scale factor from Mrs. Fickle's drawing without units.

4. Where else have you seen or used a scale?

5. To determine the length of Mrs. Fickle's classroom, you can make and use a scale ruler. To do this, use a strip of paper.

- Start at a corner of the strip and mark every centimeter along one edge of the strip.

- The corner is 0 ft.; label the first mark 3 ft, the next 6 ft, the next 9 ft, and so on, counting by 3's because the scale factor is 1 cm:3 ft. The strip is now a scale ruler.

- Use the scale ruler to measure the length of the room on the drawing.

6. How could you use a regular ruler to find the actual length of the room?

7. Mrs. Fickle forgot to draw the space where the whiteboard goes. If the whiteboard is 8 ft long, how long should it be in the drawing? Explain how you found your answer.

8. How does using scales involve proportional reasoning?

Using Scale
Fickle About Furniture

My Notes

For Question 9 you will work in a group to plan a new arrangement for your classroom. First you will work together to make a group floor plan of your classroom showing doors, shelves, and other things that cannot be moved on one piece of grid paper. All of you will then make your own copies of the floor plan.

Next you will work together to measure any classroom furniture that can be moved. The group will draw and cut out top views of the classroom furniture and use these pieces to try out new arrangements for your classroom. When your group decides on a plan, you will make a group copy and each member of the group will also make a copy of the arrangement.

9. Follow each step. Show how to write and solve any proportions needed to make your floor plan. Group members should work together, but everyone must make a drawing.

   a. Start with the scale drawing for the floor plan of the room.

   Step 1:   *Measure the length and width of the room.*

   Length: _____ Width: _____

   Step 2:   *Create a scale factor. How did you determine the scale factor?*

   Step 3:   *Use grid paper to draw the dimensions of the floor. Be sure to include the scale on the drawing. Plan so that the floor plan takes up most of the paper. Show your conversions below.*

   Step 4:   *Measure and label items such as doors, closets, bulletin boards, and whiteboards that may affect placement of furniture. Show your conversions below.*

My Notes

b. Make scale drawings of the classroom furniture on a second sheet of grid paper.

Step 5:   *Measure furniture. Objects you might include are student desks, teacher desk, tables, bookcases, and so on. You do not need to include every object in the room. List the items you measure and their measurements below.*

Step 6:   *Convert each measurement using your scale factor and draw these dimensions on a separate piece of grid paper. Show your conversions below.*

MATH TIP

As a group, cut out only one shape for each piece of classroom furniture. If your classroom has 25 desks and there are 5 people in your group, you should each cut out 5 student desks.

Step 7:   *In your group, cut out and arrange the classroom objects on the group floor plan of the room. When everyone is happy with the arrangement, draw the furniture on the floor plan. Then create your own scale drawing of your group's furniture arrangement.*

SUGGESTED LEARNING STRATEGIES: Create
Representations, Identify a Subtask, Use Manipulatives,
Vocabulary Organizer, Quickwrite

My Notes

The floor plan you made is a scale drawing. It is a model of your classroom in two-dimensions. To make a **scale model** of your classroom, you need to add the third dimension of height.

10. Now that you have each created a floor plan, work together to measure things on the walls of your classroom. Divide the work among the members of your group to create each wall. Continue to use the same scale factor as you used for the scale drawing of the floor plan.

Be sure to include all large items such as whiteboards, doors, windows, bulletin boards, pictures, and so on. Record your work in this table.

Objects	Measurements	Conversions

11. The students working on a wall should make a scale drawing of their wall on another sheet of grid paper. Then the group members cut out and tape the drawings of the four walls together and cut out and lay your group floor plan into the center of the four walls.

12. What your group has just created is called a **scale model**. Explain this term.

MATH TIP

Remember that you have already measured the length of each wall when drawing the floor plan.

My Notes

SUGGESTED LEARNING STRATEGIES: Create
Representations, Summarize/Paraphrase/Retell, Think/
Pair/Share, Quickwrite

After creating their scale models, each group of Mrs. Fickle's
students designs a logo to attach to their group model instead of
listing their names on it. When a group's floor plan is chosen for
the week, a larger version of their logo gets hung in the classroom.
Look below at some of the logos that they have made.

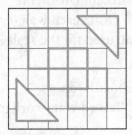 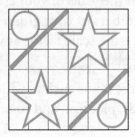 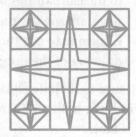

13. Choose one of the logos and create a scale drawing that is an
enlargement of it on this grid.

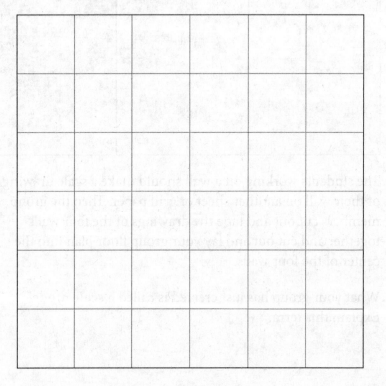

14. Describe your strategy for enlarging the logo.

SUGGESTED LEARNING STRATEGIES: Think/Pair/Share, Self/Peer Revision, Discussion Group, Quickwrite

My Notes

15. Is your enlargement proportional to the original logo? Explain.

16. What is the drawing's scale? Explain.

17. How could you enlarge this picture of a frog?

18. You have now learned two different strategies for making scale drawings.

a. Compare the strategy you used for enlarging the frog to the one you used to make the scale drawings of the floor and wall plans.

b. Could you have used the strategy used for drawing the floor plan in order to enlarge the logo? Explain.

19. Why is using scale drawings and scale models an effective method for deciding the arrangement of the classroom?

CHECK YOUR UNDERSTANDING

Write your answers on notebook paper or grid paper. Show your work.

1. On a map the distance between San Diego and San Francisco is about 5 cm. The map scale is 1 cm:110 mi. About how far is San Diego from San Francisco?

2. Write an equivalent scale factor that does not use units for 1 in.:5 ft.

3. A playground is 100 feet long by 150 feet wide. You want to make a scale drawing of the playground on an 8.5″ × 11″ paper. What scale could you use? Explain.

4. A scale model of the Statue of Liberty was built for a class project. The actual height of the Statue of Liberty is about 151 feet. What is the height of the model if its scale factor is 1:30?

5. A tarantula is being enlarged for a movie. Its actual leg span is 8 inches. The movie model of this tarantula has a leg span of 32 feet. What is the scale of the model?

6. Determine whether each scale represents a scale model that is smaller or larger than the actual object. Explain your thinking.

   a. 3:1   **b.** 1:0.5   **c.** 1:9

7. Use this picture of a ladybug on a grid.

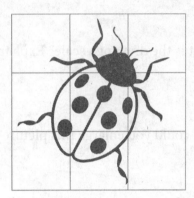

   a. Draw a reduction of the ladybug on grid paper.

   b. Approximately what scale did you use?

8. **MATHEMATICAL REFLECTION** How and why are scale drawings and scale models used in the real world?

Similar Figures
The Same but Different

SUGGESTED LEARNING STRATEGIES: Quickwrite

My Notes

The Pentagon, the headquarters of the United States Department of Defense, is located in Arlington County, Virginia. This building is named for its shape.

1. Study these two photos of the Pentagon.

Photo 1

Photo 2

a. How are the photos alike?

b. How are the photos different?

My Notes

MATH TIP

The shape of the Pentagon building is actually a regular pentagon, but the perspective in this picture makes the lengths appear to be different.

2. Use a protractor and ruler to measure the indicated line segment or angle in both photos. Measure segments to the nearest millimeter and angles to the nearest degree.

a. $AB =$ _____

b. $m\angle A =$ _____

c. $BC =$ _____

d. $m\angle B =$ _____

e. $CD =$ _____

f. $m\angle C =$ _____

g. $DE =$ _____

h. $m\angle D =$ _____

i. $EA =$ _____

j. $m\angle E =$ _____

k. $FG =$ _____

l. $m\angle F =$ _____

m. $GH =$ _____

n. $m\angle G =$ _____

o. $HI =$ _____

p. $m\angle H =$ _____

q. $IJ =$ _____

r. $m\angle I =$ _____

s. $JF =$ _____

t. $m\angle J =$ _____

SUGGESTED LEARNING STRATEGIES: Look for a Pattern, Quickwrite

My Notes

3. Use the information from Question 2 to find the following ratios to the nearest tenth.

a. $\dfrac{AB}{FG} = $ _____

b. $\dfrac{BC}{GH} = $ _____

c. $\dfrac{CD}{HI} = $ _____

d. $\dfrac{DE}{IJ} = $ _____

e. $\dfrac{EA}{JF} = $ _____

4. What can you conclude about the ratio of the segments and the measures of the angles in the photos?

5. The two photographs of the Pentagon are *similar* to each other. A scale model is similar to the original object because it is a representation or copy of that object. What does that mean mathematically?

> **MATH TERMS**
> **Similar figures** are figures in which the lengths of the corresponding sides are in proportion and the corresponding angles are congruent.

Corresponding parts of similar figures are the sides and angles that match. The smallest side or angle of one figure will always correspond to the smallest side or angle of a similar figure, the next smallest side or angle of the first will correspond to the next smallest side or angle of the similar figure, and so on.

6. For each pair of figures on pages 210 and 211:

- Measure and label all the angles in the two figures.
- Measure and label all the sides in the two figures.
- Circle *similar* or *not similar* and explain how you decided that the figures were similar or not similar.

My Notes

a.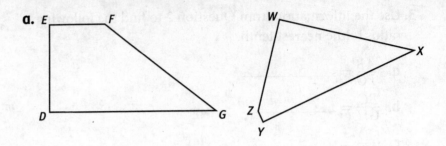

The figures are similar   not similar   because

b.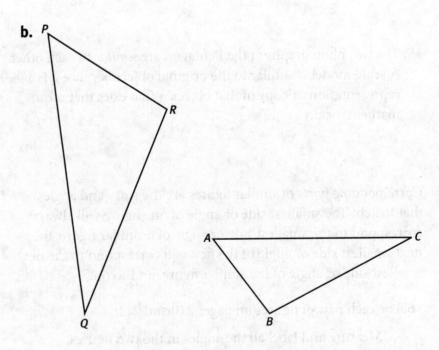

The figures are similar   not similar   because

Similar Figures
The Same but Different

SUGGESTED LEARNING STRATEGIES: Use Manipulatives, Group Presentation, Quickwrite

c.

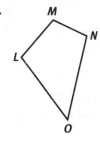
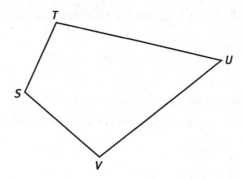

The figures are similar not similar because

d.

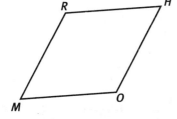
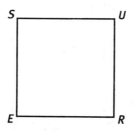

The figures are similar not similar because

7. Describe in your own words the conditions necessary for two figures to be similar.

My Notes

8. Are all rectangles similar? Explain.

When two figures are similar the common ratio of the corresponding sides is called the scale factor of one figure to the other.

9. Use the grid.

a. Graph each point and then connect them to form triangle *ABC*. Label the points on your graph.
$A(1, 2)$, $B(-2, 1)$, $C(3, -2)$

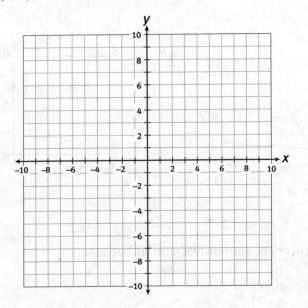

b. Multiply each *x*-coordinate and each *y*-coordinate in Part a by 3 and list them below. Graph the points and connect them to form triangle *A′B′C′*. Label the points *A′*, *B′*, and *C′*.
$A'(\underline{\quad}, \underline{\quad})$, $B'(\underline{\quad}, \underline{\quad})$, $C'(\underline{\quad}, \underline{\quad})$

c. Are the triangles similar? Explain.

d. If the triangles are similar, what is the scale factor?

Similar Figures
The Same but Different

SUGGESTED LEARNING STRATEGIES: Create Representations

My Notes

> **MATH TIP**
>
> $\triangle ABC \sim \triangle DEF$ is read as "Triangle *ABC* is similar to triangle *DEF*."

In a similarity statement such as $\triangle ABC \sim \triangle DEF$, the order of the vertices shows what the corresponding angles are. The statement $\triangle ABC \sim \triangle DEF$ shows that $\angle A$ corresponds to $\angle D$, $\angle B$ corresponds to $\angle E$, and $\angle C$ corresponds to $\angle F$.

10. In the figures below $\triangle ABC \sim \triangle DEF$.

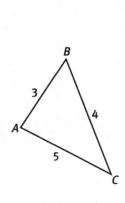
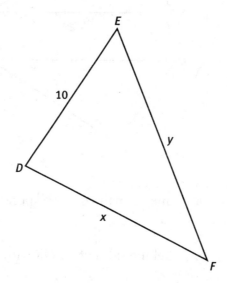

a. Name the corresponding sides.

b. Find the ratios of the corresponding sides.

c. What is the scale factor?

d. Write and solve a proportion to find the value of *x*.

e. Write and solve a proportion to find the value of *y*.

> **CONNECT TO AP**
>
> Similar figures are often used in a type of calculus problem known as related rates.

SUGGESTED LEARNING STRATEGIES: Create Representations, Quickwrite

My Notes

11. In this drawing, $\triangle XYZ \cong \triangle PQR$.

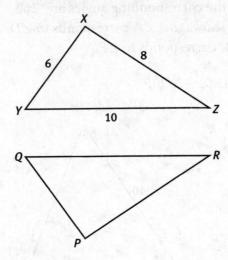

a. Name the pairs of corresponding sides.

b. Label the sides of $\triangle PQR$ with their side lengths.

c. Write the ratios of the corresponding side lengths.

d. What do you notice about these ratios?

12. Are all pairs of congruent triangles similar to each other? Explain.

13. Are all pairs of similar triangles congruent to each other? Explain.

SUGGESTED LEARNING STRATEGIES: Close Reading, Marking the Text, Question the Text

Similar triangles can be used in real life to measure indirectly the heights of objects too tall to measure conventionally. The height of a building or a flagpole or a tower can be measured using similar triangles and comparing the lengths of the shadows of objects at the same time of day.

14. In the drawing below the ratio of the height of the flagpole to the height of the yardstick is equal to the ratio of the shadow of the flagpole to the shadow of the yardstick. The yardstick is 3 feet high and its shadow is 2 feet long. The shadow of the flagpole is 8 feet long.

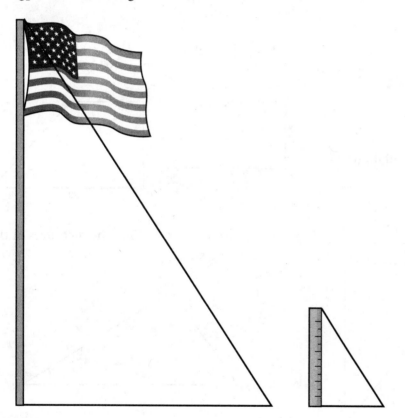

a. Label the picture with the lengths.

b. Write and solve a proportion to find the height of the flagpole.

My Notes

CHECK YOUR UNDERSTANDING

**Write your answers on notebook paper.
Show your work.**

1. Measure the sides and the angles of the two triangles below. Are the triangles similar? Explain.

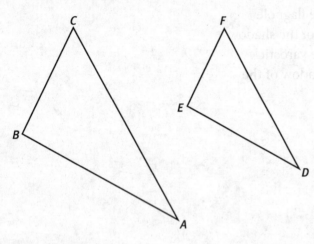

2. Sketch two similar rectangles. Explain why they are similar.

3. In the triangles below are the ratios of the corresponding sides equal? Explain.

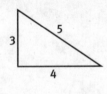

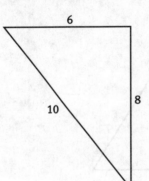

4. Rectangle *ABCD* ~ Rectangle *WXYZ*. Find the measures of the missing sides.

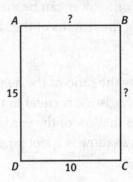 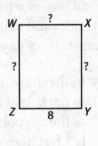

5. Trapezoid *QRST* ~ Trapezoid *EFGH*. Find the measures of the missing sides.

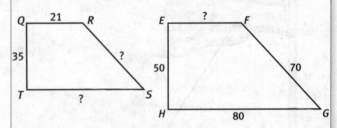

6. △*LMN* ~ △*TUV*. Find the measures of the missing sides.

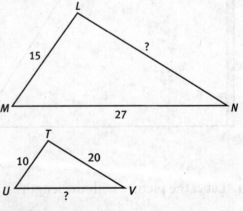

7. **MATHEMATICAL REFLECTION** How is the mathematical meaning of the word "similar" the same or different from the word "similar" in everyday conversation?

Pythagorean Theorem
Stop the Presses

SUGGESTED LEARNING STRATEGIES: Marking the Text, Predict and Confirm, Shared Reading

Jayla and Sidney are co-editors-in-chief of the school yearbook. They have just finished the final layouts of this year's edition. It is due at the print shop before it closes at 4 o'clock. The print shop is on her way home, so Jayla agrees to drop off the layouts at the print shop on the corner of 7th Avenue and Main Street. Sidney has a copy of the layouts with him to check one more time.

Jayla and Sidney part company at the front door of their school, which is located on the corner of 7th Avenue and D Street. Jayla walks towards the print shop on 7th Avenue and Sidney bikes towards his home on D Street.

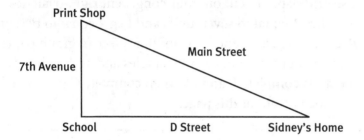

When Jayla gets to the print shop, she notices that the set of layouts is missing the last three pages. She calls Sidney at home to see whether he can quickly bring his copy of the layouts to the print shop.

Sidney leaves his house at 3:45 p.m. and starts biking down Main Street to the print shop. As he is pedaling, he wonders how far it is to the print shop. His house is 12 blocks away from the school and the print shop is five blocks away from the school. He can travel, at the most, one block per minute on his bike.

1. Predict whether Sidney makes it to the print shop before it closes.

The lengths of the three sides of any right triangle have a relationship that you could use to answer Question 1. It is one of the most useful properties you will use as you study mathematics.

My Notes

> **MATH TIP**
>
> It does not matter which leg on a right triangle is labeled Leg 1 and which is labeled Leg 2.

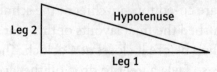

2. The **hypotenuse** of a right triangle is the side that is opposite the right angle. It is always the longest side of the triangle. The **legs** of a right triangle are the sides that form the right angle. Both Figures 1 and 2 have been formed using four congruent right triangles like the one above.

a. Use grid paper to cut out four congruent right triangles with Leg 1 equal to seven units and Leg 2 equal to two units. Recreate Figures 1 and 2 on another piece of graph paper by tracing your four congruent triangles and adding line segments to complete L and M. Then complete Case 1 in Table A at the bottom of this page.

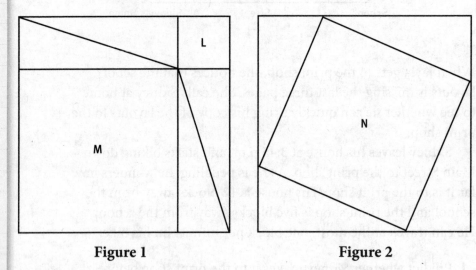

Figure 1   Figure 2

Table A

Case	Length Leg 1	Length Leg 2	Width Figure 1	Length Figure 1	Area Figure 1	Width Figure 2	Length Figure 2	Area Figure 2
1	7	2						
2	6	3						
3	4	3						
4								

My Notes

b. Complete Cases 2 and 3 in Table A by cutting out triangles with the lengths in the table.

c. Complete Case 4 in Table A by choosing your own leg lengths for a right triangle.

d. What do you notice about Figure 1 and Figure 2 in each case?

3. Now use the figures you drew for Cases 1 through 4 to complete the first seven columns (Case through Area of Shape M) of Table B. For Case 5, use the variables *a* and *b* as the lengths of Leg 1 and Leg 2.

Table B

Case	Length Leg 1	Length Leg 2	Dimensions Shape L	Area Shape L	Dimensions Shape M	Area Shape M	Area Shape N
1	7	2					
2	6	3					
3	4	3					
4							
5	*a*	*b*					

4. Describe the relationship between the areas of shapes L, M, and N and complete the eighth column of Table B.

5. Describe the lengths of the sides of shapes L, M, and N in terms of the sides of the right triangles.

6. Find the area of shapes L, M, and N in terms of the lengths of the sides of the right triangles.

My Notes

SUGGESTED LEARNING STRATEGIES: Think/Pair/Share, Create Representations, Look for a Pattern, Identify a Subtask, Quickwrite

7. Use *a* for the length of Leg 1, *b* for the length of Leg 2, and *c* for the length of the hypotenuse to write an equation that relates the areas of shapes L, M, and N.

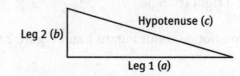

The relationship that you have just explored is called the **Pythagorean theorem**.

8. Now that you know the relationship of the lengths of the three sides of any right triangle, you can find the answer to Question 1 using the Pythagorean theorem.

 a. How many blocks is it from the school to the print shop?

 b. How many blocks is it from the school to Sidney's home?

 c. How many block lengths down Main Street will Sidney have to bike to get to the print shop?

 d. Can Sidney make it to the print shop on time? Explain your reasoning.

9. When you used the Pythagorean theorem to find the distance from Sidney's house to the print shop, the formula gave you the square of the distance. What did you have to do to get the actual distance?

ACADEMIC VOCABULARY

The Pythagorean theorem states that the sum of the squares of the lengths of the legs of a right triangle equals the square of the length of the hypotenuse.

CONNECT TO HISTORY

Although the Pythagorean theorem is named for Pythagoras, a Greek mathematician who lived about 500 BCE, the ancient Babylonians, Chinese, and Egyptians understood and used this relationship even earlier.

CONNECT TO AP

The Pythagorean theorem is fundamental to the development of many more advanced mathematical topics such as the distance formula, complex numbers, and arc length of a curve.

SUGGESTED LEARNING STRATEGIES: Marking the Text, Group Presentation, Create Representations, Identify a Subtask, Quickwrite

My Notes

10. Use the Pythagorean theorem to find the length of the hypotenuse in each of the cases in Table A. Show your work and round your answer to the nearest hundredth.

Case	Length Leg 1	Length Leg 2	Length of Hypotenuse	Work
1	7	2		
2	6	3		
3	4	3		
4				

Jayla and Sidney's parents rent cottages every summer on the opposite shores of a lake. Jayla and Sidney want to swim across the lake from one dock to the other. They need to know how far it is between the docks before they make the attempt.

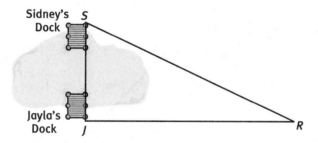

11. To approximate the distance across the lake, Jayla and Sidney stood at point *J* in front of Jayla's cottage. They walked to point *R* along a line, which they estimated was at right angles to a line connecting the cottages. They found this distance to be 300 yards. Then they walked in a straight line to point *S* in front of Sidney's cottage. They found this distance to be 600 yards. How far is it from point *J* to point *S*?

12. How does finding the distance between the two cottages differ from finding the distance from Sidney's house to the print shop?

SUGGESTED LEARNING STRATEGIES: Create Representations, Group Presentation, Quickwrite

My Notes

13. How does knowing the distance from Sidney's cottage to Jayla's cottage help estimate the distance they need to swim? What other information would Sidney and Jayla need to get an even better estimate of the distance between the two docks?

CHECK YOUR UNDERSTANDING

**Write your answers on notebook paper.
Show your work.**

1. Use the Pythagorean theorem to find the unknown length to the nearest tenth.

   a.
   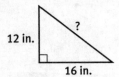
   12 in.
   ?
   16 in.

   b.
   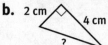
   2 cm
   4 cm
   ?

   c.

   6.3 m
   5.2 m
   ?

2. Use the Pythagorean theorem to find the length of each diagonal to the nearest tenth.

   a.
   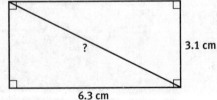
   ?
   3.1 cm
   6.3 cm

   b.
   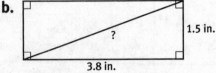
   ?
   1.5 in.
   3.8 in.

3. Tim's cousin lives 8 blocks due south of his house. His grandmother lives 6 blocks due east of him. What is the distance in blocks from Tim's cousin's house to Tim's grandmother's house?

4. Use the Pythagorean theorem to find the unknown length to the nearest tenth.

   a.
   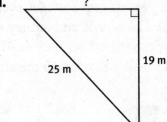
   ?
   19 m
   25 m

   b.
   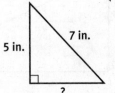
   7 in.
   5 in.
   ?

   c.
   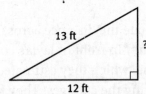
   13 ft
   ?
   12 ft

5. A ladder 3 meters long is placed against a wall so that the foot of the ladder is 0.75 meters from the wall. How high up the wall does the ladder reach? Round your answer to the nearest tenth.

6. **MATHEMATICAL REFLECTION** If you know the lengths of the sides of a triangle, how might you use the Pythagorean theorem to tell if the triangle is or is not a right triangle?

Constructions
Euclid's Arithmetic

My Notes

Euclid is known as the Father of Geometry. His great work, *Elements*, was written over 2000 years ago. One of many things Euclid explained was how to use constructions to measure lengths. Why do constructions rather than measure and calculate lengths?

The answer is surprising—the ancient Greeks could not do much arithmetic. They had only whole numbers, no zero, and no negative numbers. For example, they could not divide 3 by 2 and get 1.5, because 1.5 is not a whole number. To find the midpoint of a line, they could not measure and divide by 2. But they did know how to do constructions with compass and straightedge.

Euclid and the ancient Greeks solved problems by drawing shapes as a substitute for using arithmetic. You will explore how to do four basic constructions and use them to work on other problems.

MATH TIP

A straightedge has no markings and is used only for making straight lines—it is not a ruler. You can use a ruler as a straight-edge if you ignore the markings.

1. You will use a straightedge to draw line segments and rays, and a compass to draw arcs. Explain why the space between the point and the pencil of an opened compass is called the radius.

Construction 1
Given: ∠CAT
Construct an angle congruent to ∠CAT.

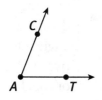

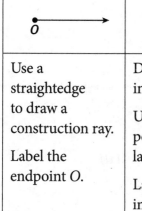	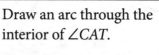	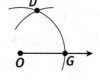	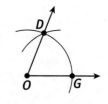
Use a straightedge to draw a construction ray. Label the endpoint *O*.	Draw an arc through the interior of ∠CAT. Using the same radius and point *O* as center, draw a large arc. Label the point of intersection with the ray *G*.	Use a compass to measure the opening of ∠CAT along the arc. Using that measure as radius and point *G* as center, draw an arc through the first arc. Label the intersection point *D*.	Draw ray *OD*. ∠DOG ≅ ∠CAT

My Notes

2. Explain why Construction 1 guarantees that the constructed angle is congruent to the original angle.

Construction 2
Given: ∠A
Construct the bisector of ∠A.

	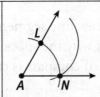		
Using point *A* as center, draw an arc through the angle. Label the intersection points *L* and *N*.	Using *L* as center and an ample radius, draw an arc in the interior of the angle.	Using *N* as center and the same radius as from *L*, draw an arc to intersect the previous arc. Label the intersection *R*.	Draw $\overrightarrow{AR}$. $\overrightarrow{AR}$ bisects ∠*LAN*. An angle bisector divides an angle into two angles of equal measure.

TRY THESE A

Use the My Notes space to show your work.

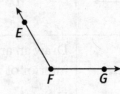

Construct each angle.
a. An angle congruent to ∠*EFG*

b. An angle with measure equal to $m\angle EFG + m\angle HIJ$

c. An angle with measure equal to half $m\angle EFG$

SUGGESTED LEARNING STRATEGIES: Create Representations, Use Manipulatives, Notetaking

Construction 3

Given: $\overline{EZ}$

Construct a segment congruent to $\overline{EZ}$.

E   Z

	C	C Q
Use a straightedge to draw a construction segment that you can see is longer than the segment you are constructing.	Mark any point on the segment and label it C. Use a compass to measure EZ.	Using C as center, draw an arc on segment. Label the intersection Q. $\overline{CQ} \cong \overline{EZ}$

Construction 4

Given: $\overline{WO}$

Construct the perpendicular bisector of $\overline{WO}$.

W   O

W O	W O	W O	G W O L
Using point W as center and a radius that you can tell by sight is greater than half WO, draw a large arc above and below the segment.	Using the same radius and point O as center, draw a large arc to intersect the other arc in two points.	Draw a line through the two intersection points.	Label two points on the line. $\overleftrightarrow{GL}$ is the perpendicular bisector of $\overline{WO}$.

3. What is the geometric term for the point of intersection of $\overline{WO}$ and $\overleftrightarrow{GL}$ in Construction 4?

My Notes

SUGGESTED LEARNING STRATEGIES:
Create Representations, Use Manipulatives

TRY THESE B

Use the My Notes space to show your work.

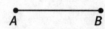

Construct and name each line segment.

a. A segment congruent to $\overline{AB}$.

b. The perpendicular bisector of AB.

CHECK YOUR UNDERSTANDING

Write your answers on unlined paper.
Show your work.

Do each construction. Do not erase your
construction marks.

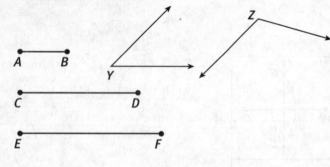

1. Construct and name an angle congruent
    to $\angle Y$.

2. Construct an angle with measure equal
    to $2\,m\angle Y$.

3. Construct an angle with measure equal
    to $\frac{1}{2}\,m\angle Z$.

4. Construct and name a segment congruent
    to $\overline{AB}$.

5. Construct the perpendicular bisector
    of $\overline{AB}$.

6. Construct and name a segment with
    length equal to $CD + EF$.

7. Use construction to locate the midpoint
    of EF.

8. **MATHEMATICAL REFLECTION** Compare and contrast
    geometric drawings with
    geometric constructions.

Scale Drawings and Right Triangles

THE BERMUDA TRIANGLE

Write your answers on notebook paper or grid paper. Show your work.

Have you ever heard of the Bermuda Triangle? It is a triangular region of the Atlantic Ocean between Bermuda; Miami, Florida; and San Juan, Puerto Rico. A number of ships and planes have disappeared in this region throughout history. People have various ideas about the Bermuda Triangle, but no one really knows why the ships and planes disappeared.

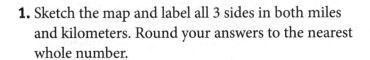

1. Sketch the map and label all 3 sides in both miles and kilometers. Round your answers to the nearest whole number.

2. Another copy of this diagram is larger in size without a scale. The triangle is similar to the one above and the length of the side from Bermuda to San Juan is 4 inches. Find the lengths to the nearest hundredth of an inch of the other two sides of the triangle. Then calculate the scale factor.

MATH TIP

1 mi = 1.61 km

3. Martha has an old hand-drawn map in which the Bermuda Triangle looks like a right triangle. She labeled the legs and hypotenuse on a sketch of the map she made so she could use math to see whether the Bermuda Triangle is a right triangle. She did not draw the sketch to scale.

   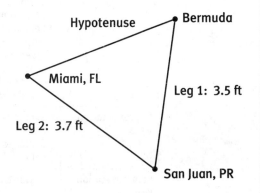

   a. What length would the hypotenuse have to be in order for it to be a right triangle? Round to the nearest tenth.

   b. Martha labeled the hypotenuse 3.8 ft. Is the Bermuda Triangle a right triangle? Explain.

4. A cruise ship travels at an average speed of 20 knots per hour. How many miles per hour is this? At this speed, how long will it take the cruise ship to travel from San Juan to Bermuda?

   MATH TIP

   1 knot = 1.151 mi

5. Mikhail did some research on the Bermuda Triangle. In order to present his research to the class, he will enlarge a diagram of the Bermuda Triangle so that it covers a sheet of grid paper. What approximate scale factor should he use? Enlarge one of the two scale drawings of the Bermuda Triangle on this page so that it fits on a sheet of grid paper.

Scale Drawings and Right Triangles

THE BERMUDA TRIANGLE

	Exemplary	Proficient	Emerging
Math Knowledge #1, 4	• Labels the map with correctly rounded miles and kilometers (1) • Calculates the correct number of miles per hour (4)	• Labels the map with correct dimensions, but does not round correctly • Uses a correct method to find the miles per hour but makes a computational error	• Labels the map with incorrect dimensions • Method used indicates a misconception.
Problem Solving #1, 2, 3a–b, 4, 5	• Measures correctly from Miami, FL to Bermuda to calculate the distance in kilometers (1) • Finds the correct lengths of the two sides to the nearest hundredth of an inch (2) • Calculates the correct scale factor, based on his/her drawing (2) • Calculates the correctly rounded length of the hypotenuse (3a) • Determines correctly whether or not the Bermuda Triangle is a right triangle (3b) • Calculates the correct length of time (4) • Gives the correct scale factor for the enlarged diagram, based on his/her diagram (5)	• Measures correctly and uses a correct method but makes an arithmetic error • Finds the correct lengths of the two sides but does not round correctly • Uses a correct method to find the scale factor, but makes a computational error • Calculates the correct length but does not round correctly • Uses the correct method to find the length of time but makes a computational error • Uses a correct method to find the scale factor, but makes a computational error.	• Measures incorrectly or uses an incorrect method to convert to kilometers • Does not find the correct lengths of the two sides • Indicates a misconception when finding the scale factor • Indicates a misconception when finding the length • Does not determine correctly whether or not the Bermuda Triangle is a right triangle • Does not find the correct length of time • Indicates a misconception when finding the scale factor
Representations #1, 5	• Sketches a correct map (1) • Sketches a correct enlarged diagram (5)	• Sketches a map that is partially correct • Sketches a diagram that is partially correct	• Sketches an incorrect map • Sketches an incorrect diagram
Communication #3b	The student gives a correct explanation of whether or not the Bermuda Triangle is a right triangle. (3b)	The student gives an incomplete explanation of whether or not the Bermuda Triangle is a right triangle.	The student gives an incorrect explanation of whether or not the Bermuda Triangle is a right triangle.

ACTIVITY 3.1

1. Classify the following angles according to their measures.

   a. 75° **b.** 38° **c.** 90° **d.** 154°

2. Find the complement of an angle that measures 42°.

3. Find the supplement of an angle that measures 115°.

4. ∠ABC and ∠TMI are complementary. m∠ABC = 32° and m∠TMI = (29x)°. Find the value of x and the measure of ∠TMI.

5. ∠SUN and ∠CAT are supplementary. m∠SUN = (2x)° and m∠CAT = 142°. Find the value of x and the measure of ∠SUN.

6. Find the measure of each angle in the figure below and explain how you found each measure.

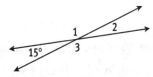

7. Two parallel lines are cut by a transversal as shown below. Find the measures of the remaining seven angles and explain how you found each measure.

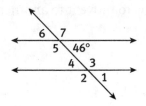

ACTIVITY 3.2

8. Draw an example of an isosceles triangle. Explain why it is classified as isosceles.

9. Draw an example of an obtuse triangle. Explain why it is classified as obtuse.

10. Draw an example of a right triangle. Explain why it is classified as a right triangle.

Find the area and perimeter or circumference of each figure.

11.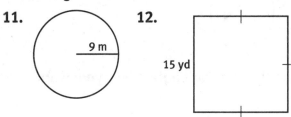
9 m

12.
15 yd

13.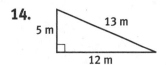
7.3 in.
12.5 in.

14.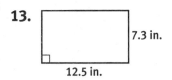
5 m 13 m 12 m

15.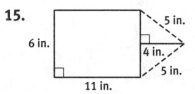
6 in. 5 in. 4 in. 5 in. 11 in.

ACTIVITY 3.3

Determine if each of the following figures is a polygon. If the figure is a polygon, determine if it is convex. Justify your answer.

16.

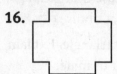

17.

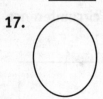

Find the missing angle. Show your work.

18.

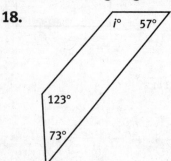

19.

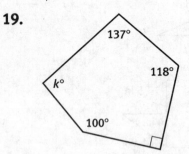

20.

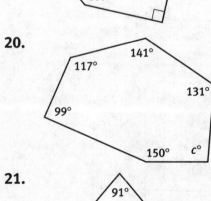

21.

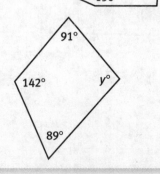

ACTIVITY 3.4

22. Consider triangle *ABC* with vertices A(−5, 3), B(1, 3) and C(−5, 6)

  a. Plot the triangle on a coordinate grid.

  b. Plot and identify the following transformation of triangle $ABC: (x, y) \rightarrow (x + 3, y − 4)$.

  c. Plot and identify the following transformation of triangle $ABC: (x, y) \rightarrow (−y −1, x − 3)$

  d. Plot and identify the following transformation of triangle $ABC: (x, y) \rightarrow (−x, −y)$

23. Beginning with triangle *DEF* (*D* (4, 4), *E* (8, 4), and *F*(8, 2). Tell the ending points of the composition of transformations: $(x, y) \rightarrow (−y, −x)$ and $(x, y) \rightarrow (x + 3, y − 1)$.

24. Plot a triangle in Quadrant IV and give directions to move it to Quadrant II.

25. Plot a square in Quadrant I and give directions to move it to Quadrant II.

26. Plot a rectangle in Quadrant I and give directions to move it to Quadrant IV.

27. Plot a trapezoid on a coordinate grid and give directions to move it to another quadrant.

ACTIVITY 3.5

28. Plot the following points on a grid and connect them to form the figure *RAFT*: $R(-2, 4)$, $A(-6, 4)$, $F(-3, 2)$, and $T(-5, 2)$.

On your grid paper, use *RAFT* to complete each transformation. Start with *RAFT* each time. Label each figure with the problem number.

29. 180° rotation

30. Translation down 8 units

31. Translation right 6 units

32. Reflection across the *x*-axis

Name each type of transformation shown below.

33.

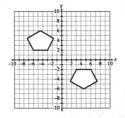

34.

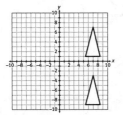

35. What side corresponds with side VN in these similar triangles?

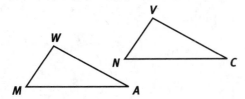

ACTIVITY 3.6

36. A total of 180 students and 35 chaperones are going on a field trip to the Smithsonian Institution, a museum in Washington, DC.

   a. Write the ratio of students to chaperones in three different ways.

   b. About how many students per chaperone is this? Show your work.

37. Consider two different mixtures of lemon iced tea: 10 cups of water to 2 scoops of mix or 8 cups of water to 1.5 scoops of mix. Which iced tea has more lemon flavor? Show how you know.

38. Trevor's recipe for pancakes says to use 2 cups of mix to make 14 pancakes. Write and solve a proportion to show how much mix he should use to make 35 pancakes.

39. A person weighing 110 pounds burns about 377 calories during an 8-hour night of sleep. At this rate, how many calories per minute is this?

40. Niagara Falls is located partly in the United States and partly in Canada. While visiting Niagara Falls, Mia wishes to convert her U.S. dollars to Canadian dollars. She knows the rate is 1 U.S. dollar = 1.07 Canadian dollars. How many Canadian dollars would Mia get if she exchanges $55 from the United States?

41. How many millimeters tall are you? Show your work.

42. A kitchen measures 250 square feet. How many square centimeters is this?

43. Proportions can be used to find the unknown in each of the following situations. Determine which situations will give exact answers, and which will give close estimates.

   a. The number of stones needed to fill a whole driveway if you know the number of stones to fill just 1 square foot.

b. The number of leaves on a tree if you know the number of leaves on just one branch.

c. The price of sending 1,000 text messages if you know the cost of sending 5 text messages.

ACTIVITY 3.7

44. The scale on a map of Texas is 1 cm:31 mi. On the map the distance between Houston and Dallas is 8 cm. What is the actual distance between Houston and Dallas?

45. An architect created a scale drawing of a concert hall. The length of the hall in the scale drawing is 12.5 inches. When the concert hall is built, the actual length will be 350 feet. What is the scale of the architect's drawing?

46. You decide to make a scale drawing of your bedroom. Your bedroom measures 12 feet wide by 20 feet long. If you are using an 8.5" × 11" paper, what scale will you use? Explain your reasoning.

47. A model airplane is built using the scale 1 cm:2.5 m. If the wingspan on the model is 24 cm, what is the actual wingspan of the airplane?

48. The sculptures of soldiers in the Korean War Memorial in Washington, D.C. were built with the scale factor of 1.26:1. If the height of an average man is 69 in., estimate the height of a soldier in the monument. Write your answer in feet and inches.

49. The table lists places that Paloma has lived and the number of years she lived in each place.

Places	Years There
Massachusetts	1981–1986
Montana	1986–1990
Tennessee	1990–1993
North Carolina	1993–1999

Make a timeline showing how long she lived in each place. Use the scale 1 cm:2 years.

50. Look at the data in the table below.

Days	Temp. (°F)	Days	Temp. (°F)
Jan. 1	1	July 1	84
Feb. 1	23	Aug. 1	99
March 1	55	Sept. 1	84
April 1	61	Oct. 1	72
May 1	69	Nov. 1	49
June 1	80	Dec. 1	22

What scale factor would be most appropriate to use when making a line graph on a grid that has 15 rows, and you want to use as much of the grid as possible? Explain your reasoning.

51. Look at the picture on the grid below.

a. Draw an enlargement of this picture on a larger grid.

b. Approximately what scale was used? Explain.

ACTIVITY 3.8

52. Measure the sides and the angles of the two figures below. Are the triangles similar? Explain.

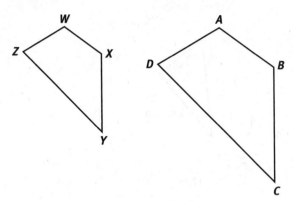

53. Sketch two similar right triangles. Explain why they are similar.

54. In the triangles below are the ratios of the corresponding sides equal? Explain.

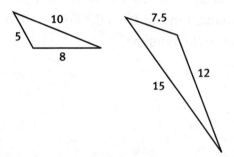

55. □ABCD ~ □WXYZ. Find the measures of the unknown sides.

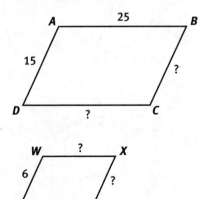

56. △LMN ~ △TUV. Find the measures of the missing sides.

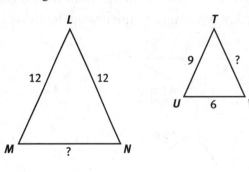

57. △QRS ~ △EFG. Find the measures of the missing sides.

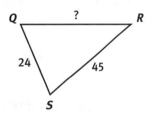

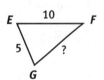

ACTIVITY 3.9

58. Use the Pythagorean Theorem to find the unknown length to the nearest tenth.

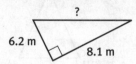

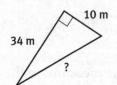

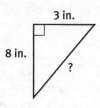

59. Use the Pythagorean Theorem to find the length of each diagonal to the nearest tenth.

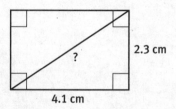

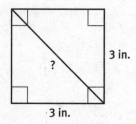

60. Use the Pythagorean Theorem to find the unknown length to the nearest tenth.

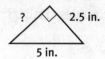

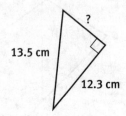

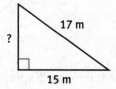

61. Jenny's father has a 6-foot plank that he wants to use as a ramp up to the back door of his house. If the back door is 2 feet from the ground, how far from the house will the bottom of the ramp be?

ACTIVITY 3.10

Use the given figures below and unlined paper to complete your answers. Do not erase your construction marks.

62. Use a straightedge to draw an acute angle. Construct an angle congruent to your acute angle.

63. Bisect the angle you drew in Question 62.

64. Use a straightedge to draw a line segment. Construct the perpendicular bisector of your segment and locate the midpoint of the segment.

65. Construct an equilateral triangle with side length congruent to segment *AB* below.

A  *B*

Reflection

An important aspect of growing as a learner is to take the time to reflect on your learning. It is important to think about where you started, what you have accomplished, what helped you learn, and how you will apply your new knowledge in the future. Use notebook paper to record your thinking on the following topics and to identify evidence of your learning.

Essential Questions

1. Review the mathematical concepts and your work in this unit before you write thoughtful responses to the questions below. Support your responses with specific examples from concepts and activities in the unit.

   - Why is it important to understand properties of angles and figures to solve problems?

   - How can diagrams be used to interpret solutions to real-world problems?

Academic Vocabulary

2. Look at the following academic vocabulary words:

   - angle
   - coordinate plane
   - polygon
   - Pythagorean Theorem
   - ratio

   Choose three words and explain your understanding of each word and why each is important in your study of math.

Self-Evaluation

3. Look through the activities and Embedded Assessments in this unit. Use a table similar to the one below to list three major concepts in this unit and to rate your understanding of each.

Unit Concepts	Is Your Understanding Strong (S) or Weak (W)?
Concept 1	
Concept 2	
Concept 3	

   a. What will you do to address each weakness?

   b. What strategies or class activities were particularly helpful in learning the concepts you identified as strengths? Give examples to explain.

4. How do the concepts you learned in this unit relate to other math concepts and to the use of mathematics in the real world?

1. Identify the location of point *F* after a rotation of 180° about the origin.

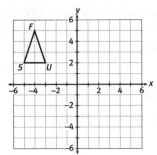

1. Ⓐ Ⓑ Ⓒ Ⓓ

   A. (5, 4)   **C.** (−4, 5)

   B. (−5, −4)   **D.** (4, −5)

2. A sporting goods store has models of several of the tents they sell. The model of the four-person tent is 12 in. by 15 in. The shortest side of the actual tent is 8 feet. Find the length in feet of the longest side.

2.

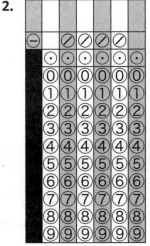

Read

Solve

Explain

3. Triangle *ABC* is similar to triangle *DBE*. The length of *AC* is 15 units, the length of *DE* is 10 units and the length of *DB* is 28 units.

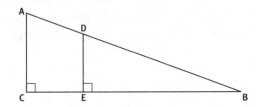

Part A: Find the length of *AB*. Explain your reasoning.

Answer and Explain

_____

_____

_____

_____

Part B: If ∠*CAB* = 78°, determine the measure of ∠*EDB*. Explain your answer.

Answer and Explain

_____

_____

_____

_____

Read

Solve

Explain

4. Laura and Jon Sever are planning a trip to San Antonio from Tallahassee. Jon records the distance they traveled and the time it took to travel the distance at each stop. He also records the driver during that time period.

Driver	Laura	Jon	Jon	Laura
Miles driven	197	257	270	197
Time in hours	2.6	3.0	3.4	3.0

Part A: Compare Jon's average speed in miles per hour to Laura's average speed in miles per hour.

Answer and Explain

_____

_____

_____

_____

Part B: If the Severs want to return to Tallahassee as quickly as possible who should drive? How much time will that save compared to the slower driver making the entire return trip?

Answer and Explain

_____

_____

_____

Part C: Laura decides to drive home to Tallahassee, but there is road work on Interstate 10 in Florida. She must drive 55 mi/h for the last 201 miles of the trip. Find the time it will take her to drive from San Antonio to Tallahassee.

Answer and Explain

_____

_____

_____

_____

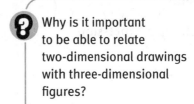

Three-Dimensional Geometry

Unit 4

Unit Overview

In this unit you will analyze the characteristics of two- and three-dimensional figures to formulate statements relating them, sketch solids from different perspectives, and investigate the concepts of surface area and volume as ways to measure three-dimensional figures. Building on the concepts of similarity that you have learned, you will use ratios to determine the surface area and volume of similar solids.

Academic Vocabulary

As you work through this unit, add these terms to your vocabulary notebook.

- area
- net
- similar
- solid
- volume

Essential Questions

? Why is it important to be able to relate two-dimensional drawings with three-dimensional figures?

? How can surface area and volume be used to find answers to real-world problems?

EMBEDDED ASSESSMENTS

These assessments, following Activities 4.3 and 4.5, will give you an opportunity to demonstrate your ability to make and use representations of solids and to apply your understanding of surface area and volume of solids to real-world problems.

Embedded Assessment 1

Surface Area and
Volume   p. 265

Embedded Assessment 2

Surface Area and
Changes in Dimension   p. 287

Write your answers on notebook paper or grid paper. Show your work.

1. Compare and contrast the terms *surface area* and *volume*.

2. Given $e^2 = 100$, explain how to determine the value of e.

3. Rewrite the expression $b \cdot b \cdot b$ using exponents.

4. Evaluate each expression.
   a. $6 \cdot 8^2$
   b. $2(11 \cdot 5 + 6 \cdot 4)$
   c. 5^3

5. Simplify the ratio $\dfrac{28\pi}{100\pi}$.

6. Determine what fraction of the circle has been shaded. Explain how you arrived at your answer.

7. Solve for r.
$$2\pi r = \frac{4}{5}(35\pi)$$

8. Determine the area of each plane figure described or pictured below.
   a. Circle with radius 5 inches. Round your answer to the nearest tenth.
   b. Right triangle with leg lengths 4 inches and 7 inches.
   c. Rectangle with length 6 inches and width 10 inches.
   d. Trapezoid with base lengths 3 inches and 7 inches and height 12 inches.
   e.

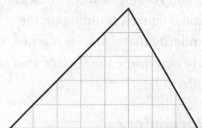

SUGGESTED LEARNING STRATEGIES: Activating Prior Knowledge, Use Manipulatives, Visualization, Group Presentation, Think/Pair/Share

The shape in Figure 1 is a **net**. A net is a two-dimensional drawing used to represent or form a three-dimensional object or solid.

Figure 1

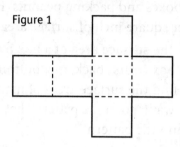

1. Cut out Figure 1 on page 249 and fold it along the dotted lines to form a box. The figure formed is a cube. Describe the characteristics that make it a cube.

2. The net below will also form a cube. If face number 1 is the bottom of the cube, which numbered face is the top of the cube?

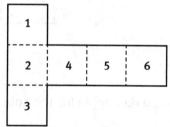

3. Many other nets can be used to represent a cube.

   a. Use graph paper to draw as many of these other nets as you can find. Cut out each net and fold it to verify that a cube can be formed.

   b. Sketch the nets you found that form a cube in the My Notes space.

   c. Sketch below two nets made up of six squares that do not form a cube.

My Notes

ACADEMIC VOCABULARY

The **area** of a plane figure is the measure in square units of its interior region.

In Elaine's new business, All Boxed Up, she sells shipping materials, including boxes and packing peanuts. Her box supplier charges her $\frac{1}{2}$ cent per square inch of surface area for each box. Elaine can determine the **surface area** of a box by adding the areas of the six faces of the box (front, back, top, bottom, left, and right).

Elaine must now find the surface areas of many boxes of different sizes, so she wants to find a pattern that will help shorten this work. Help her find the pattern.

4. One type of box that Elaine will keep in stock at All Boxed Up is a cube. For one of the cube-shaped boxes, the length of each edge is 5 inches.

   5 inches

   a. Find the area of each face.

   b. Find the total surface area of the cube.

5. Elaine wants to make a data table for the cube-shaped boxes.

   a. Record your answer from Item 4. Then complete the table for other cube-shaped boxes that will be in stock.

Length of Edge (in.)	Number of Faces	Area of One Face (in.^{2})	Surface Area (in.^{2})
5			
6			
7			
8			
		100	
			1350

   b. Describe any patterns you see in the table above.

   c. For each box, how does the area of one face relate to the surface area?

Volume and Surface Area of Rectangular Prisms
All Boxed Up

SUGGESTED LEARNING STRATEGIES: Create Representations, Group Presentation, Identify a Subtask, Interactive Word Wall, Use Manipulatives

My Notes

6. You can use a variable to represent the length of the edge of a cube.

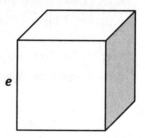

e

a. In the figure to the right, what variable is used to represent the length of the edge of the cube?

b. Write a rule, in terms of the variable, for finding the surface area of a cube.

7. Cube-shaped boxes with 12-inch edges are kept in stock at All Boxed Up.

a. Determine the surface area of a box with 12-inch edges.

b. The supplier charges Elaine $\frac{1}{2}$ cent per square inch of surface area for each box. Determine how much profit Elaine will make on a 12-inch cube-shaped box if she sells it for $4.95. Show your work.

8. Another type of box is a **rectangular prism**. In a rectangular prism, all the faces are rectangles but not necessarily squares. Look at Figure 2, which is a rectangular prism, on page 249. Show the calculations to find the area of each face. Then find the surface area of the prism.

MATH TERMS

A **prism** is a solid with parallel congruent bases which are both polygons. The faces (sides) of a prism are all parallelograms or rectangles. A prism is named according to the shape of its bases.

Face	Calculation	Area (in.²)
1		
2		
3		
4		
5		
6		

Surface area of Figure 2 = _____

My Notes

9. Cut out Figure 2 on page 249. Fold it to form a rectangular prism. Make folds so that the measurements are on the outside.

   a. Label the length, width, and height of the rectangular prism you formed on this diagram.

   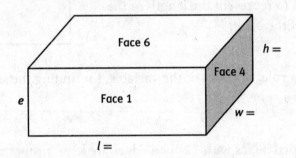

   b. Faces 2, 3, and 5 cannot be seen in the diagram above. Describe the location of each of these hidden faces.

   Face 2:

   Face 3:

   Face 5:

   c. Which pairs of faces have the same area?

10. Calculate the surface area of each rectangular prism. Show your work.

   a.

   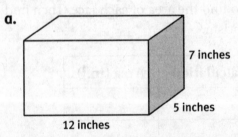

   b.

   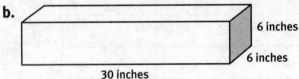

SUGGESTED LEARNING STRATEGIES: Create Representations, Identify a Subtask, RAFT

My Notes

11. Write a rule that Elaine can use to determine the surface area of a rectangular prism with the length, width, and height represented by the variables *l*, *w*, and *h*. Explain how you found the rule.

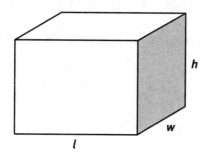

12. Elaine is stocking a new box that is 24 inches long, 12 inches wide, and 10 inches high. Make a recommendation to Elaine regarding a price for this size box. Remember that her box supplier charges her $\frac{1}{2}$ cent per square inch of surface area for each box. Be certain to explain how you arrived at your recommendation.

Elaine plans to sell packing peanuts at All Boxed Up. She knows that surface area will not tell her how many packing peanuts she needs to fill a box. She knows the **volume** of a box will help in estimating the number of packing peanuts needed to fill the box. Volume is measured in cubic units.

Cubes are named for the lengths of their edges. A 1-inch cube is a cube with edges that are 1 inch in length. A 2-inch cube is a cube with edges that are 2 inches in length. Any size cubes can be used to build larger cubes.

ACADEMIC VOCABULARY

Volume is the measure of the space occupied by a solid. It is measured in cubic units such as cubic inches (in.^{3}).

My Notes

13. Elaine uses unit cubes, similar to the ones your teacher has given you, as models of 1-inch cubes.

   a. Use your unit cubes to build models of 2-inch cubes and 3-inch cubes. Then complete this table.

Length of Edge (in.)	Area of Face (in.²)	Volume of Cube (in.³)
1		
2		
3		

   b. Describe any relationships you see in the table.

14. Describe how you can determine the volume of a cube when you do not have enough cubes to build the box.

15. Use the variable *e* to represent the length of the edge of a cube. Write a rule, in terms of *e*, for calculating the volume of a cube.

16. Determine the volume of a cube with edge length 8 inches.

17. Now think about boxes that are rectangular prisms.

   a. Complete this table. Use cubes to build boxes as needed.

Length (in.)	Width (in.)	Height (in.)	Volume (in.³)
2	1	4	
4	3	2	
5	2	3	
3	4	5	

My Notes

b. Describe any pattern you see in the table for finding the volume of rectangular prisms (on the previous page).

c. Use the variables *l*, *w*, and *h* to represent the length, width, and height of a box. Write a rule, in terms of *l*, *w*, and *h*, for finding the volume of a box.

18. Elaine has a customer who needs a box with a volume of 12 cubic inches. The customer wants to know what size box is the least expensive to buy.
  - The price will be based on surface area. The supplier charges $\frac{1}{2}$ cent per square inch.
  - The dimensions of the box are whole numbers.

What size box do you recommend that Elaine's customer buy? Write a report to Elaine that shows your work and explains your recommendation.

CHECK YOUR UNDERSTANDING

Write your answers on notebook paper.
Show your work.

1. Determine whether the net can be cut out and folded to form a cube.

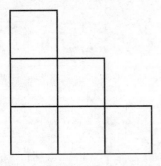

2. What is the surface area of a cube that measures 4 cm on each edge?

3. Determine the length of one edge of a cube that has a surface area of 864 square inches.

4. Find the surface area of this prism.

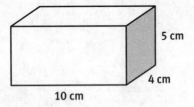

5. A swimming pool, in the shape of a rectangular prism, is 50 meters long, 25 meters wide and 3 meters deep. A liter is the same as 0.001 cubic meters. How many liters of water are needed to completely fill the pool?

6. Danny needs to buy sand for this box. He wants to nearly fill the box, leaving only 6 inches empty at the top. How much sand does Danny need?

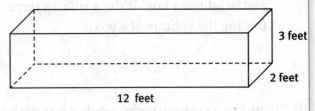

7. A hole shaped like a rectangular prism is 3 feet wide, 5 feet long, and 3 feet deep. If the hole is made 2 feet deeper, how much will the volume of the hole increase?

8. What is the maximum number of cubes with a side length of 2 inches that can fit in this box?

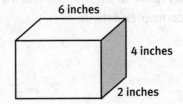

9. Determine the length of a rectangular prism whose width is 5 mm and whose height is 18 mm, if the volume of the prism is 540 mm^3.

10. **MATHEMATICAL REFLECTION** You are to design a box that will hold 24 2-inch cubes. Describe two possible designs for the box if there is no empty space left in the box after you have put in all of the cubes. Sketch each of your designs and give their surface areas and volumes.

Figure 1

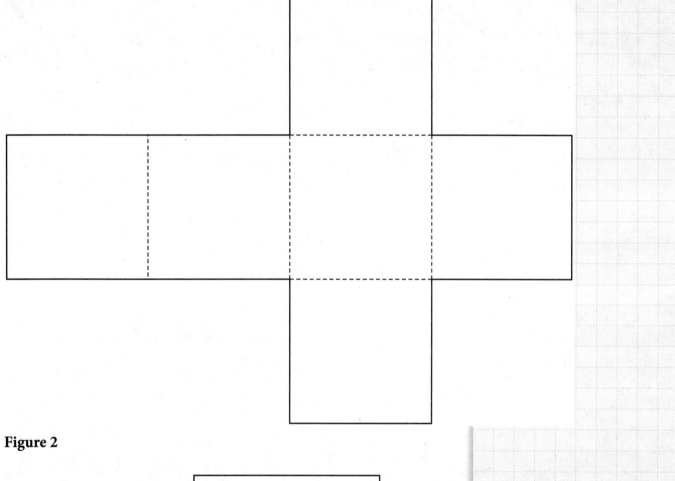

Figure 2

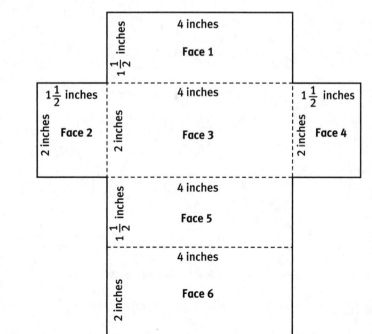

Sketching Solids
Putt-Putt Perspective

SUGGESTED LEARNING STRATEGIES: Activating Prior Knowledge, Look for a Pattern, Visualization

The Community Service Club at Greenway Park Middle School is designing a miniature golf course to use to raise funds for a food bank. The theme of the golf course is interesting structures around the world. Some buildings that will be included are the Washington Monument, the Flatiron Building, the Louvre Pyramid, and the Pentagon Building.

1. Compare and contrast the shapes of these four buildings.

2. Three or more planes can intersect in a point. In the photos above, find and circle a point where three or more planes intersect.

3. Two or more planes can intersect in a line. In the photos above, find and draw a rectangle around a line where two or more planes intersect.

My Notes

CONNECT TO GEOGRAPHY

The Washington Monument is located in Washington, DC. The Pentagon is nearby in Arlington County, VA. The Flatiron Building is in New York, NY. The Louvre Pyramid is the entrance to the Louvre Museum in Paris, France.

MATH TERMS

A **pyramid** is a three-dimensional figure whose base is a polygon and whose other faces are triangles that share a common vertex.

MATH TERMS

A **plane** is a flat surface that extends infinitely in all directions. A parallelogram is usually used to model a plane in two dimensions.

My Notes

4. Find an example in your classroom of two or more planes that do not intersect.

5. The Flatiron Building is in the shape of a triangular prism.

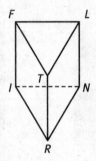

a. Name two parallel segments.

b. **Skew** lines are not parallel but do not intersect. Name two skew segments in the triangular prism.

The club members do not know how to draw three-dimensional shapes, so they ask their math teacher to explain the process. To prepare them for learning how to draw the buildings for their mini-golf course plans, their teacher helps them investigate relationships between shapes, views of shapes, and drawings of shapes.

6. Use unit cubes to build a model of the solid with these top, side, and front views.

Top View

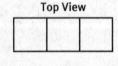

Front View   **Side View**

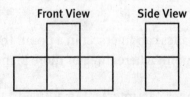

Sketching Solids
Putt-Putt Perspective

SUGGESTED LEARNING STRATEGIES: Create Representations, Look for a Pattern

My Notes

> **MATH TIP**
>
> Isometric dot paper has a different arrangement of dots than square dot paper.

ACADEMIC VOCABULARY

A **solid** is a three-dimensional figure, having length, width, and height.

7. Their teacher coached them through the following steps for sketching the **solid** on isometric dot paper.

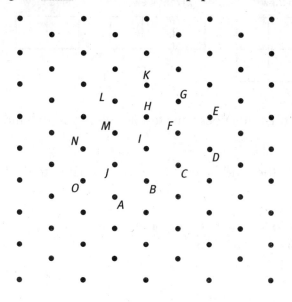

a. Use a ruler or the edge of an index card to connect A–B–C–D–E–F–G–H–I–J–A in that order.

b. Connect B–I, next connect C–F, and then connect I–F to complete the four squares.

c. Explain how the figure made in Parts a and b relates to the solid you built in Question 6.

d. Connect E–G–K–L–M–N–O–A in that order.

e. Connect the remaining dots to complete the isometric drawing of the solid.

f. Explain how the three views in Question 6 compare to the isometric drawing you just completed.

My Notes

8. These drawings are the top, side, and front views of a solid.

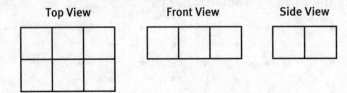

Top View   Front View   Side View

a. Use the unit cubes your teacher gives you to build the solid.

b. Draw the solid on the isometric dot paper to the left.

9. A prism is a solid with two parallel bases and rectangles or parallelograms as sides.

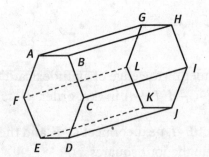

a. What would be the most appropriate name for the prism in this drawing? Explain how you determined your answer.

b. Why do you think some of the lines are dotted?

c. Imagine making a slice through points *B*, *D*, *H* and *J* of the prism. What would be the shape of the two-dimensional slice?

10. In the My Notes space, redraw the prism in Item 9. Explain the steps used to create your drawing.

SUGGESTED LEARNING STRATEGIES: Create Representations, Visualization

My Notes

11. Sketch an octagonal prism. Dot the appropriate lines.

12. What is a name for a solid whose two parallel bases are circles? Draw the solid.

13. What would be the most appropriate name for the pyramid drawn below? Explain how you determined your answer.

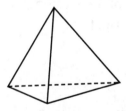

14. Look at the net for a solid in the My Notes space.

   a. If the net were folded along the dotted lines, what would be the most appropriate name for the solid formed?

   b. Sketch a three-dimensional drawing of the solid that could be formed with the net.

My Notes

15. What is a name for a solid with features similar to a pyramid whose base is a circle? Draw the solid.

16. Compare and contrast the features of a prism and a pyramid.

17. The Washington Monument is an example of a **complex solid**.

    a. Which geometric solids appear to make up the Washington Monument?

    b. Sketch a drawing of the Washington Monument at the right.

18. One member of the Community Service Club has been doing research on other landmark buildings. The Lighthouse of Alexandria, one of the seven wonders of the ancient world, had three different levels built on a large foundation. Use the information in each part to sketch the lighthouse.

    a. The bottom level was the largest and had the views shown in the My Notes space. Sketch the bottom level below.

> **MATH TERMS**
> In two-dimensional geometry, you studied composite figures. Composite figures are made up of more than one shape. In three-dimensional geometry, a **complex solid** is formed when two or more solids are put together.

Top, Side, and Front

SUGGESTED LEARNING STRATEGIES: Create Representations

b. The middle level was a regular octagonal prism. The height of this level was $\frac{1}{2}$ the height of the bottom level and the length of each side of the octagon was $\frac{1}{3}$ the width of the lower level. Sketch the middle level.

c. The top level was about half the height and half the width of the middle level. It is often shown as a complex solid consisting of a cylinder with a cone on top. Sketch the top level of the lighthouse.

d. Sketch the Lighthouse of Alexandria.

19. Choose a building you have seen in your town, when traveling, or in a film, book, or magazine that would be an interesting addition to the miniature golf course the Community Service Club is building. Describe the shape of the building as a solid figure or as a complex solid. Sketch the front, side, and top views of the building. Then make a drawing of the building on isometric dot paper.

CHECK YOUR UNDERSTANDING

Write your answers on notebook paper or isometric dot paper. Show your work.

1. Use the rectangular prism to answer the following.

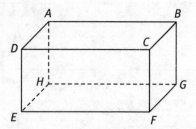

   a. Name two parallel line segments.

   b. Name two skew line segments.

   c. What is the intersection of the two planes: *ABCD* and *FGBC*?

   d. What is the intersection of the three planes: *ABCD*, *ADEH*, and *CDEF*?

   e. Imagine slicing through points *A*, *D*, *F*, and *G*. What would be the shape of the two-dimensional slice?

2. Use the top, front and side views to sketch the solid.

Top View

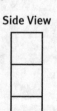

Side View

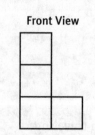

Front View

3. Sketch the front, side, and top views of the solid.

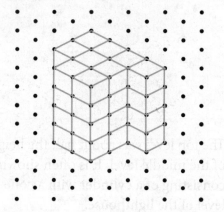

4. Sketch a drawing of a triangular prism.

5. Sketch a square pyramid.

6. **MATHEMATICAL REFLECTION** Think of a common object or building that is a complex solid. Identify the solids that make up the object or building.

Volume
Berneen Wick's Candles

SUGGESTED LEARNING STRATEGIES: Activating Prior Knowledge, Create Representations, Use Manipulatives, Quickwrite

Berneen makes all the candles that she sells in her shop, Wick's Candles. Her supplies cost $0.10 per cubic inch of a candle, so knowing the volume of a candle will help Berneen find the cost of making that candle. She has to do this for every shape of candle, so she wants to find a pattern that will make the computation easier.

The first candle shapes to investigate are prisms and cylinders.

1. Berneen begins by reviewing rectangular prisms because most of the candles she makes are this shape.

   a. Sketch a rectangular prism in the My Notes space.

   b. Explain how to find the volume of a rectangular prism.

2. The length and width of a candle are the dimensions of its base, or bottom.

   a. Complete this table.

Dimensions of Candle (in.)	Area of Base (in.²)	Candle Height (in.)	Candle Volume (in.³)
$l = 4$ $w = 2$ $h = 1$			
$l = 4$ $w = 2$ $h = 2$			
$l = 4$ $w = 2$ $h = 3$			
$l = 4$ $w = 2$ $h = 4$			
$l = 5$ $w = 3$ $h = 1$			
$l = 5$ $w = 3$ $h = 2$			

   b. Describe any pattern you see for finding volume.

My Notes

3. Use the variable B to represent the area of the base and h to represent the height of the candle.

  a. Write an equation, in terms of the variables, for finding the volume of the candle.

  b. Explain how the equation you just wrote in Part (a) and the equation you wrote in Item 1(b) are related.

Berneen knows that the volume equation for all prisms is the same as the equation you explored in Item 3.

4. The candle shown below is very popular with many of Berneen's customers because of its interesting shape.

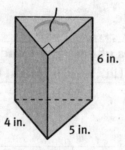

6 in.

4 in.   5 in.

  a. What is the most appropriate name for its shape?

  b. Apply the equation from Item 3 to find the volume of the candle. Be sure to include units with your answer.

  c. Remember that the cost of the supplies for a candle is $0.10 per cubic inch. Determine how much profit Berneen will make if she sells this candle for $8.99.

There are similarities between cylinders and prisms. The formula written in Item 3 can also be used to determine the volume of a cylinder.

CONNECT TO AP

Much of the work done in calculus is based on the fact that the volume of a prism is equal to the area of the base times the height of the prism.

SUGGESTED LEARNING STRATEGIES: Create Representations, Group Presentation, Think/Pair/Share, Identify a Subtask, Quickwrite

My Notes

5. Use the variables *r* and *h* to represent the radius and height of the cylinder. Write an equation, in terms of *r* and *h*, for determining the volume of a cylinder.

6. Berneen has created a new candle to stock in her store. It is in the shape of a cylinder with radius 1.5 inches and height 8 inches.

   a. Sketch a drawing of the candle. Label the radius and height of the candle on your drawing.

   b. Recommend a price for this candle to Berneen. Remember supplies cost $0.10 per cubic inch. Show how you found the volume. Explain how you arrived at your price recommendation.

> **WRITING MATH**
>
> You may use either of two symbols to represent inches in drawings and technical writing: in. or ".

7. Other candles in Wick's Candles are in the shape of pyramids and cones. To determine their volumes, Berneen wants to make models of some candle molds so she can look for a relationship between the volume of a prism and the volume of a pyramid.

   a. Make a model of the prism candle mold.

   - Use the index cards or cardstock your teacher has given you to cut out 1 square with side length 2.5" and 4 rectangles with length 2.5" and width 2.75".
   - Tape them together to form a net for the rectangular prism with no top shown below.

> **MATH TIP**
>
> When π is used in a calculation, the answer may be left in terms of π or is given an approximate answer by using an approximation of π (3.14 or $\frac{22}{7}$). Often a problem will say what value to use for π or say to round the answer. If it does not, leave the answer in terms of π.

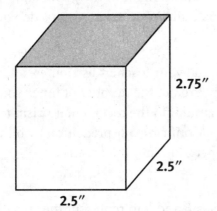

2.75"

2.5"

2.5"

   - Fold the net and tape it together to form a rectangular prism with no top.

My Notes

b. Make a model of the pyramid candle mold.

- Use the index cards or cardstock your teacher has given you to cut out 4 isosceles triangles with the dimensions shown in this diagram.

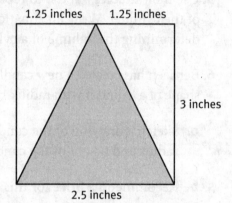

1.25 inches   1.25 inches

3 inches

2.5 inches

- Tape them together along the congruent sides of the triangles to form the net shown below for an open square pyramid.

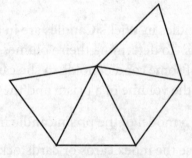

- Tape the last pair of sides together to form a square pyramid.

c. Compare the dimensions of the prism and the square pyramid you built. What relationships do you notice?

8. Using the material your teacher distributes, fill your pyramid level to the top. Predict the number of times you can fill and empty the pyramid into the rectangular prism to fill the prism level to the top. Confirm your prediction by filling and emptying the pyramid into the prism.

9. Use the variables *B* and *h* to represent the area of the base of the pyramid and the height of the pyramid. Write an equation, in terms of the variables, for finding the volume of the pyramid.

Volume
Berneen Wick's Candles

SUGGESTED LEARNING STRATEGIES: Quickwrite, Identify a Subtask, Create Representations, Think/Pair/Share Interactive Word Wall, RAFT

My Notes

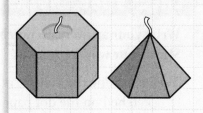

10. Two of Berneen's candles are shown to the right. They have the same base and height. What seems to be true about the relationship between the volumes of the candles?

11. Determine the volume and cost to make a candle in the shape of a square pyramid whose base edge is 6" and height is 4". Show your work.

12. You have learned that a cone is similar in some ways to a pyramid. Use the variables r and h to represent the radius and height of a cone. Write an equation, in terms of r and h, for determining the volume of a cone.

13. Determine the volume of a cone with diameter 8" and height 3". Show the calculations that lead to your answer and round your answer to the nearest tenth.

14. The volume of a **sphere** with radius r can be determined using the equation $V = \frac{4}{3}\pi r^3$. Determine the volume of a sphere with radius 6".

> **MATH TERMS**
>
> A **sphere** is the set of all points that are the same distance from a given point.

15. Berneen Wick wants to offer a gift set containing the five candles shown below. Remember: the cost per cubic inch of candle is $0.10. On a separate sheet of paper, prepare a report for Berneen in which you provide her with this information:
    - a name and a cost for each candle and the method of calculating each cost
    - your recommendation for the price of the gift set
    - your reasons for the recommendation

> **MATH TIP**
>
> Since you need to find a price, use 3.14 instead of $\frac{22}{7}$ as an approximation of π.

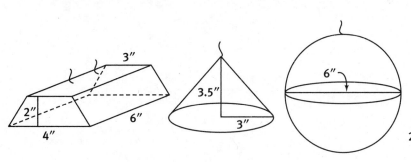

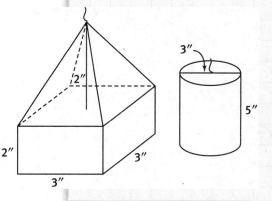

CHECK YOUR UNDERSTANDING

Write your answers on notebook paper.
Show your work.

1. Determine the volume of the figure sketched on the dot paper.

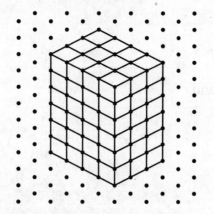

2. Find the volume of the cylinder.

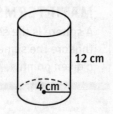

12 cm

4 cm

3. Find the volume of the triangular prism.

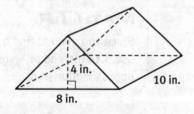

4 in.

10 in.

8 in.

4. What is the volume of a cone with a radius of 12 inches and a height of 11.2 inches?

5. The area of the base of a pyramid is 85 square centimeters. If its volume is 255 cubic centimeters, find the height of the pyramid.

6. Calculate the volume of the complex solid.

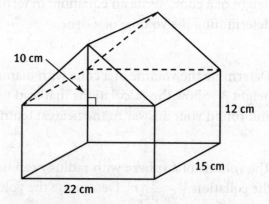

10 cm

12 cm

15 cm

22 cm

7. **MATHEMATICAL** **REFLECTION** How are the area of the base of a solid and the volume of that solid related? How is the shape of a solid related to its volume?

Surface Area and Volume

UNDER THE SEA

**Write your answers on notebook paper or isometric dot paper.
Show your work.**

Mack Finney is creating a new aquarium named Under the Sea. Because of his love of sea animals, he plans to include several different style tanks to house the aquatic life.

   He begins by designing the smallest fish tank. This tank is a rectangular prism with dimensions 4 feet by 3 feet by 2 feet.

1. Sketch a picture of the prism on isometric dot paper.

2. Draw a net that could be cut out and folded to represent the rectangular prism.

3. Determine the surface area and volume of the fish tank. Show the calculations that lead to your answer.

Near the main entrance to the aquarium, Mack has decided to locate a larger pool for four dolphins. Its shape is shown below.

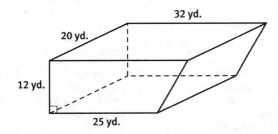

4. Determine the amount of water needed to fill the pool. Show the calculations that lead to your answer.

5. A drawing of the exotic fish center is shown below. Calculate the volume of the building.

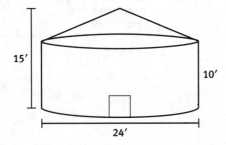

6. Mack designed a water fountain with a square pyramid flowing into a cube, as shown to the right. The edges of the bases of the pyramid and the cube have the same length and the heights of the pyramid and the cube are the same. Describe the relationship between the volume of the cube and the volume of the pyramid.

Surface Area and Volume

UNDER THE SEA

	Exemplary	Proficient	Emerging
Math Knowledge #3, 5	• Determines the correct surface area and volume of the tank (3) • Calculates the correct volume of the building (5)	• Determines the correct surface area or volume of the tank but not both • Uses the correct method to calculate the volume but makes a computational error	• Determines neither the correct surface area nor the volume • Shows evidence of a misconception when calculating the volume
Problem Solving #2, 4, 6	• Draws a net that correctly represents the prism (2) • Determines the correct amount of water needed to fill the pool (4) • Finds the correct relationship between the volume of the cube and the volume of the pyramid (6)	• Draws a partially correct net for the prism • Uses a correct method to find the amount of water but makes a computational error	• Draws an incorrect net for the prism • Determines an incorrect amount of water • States a relationship between the volumes that is incorrect
Representations #1, 2	• Makes a correct sketch of the prism (1) • Draws a correct net (2)	• Makes a partially correct sketch of the prism • Draws a partially correct net	• Makes an incorrect sketch of the prism • Draws an incorrect net
Communication #3, 5, 6	• Shows correct calculations for the surface area and the volume (3) • Shows correct calculations for the amount of water (4) • Shows correct calculations for the volume of the building (5) • Gives a complete description of the relationship between the volume of the cube and the volume of the pyramid (6)	• Shows correct calculations for either the surface area or volume but not both • Shows some, but not all of the correct calculations for the amount • Shows some, but not all of the correct calculations for the volume • Gives an incomplete description of the relationship	• Shows correct calculations for neither the surface area nor the volume • Shows incorrect calculations • Shows incorrect calculations • Gives an incorrect description of the relationship

Surface Area
Think Green

My Notes

The Horticulture Club has been given some land to build a greenhouse. The club president, Lillie, has to design a greenhouse and determine how much building material is needed. She will investigate possible designs by building models. Her teacher has provided several nets for the models Lillie wants to explore.

Lillie decides to begin her investigation with prisms.

1. Cut out Net 1, Net 2, and Net 3 on pages 273 and 275. Build the models. Write the best name for each prism.

2. Compare and contrast the characteristics of the prisms built from the nets provided.

3. Explain how to calculate the surface area of a prism.

4. Measure the nets to determine the surface area of each prism. Explain how you found the surface area.

> **CONNECT TO SCIENCE**
>
> *Horticulture* is the science and art of growing fruit, flowers, ornamental plants, and vegetables.

> **MATH TIP**
>
> Measure the Net 1 prism by using the square units on its surface.
>
> Measure the Net 2 prism by using the measures given on its surface.
>
> Measure the Net 3 prism with an inch ruler.

While doing online research about greenhouse designs, Lillie found the formula $SA = Ph + 2B$ for determining surface area of a prism where P represents the perimeter of the base, B represents the area of the base, and h represents the height of the prism.

5. Verify that the formula Lillie found will correctly calculate the surface area of the prisms you made in Item 1. Record the measures in this table and use the formula to find the surface areas. Then compare them to those you found in Item 4.

Net	P	h	B	SA
1				
2				
3				

6. Use the formula Lillie found ($SA = Ph + 2B$) to determine the surface area of this triangular prism.

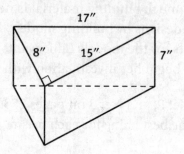

On page 277 are nets of pyramids that Lillie's teacher gave her.

7. Compare and contrast the characteristics of the pyramids that could be built from Net 4 and Net 5.

8. Cut out Net 5 and fold it to make a model of a square pyramid.

The surface area of a pyramid is the sum of the areas of the triangular faces and the area of the base. The height of a triangular face is the **slant height** of the pyramid.

9. Consider the slant height of the square pyramid.

   a. Draw the slant height on the faces of the pyramid you made.

   b. Why do you think it is called the slant height?

   c. How could you use your model to show the height of the pyramid?

10. Use the net to calculate the surface area of the square pyramid you built. Show the calculations that lead to your answers.

My Notes

11. Determine the number of triangular faces on a pyramid whose base has *n* sides.

12. A formula for finding the surface area of a **regular pyramid** uses four variables:

B to represent the area of the base,

l to represent slant height,

s to represent length of a base edge and

n to represent the number of sides on the base.

Write an equation, in terms of these variables, for finding the surface area of a regular pyramid.

13. Use the equation you wrote in Item 12 to calculate the surface area of the model you made of the square pyramid. Confirm that your answer agrees with the answer you got in Question 10.

In her research, Lillie discovers that The Myriad Botanical Gardens in Oklahoma City has a greenhouse in the shape of a cylinder. She wants to consider a cylindrical shape for their greenhouse. Help Lillie investigate the surface area of a cylinder.

14. Trace the top and bottom of a can on grid paper. Cut out the shapes drawn.

15. What shape is a piece of paper that would cover the side of the can?

16. Describe the relationship between the circumference of the base of the can and the length of the paper that covers the side of the can.

17. From the grid paper cut out a piece of paper that would cover the side of the can.

18. Use the shapes you have cut out to make a net that could be used to make a cylinder.

> **MATH TERMS**
> A **regular polygon** is a polygon whose sides are all congruent and whose angles are all congruent.
>
> A **pyramid** is a three-dimensional figure whose base is a polygon and whose other faces are triangles that share a common vertex.
>
> A **regular pyramid** has a base that is a regular polygon.

My Notes

19. Use your net to estimate the surface area of the cylindrical can.

20. Explain how to determine the surface area of a cylinder.

21. Use the variables r and h to represent the radius and height of a cylinder. Write an equation, in terms of r and h, for determining the surface area of a cylinder.

22. The greenhouse at the Myriad Botanical Gardens in Oklahoma City is a large cylinder with a diameter of 70 feet and a height of 224 feet. Lillie thinks that the club might build a smaller version that would have a diameter of 10 feet and a height of 20 feet. Determine the surface area of these two cylinders.

After considering prisms, pyramids, and cylinders, Lillie wants to study one last solid before designing the greenhouse. One of the nets her teacher gave her was for a cone. It looks like this:

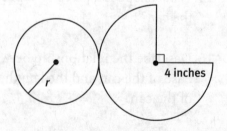

MATH TERMS

A **sector** is a part of a circle that is formed by 2 radii and part of the circumference of the original circle.

23. Cut out Net 6 on page 279, and build the cone.

24. The larger figure in the net is a **sector**. It looks like a circle that is missing a part. Why is the sector part of the net?

SUGGESTED LEARNING STRATEGIES: Identify a Subtask, Quickwrite

My Notes

25. How much of the circle remains in the sector? Explain your answer.

26. How is the circumference of the smaller circle related to the curved edge of the sector?

27. Calculate the circumference of the smaller circle. Give the answer in terms of π. Then find the radius of the smaller circle.

28. Determine the surface area of the cone. Show your work. Give the answer in terms of π.

Lillie knows that she will have to use three railroad ties to build steps up to the piece of land on which the greenhouse will be built. The ties are assembled as shown to the right and form a complex solid.

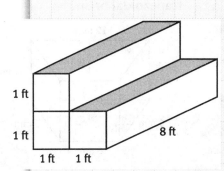

1 ft

1 ft

8 ft

1 ft   1 ft

29. If each railroad tie measures 1 ft by 1 ft by 8 ft, what is the surface area of the assembled steps?

30. Write a letter to Lillie giving her your suggestion for the design of a greenhouse. In your letter tell her what solids you would use and why you selected them. Include a drawing or sketch showing the dimensions of the greenhouse along with calculations for surface area.

My Notes

CHECK YOUR UNDERSTANDING

**Write your answers on notebook paper.
Show your work.**

1. The surface area of a rectangular prism is 96 square feet. Give one possible set of dimensions for this prism. You can use either of two formulas to find the surface area of a rectangular prism:
$SA = 2lw + 2lh + 2hw$ or $SA = Ph + 2B$.

2. Determine the surface area of the trapezoidal prism.

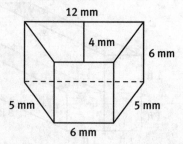

3. A tent with canvas sides and floor is shown below. How much canvas is in the sides and floor of the tent?

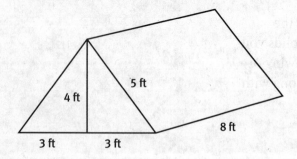

4. Determine the surface area of the pyramid.

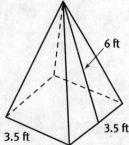

5. Find the surface area of the cylinder to the nearest tenth of an inch. Use 3.14 to approximate π.

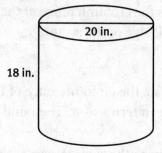

6. Find the surface area of the cone that can be formed from the net below. The sector is $\frac{4}{5}$ of a circle.

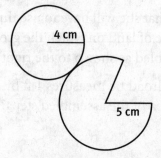

7. This composite figure consists of a regular pyramid and a cube. The edge of the cube is 4 inches. The height of each triangular face of the pyramid is 3 inches. What is the surface area of the figure?

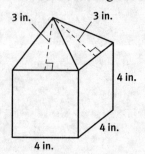

8. **MATHEMATICAL REFLECTION** What are some real-world situations for which it would be important to know the surface area of an object.

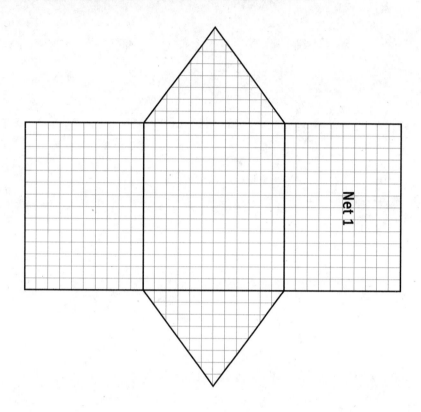

Net 1

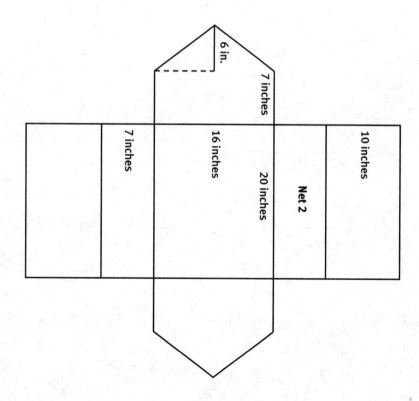

Net 2

6 in.

7 inches

16 inches

20 inches

7 inches

10 inches

Net 3

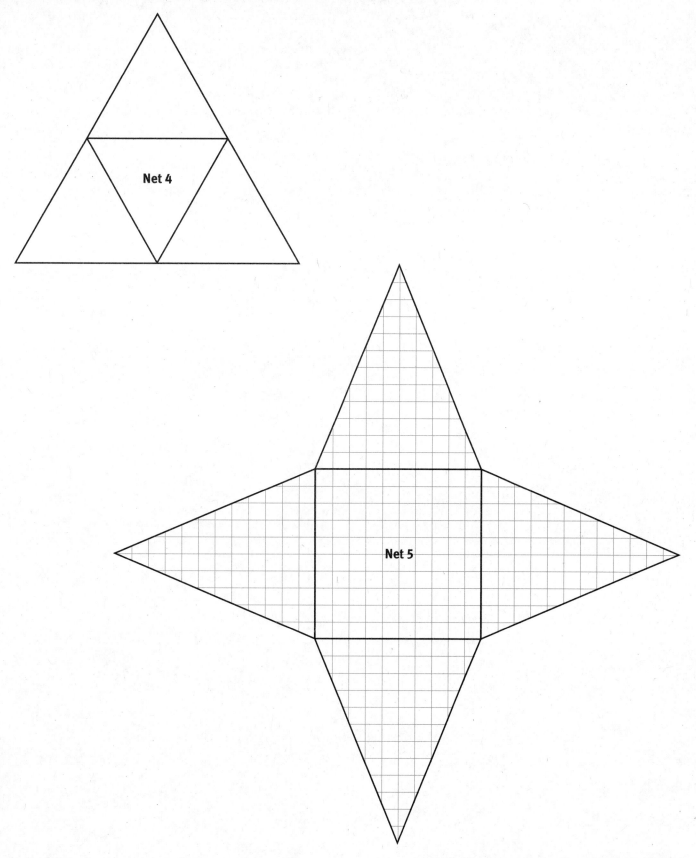

Net 4

Net 5

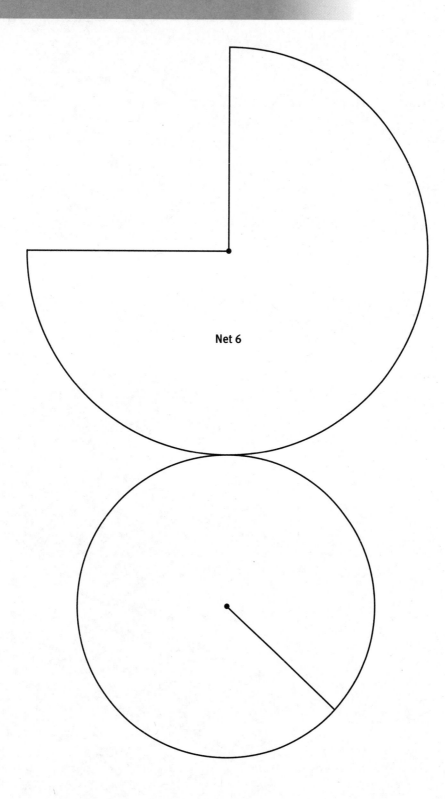

Net 6

Changing Dimensions
Crystal Globes

SUGGESTED LEARNING STRATEGIES: Activating Prior Knowledge, Summarize/Paraphrase/Retell, Discussion Group, Look for a Pattern, Quickwrite

The Crystal Globe Company uses special glass-blowing techniques to make decorative spheres of various diameters. Each crystal globe is packed in a distinctive cube-shaped gift box. The company has hired Heracio to investigate the different sizes of the spheres and the boxes so he can determine the volume of each box and how much material is needed to construct it.

1. Each decorative box has a special design on the top that is added after the sphere has been packed. This design (shown below) is made by gluing squares and circles on top of each other.

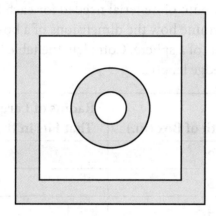

   a. The squares in the design have side lengths of 9 inches and 12 inches. Determine the perimeter and area of each square.

   b. Calculate the ratio of the side length of the smaller square to the larger square.

   c. Calculate the ratio of the perimeter of the smaller square to the larger square. What do you notice?

   d. Calculate the ratio of the area of the smaller square to the larger square. What do you notice?

2. The circles in the design have diameters 2 inches and 5 inches. Give each answer as a ratio of integers in terms of π.

   a. Determine the circumference and area of each circle.

My Notes

b. Calculate ratios for the larger circle to the smaller circle of:
- the diameters
- the circumferences
- the areas

c. What patterns do you notice for each ratio written in Part b?

3. To find the amount of material needed for each box, Heracio needs to determine how the dimensions of a box compare to the dimensions of a sphere. Complete the table below for boxes with various edge lengths.

Edge Length of Box (in.)	Radius of Largest Sphere That Fits in the Box (in.)
2	
3	
4.5	
e	

Heracio also needs to see if there are patterns that occur relating the surface area and volume of cubical boxes. He begins by investigating boxes in which the length of each edge is double the length of the previous edge.

4. Complete this table.

Length of Edge (in.)	Surface Area of Cube (in.²)	Volume of Cube (in.³)
1		
2		
4		

My Notes

5. As the length of an edge increases, so does the resulting surface area.

   a. Make a conjecture about the way the surface area changes when the edge of a cube is doubled.

   b. Use your conjecture to predict the surface area of a cube whose edge is 8 inches and then verify or revise your conjecture from Part a.

6. As the length of an edge increases, so does the resulting volume.

   a. Make a conjecture about the way the volume changes when the edge of a cube is doubled.

   b. Use your conjecture to predict the volume for a cube whose edge is 8 inches and verify or revise your conjecture from Part a.

7. Heracio now wants to focus on what happens when edges triple in length. Complete the following table.

Length of Edge (in.)	Surface Area of Cube (in.²)	Volume of Cube (in.³)
1		
3		
9		

8. As the edges of a cube are tripled, the surface area and volume increase. In addition to the increase, what other relationship exists between change in surface area and the change in volume?

My Notes

9. Heracio is now ready to make two conjectures.

   a. If a cube is built from 1-inch cubes, and if each new cube has an edge N times as long as the previous model, what would be true of consecutive surface areas?

   b. If a cube is built from 1-inch cubes, and if each new cube has an edge N times as long as the previous model, what would be true of consecutive volumes?

10. Apply the conjectures from Item 9 to a cube whose edge measures 27 inches.

   a. What amount of material is in this box?

   b. What would be the volume of this box?

11. Heracio now wants to determine if the relationship discovered in Item 9 is also true for the spherical crystal globes. Complete the table for spheres with various radii. Give the measures in terms of π.

Radius of Sphere (in.)	Surface Area of Sphere (in.^{2})	Volume of Sphere (in.^{3})
3		
6		
12		

12. Does it appear that the same conjecture you made for cubes in Item 9 applies to spheres as well? If *yes*, explain your answer in terms of the value of N that you identify. If *no*, give a counterexample that supports your explanation.

MATH TiP

In a sphere with radius r:

Surface area $= 4\pi r^2$

Volume $= \frac{4}{3}\pi r^3$

SUGGESTED LEARNING STRATEGIES: Interactive Word Wall, Quickwrite, Think/Pair/Share, Identify a Subtask

Similar two-dimensional and three-dimensional figures are those that have the same shape but not necessarily the same size.

13. Does this statement imply that all cubes are similar to all other cubes, and that all spheres are similar to all other spheres? Explain below.

14. The Crystal Globe Company has just begun making crystal sculptures in the shape of a tetrahedron. A **tetrahedron** has four faces, each of which is an equilateral triangle. The diagram below shows two tetrahedrons. Suppose the tetrahedron on the right has 4-inch edges and the tetrahedron on the left has 6-inch edges.

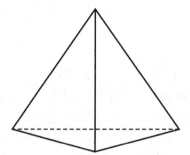
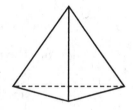

   a. Explain why the sculptures above are similar figures.

   b. What is the ratio of the surface area of the smaller tetrahedron to the surface area of the larger tetrahedron?

   c. What is the ratio of the volume of the smaller tetrahedron to the volume of the larger tetrahedron?

15. In addition to consulting for Crystal Globe, Heracio works on his family farm where grain is stored in silos. One silo has a diameter of 8 feet and the second silo has a diameter of 10 feet.

   a. Predict how the surface areas of the two silos compare. Explain how you arrived at your conclusion.

My Notes

ACADEMIC VOCABULARY

similar

CONNECT TO SOCIAL STUDIES

Silos are seen on many farms. A silo is usually quite tall and looks like a cylinder with a hemisphere on top.

My Notes

b. Predict how the volumes of the two silos compare. Explain how you arrived at your conclusion.

c. The volume of the smaller silo is 512π cubic feet. Use ratios to determine the volume of the larger silo.

CHECK YOUR UNDERSTANDING

Write your answers on notebook paper. Show your work.

1. The side length of a square is doubled.

    a. What will happen to the perimeter?

    b. What will happen to the area?

2. The radius of a circle is tripled.

    a. What will happen to the circumference?

    b. What will happen to the area?

3. A 5 × 7 photo is enlarged so that its new dimensions are 10 × 14. How does the area of the enlarged photo compare to the area of the original photo?

4. The ratio of the areas of two squares is 16:25. What is the ratio of the perimeters?

5. Each edge of a cube is 3 inches long. If the length of the edge is multiplied by four,

    a. What will happen to the surface area?

    b. What will happen to the volume?

6. The ratio of the volumes of two cubes is 8:27. If the length of the edge of the smaller cube is 2 centimeters, what is the length of the edge of the larger cube?

7. The radius of a sphere is multiplied by five.

    a. What will happen to the surface area?

    b. What will happen to the volume?

8. The surface areas of two similar pyramids are 100 cm² and 144 cm².

    a. What is the ratio of the heights?

    b. What is the ratio of the volumes?

    c. If the volume of the larger pyramid is 216 cm³, what is the volume of the smaller pyramid?

9. **MATHEMATICAL REFLECTION** Describe how the surface areas and volumes of solids are related to their linear dimensions. Use two different types of solids as examples.

Surface Area and Changes in Dimension

BIRD'S EYE VIEW

Write your answers on notebook paper. Show your work.

The Bird's Eye View Company designs and manufactures birdhouses.

1. The net for one birdhouse is shown below.

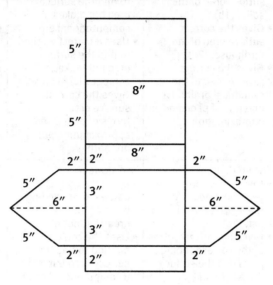

a. What is the appropriate geometric name for the solid formed by the net?

b. What is the total surface area of the solid? Show the calculations that lead to your answer.

2. The company also makes birdhouses in the shape of square pyramids. One of these birdhouses is shown to the right.

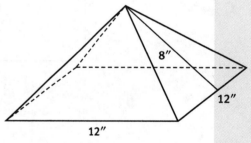

a. Determine the surface area of the birdhouse.

b. A larger birdhouse in the shape of a square pyramid is similar to the birdhouse shown. The length of the base edge of the larger birdhouse is 24". What is the ratio of the corresponding parts of the two pyramids?

c. What is the ratio of the surface areas of the two birdhouses?

d. Use the ratio given in Part c, to find the surface area of the larger birdhouse.

3. The company makes a bird feeder that is in the shape of a cylinder. The base has a 3-inch radius, and the height of each cylinder is 15 inches. What is the surface area of the cylindrical bird feeder? Give the answer in terms of π and as an approximation using 3.14 for π.

Surface Area and Changes in Dimension

BIRD'S EYE VIEW

	Exemplary	Proficient	Emerging
Math Knowledge #1b, 2a, 3	The student: • Gives the correct surface area of the solid. (1b) • Gives the correct surface area of the birdhouse. (2a) • Gives the correct surface area of the cylindrical birdhouse in terms of pi and as an approximation. (3)	The student: • Uses a correct method to find the surface area but makes a computational error. • Uses a correct method to find the surface area but makes a computational error. • Gives the correct surface area in terms of pi or as an approximation but not both.	The student: • Uses an incorrect method to find the surface area. • Uses an incorrect method to find the surface area. • Does not determine the correct surface area.
Problem Solving #1a, 2b-d	The student: • Gives the appropriate geometric name for the solid formed by the net. (1a) • Gives the correct ratios of the corresponding parts and the surface areas. (2b, c) • Finds the correct surface area of the larger birdhouse, based on the ratio given in 2c. (2d)	The student: • Gives the correct ratio of the corresponding parts or the surface areas but not both. • Uses the correct method to find the surface area but makes a computational error.	The student: • Gives the incorrect name for the solid formed by the net. • Gives the correct ratio for neither the corresponding parts nor the surface areas. • Does not find the correct surface area.
Communication #1b	The student shows correct calculations for the surface area. (1b)	The student shows some correct calculations for the surface area.	The student shows no correct calculations that would lead to the correct surface area.

ACTIVITY 4.1

1. Determine the surface area of a cube with edge length 15 cm.

2. The surface area of a cube is 726 in². Determine the length of one edge.

3. Rosie is making a stadium cushion in the shape of a rectangular prism with length 1.5 ft, width 1.5 ft, and height 0.5 ft. The foam for the cushion costs $2.50 and the fabric costs $0.75 per square foot. How much does it cost to make the cushion?

4. A room is 12 feet long, 11 feet wide and 10 feet high. In the room, four windows are each 3 feet wide and 4 feet tall. A gallon of paint covers 350 square feet. How many gallons of paint do you need to paint the four walls, not including the windows? Explain your answer.

5. Determine the length of one edge of a cube with volume 8000 ft³.

6. Calculate the volume of the prism shown.

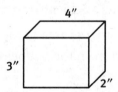

7. An office is 20 feet wide, 18 feet long and 10 feet high. If it costs on average $0.12 per year for air conditioning one cubic foot, how much does it cost to air condition the office for one year?

8. An aquarium shaped like a rectangular prism has length 30 inches, width 12.5 inches, and height 12.5 inches. How much water is needed to fill the tank 0.5 inches from the top of the tank?

ACTIVITY 4.2

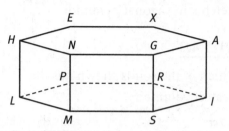

9. Use the prism to fnd each answer.

   a. Name two parallel segments.

   b. Name two skew segments.

   c. What is the intersection of the two planes: *HNML* and *NGSM*?

   d. What is the intersection of the three planes: *HNML*, *HEXAGN*, and *NGSM*?

10. Use the top, front and side views to draw the solid.

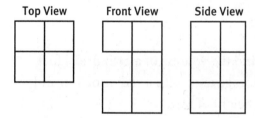

11. Draw the top, side and front views of the solid.

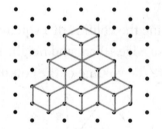

12. Draw a top, side and front view of the solid below.

Practice

13. Sketch a pentagonal prism.

14. Sketch a hexagonal pyramid.

ACTIVITY 4.3

15. Which of the solids shown has the greatest volume?

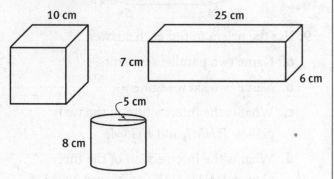

10 cm

25 cm

7 cm

6 cm

5 cm

8 cm

16. Determine the volume of the solid.

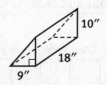

10"

18"

9"

17. Find the volume of a cylindrical fuel storage tank with a radius of 9 m and a height of 15 m.

18. How deep is a cylindrical swimming pool with a diameter of 14 ft and a volume of 1077.6 ft³?

19. Determine the volume of a square pyramid with base edge 10 cm and height 12 cm.

20. Calculate the volume of the complex solid.

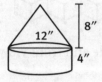

12"

8"

4"

ACTIVITY 4.4

21. Find the surface area of the prism.

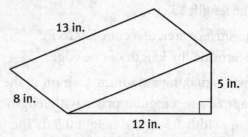

13 in.

5 in.

8 in.

12 in.

22. Determine the surface area of a regular hexagonal prism with base edge 10 cm, height 8 cm, and area of the base 259.8 cm².

23. Determine the surface area of a square pyramid with slant height 5 cm and perimeter of the base 32 cm.

24. Calculate the surface area of a regular triangular pyramid with slant height 8.3 inches, base edge 6 inches, and area of the base 15.6 square inches.

25. A vinyl liner covers the inside walls and bottom of a cylindrical pool that has a diameter 12 feet and height 3 feet. Find the area of this liner to the nearest tenth.

26. Calculate the surface area of the cone that can be formed from the net below.

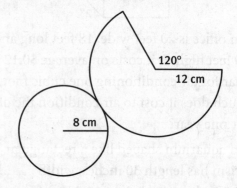

120°

12 cm

8 cm

ACTIVITY 4.5

27. If the length and width of a rectangle is doubled, what will happen to its area?

28. The areas of two circles are 16π in.² and 25π in.², what is the ratio of the circumference of the smaller circle to the larger circle?

29. The side measurements of a cube are tripled. What is the ratio of the surface area of the original cube to the surface area of the larger one?

30. The volumes of two spheres are 8π ft³ and 125π ft³.

   a. What is the ratio of the radii?

   b. What is the ratio of the surface areas?

31. Two similar prisms are shown.

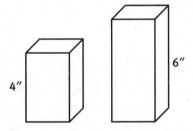

   a. If the surface area of the smaller prism is 52 in.², determine the surface area of the larger prism.

   b. If the volume of the smaller prism is 24 in.³, determine the volume of the larger prism.

32. The radius of a cone is 6 inches. The height is 12 inches. If the radius and height of the cone are tripled, what is the volume of the new cone?

33. A rugby ball is shaped like an elongated sphere (an ellipsoid). The ball used in official rugby has a length of 30 cm and a width of 18 cm. Younger children will use a ball whose length is 18 cm, but of the same shape as an official rugby ball.

   a. Determine the ratio of the size of the smaller rugby ball to the larger rugby ball.

   b. What are the ratios of the surface areas of the two rugby balls?

   c. What are the ratios of the volumes of the rugby balls?

An important aspect of growing as a learner is to take the time to reflect on your learning. It is important to think about where you started, what you have accomplished, what helped you learn, and how you will apply your new knowledge in the future. Use notebook paper to record your thinking on the following topics and to identify evidence of your learning.

Essential Questions

1. Review the mathematical concepts and your work in this unit before you write thoughtful responses to the questions below. Support your responses with specific examples from concepts and activities in the unit.

   - Why is it important to be able to relate two-dimensional drawings with three-dimensional figures?

   - How can surface area and volume be used to find answers to real-world problems?

Academic Vocabulary

2. Look at the following academic vocabulary words:
   - area
   - solid
   - net
   - volume
   - similar

   Choose three words and explain your understanding of each word and why each is important in your study of math.

Self-Evaluation

3. Look through the activities and Embedded Assessments in this unit. Use a table similar to the one below to list three major concepts in this unit and to rate your understanding of each.

Unit Concepts	Is Your Understanding Strong (S) or Weak (W)?
Concept 1	
Concept 2	
Concept 3	

   a. What will you do to address each weakness?

   b. What strategies or class activities were particularly helpful in learning the concepts you identified as strengths? Give examples to explain.

4. How do the concepts you learned in this unit relate to other math concepts and to the use of mathematics in the real world?

1. What is the surface area of the triangular prism?

    F. 132 cm²

    G. 144 cm²

    H. 147 cm²

    I. 660 cm²

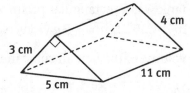

2. What is the volume of the figure?

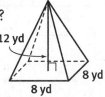

2.

Read
Solve
Explain

3. Elisabeth is creating a cake in the shape of a house shown at right for her Family and Consumer Science class. She must include information on how much cake and icing she used for the design.

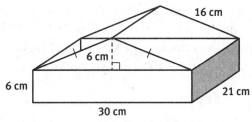

Part A: Calculate the amount of cake that is in Elisabeth's design (in cubic centimeters).

Answer and Explain

_____

_____

_____

Part B: Find the volume of icing Elisabeth used to frost the outside of the cake if all the icing is 2 cm thick. There is no icing under the cake. Explain your reasoning.

Answer and Explain

_____

_____

_____

_____

_____

_____

Read
Solve
Explain

4. Roger bought a fish tank for the puffer fish he received for Christmas. The tank was a rectangular prism with dimensions 12" by 10" by 10". It holds 5 gallons of water.

Part A: What is the volume of the tank in cubic inches?

Answer and Explain

_____

_____

_____

Part B: Roger receives another puffer fish for his birthday. The fish are very aggressive so he needs a 10-gallon tank. He is looking for a tank that is 24" × 20" × 20" because he thinks that this is double the size of his first tank. Is Roger's assumption accurate? Explain your reasoning.

Answer and Explain

_____

_____

_____

_____

Part C: Select a set of dimensions for a new tank that would double its holding capacity. Explain your reasoning.

Answer and Explain

_____

_____

_____

_____

Data and Probability

Unit Overview

In this unit you will formulate statements and answer questions about small populations by collecting, organizing, and analyzing data including bivariate data. You will determine sample space and calculate the probabilities for events, both dependent and independent.

Academic Vocabulary

As you work through this unit, add these terms and others you think are important to your vocabulary notebook.

- bivariate data
- event
- five-number summary
- measures of center
- random
- trend line

Essential Questions

? Why is it important to be able to represent data using graphs and measures of central tendency?

? How can data and probabilities be used to predict the outcome of future events?

EMBEDDED ASSESSMENTS

These assessments, following Activities 5.3 and 5.5, will give you an opportunity to demonstrate your ability to create and interpret data displays, as well as to calculate the probability of independent events, dependent events, and compound events and to determine mutual exclusivity.

Embedded Assessment 1

Data Display and Interpretation
p. 319

Embedded Assessment 2

One- and Two-Stage Probability
p. 335

Write your answers on notebook paper. Show your work.

1. Explain how to determine the mean, median, mode, and range of a set of data.

2. Use the data below to determine each measure of central tendency.

   3, 4, 6, 6, 7, 9, 9, 9, 14, 15

   a. Mean
   b. Median
   c. Mode

3. There are 2 white, 8 red, and 5 blue marbles in a bag. What is the probability of choosing a red marble?

4. The math club had 25 members and now has 30 members. What is the percent increase?

5. Apples cost $3.99 per pound. At that rate, what is the cost of a 3 pound bag?

6. A circle has 360°. What is the measure of an angle that represents 25% of the degrees in a circle?

7. Maddie is taking guitar lessons and has registered for private lessons with a music teacher. The cost of the lessons is shown in the graph below.

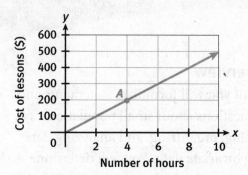

   a. Explain the meaning of point A on the graph.
   b. Use the graph to determine the cost of 2 hours of lessons. Explain how you determined your answer.
   c. Use the graph to determine how many hours of lessons Maddie received for $400.

8. Draw a ray like the one below. Use your ray and a protractor to draw an angle that measures 35°.

Data Displays
Batter Up

SUGGESTED LEARNING STRATEGIES: Activating Prior Knowledge, Marking the Text, Group Presentation, Interactive Word Wall

My Notes

Henry "Hank" Aaron and Harmon Killebrew are among the all-time leaders in home runs in Major League Baseball. As a tribute to their outstanding performance during their careers, both were elected to the Hall of Fame in the 1980s. To help compare the noteworthy achievements of these two players, their home run statistics are listed below.

CONNECT TO SPORTS

A 2007 study indicated that the average career span for a major league baseball player is 5.6 years. Statistics also indicate that the average home run production for a full time player per season is approximately 14 home runs.

Total Number of Home Runs Hit by Year

Year	Aaron	Killebrew	Year	Aaron	Killebrew
1954	13	0	1966	44	39
1955	27	4	1967	39	44
1956	26	5	1968	29	17
1957	44	2	1969	44	49
1958	30	0	1970	38	41
1959	39	42	1971	47	28
1960	40	31	1972	34	26
1961	34	46	1973	40	5
1962	45	48	1974	20	13
1963	44	45	1975	12	14
1964	24	49	1976	10	
1965	32	25			

1. In this table, is it easy to compare the home run data for Hank Aaron and Harmon Killebrew? Why or why not?

ACADEMIC VOCABULARY

The mean, median, and mode are referred to collectively as **measures of center** or **measures of central tendency**.

2. For each player's data, find the mean, median, mode and range.

Aaron	Killebrew
Mean:	Mean:
Median:	Median:
Mode:	Mode:
Range:	Range:

My Notes

3. Considering this data, why do you think the home run data for Hank Aaron and Harmon Killebrew is said to be exceptional?

4. Describe any similarities or differences in the home run data of the two baseball players.

To organize data so that it can be interpreted more easily, a **stem plot** can be used.

MATH TERMS

A **stem plot**, also called a **stem-and-leaf plot**, displays each data value in a set in two parts according to place value, where the stem represents the first digit or digits and the leaf represents the last digit of the number. A key shows how to read the values in a stem plot:
Examples:
1 | 4 represents 14
21 | 0 represents 210

EXAMPLE 1

Draw a stem plot for this set of data.

$$\{53, 84, 55, 70, 77, 63, 51, 53, 75, 82, 72\}$$

Step 1: Draw a vertical line. On the left side of the line write the tens digit of each number (without repeating) in the data set. This is the **stem**.

```
5 |
6 |
7 |
8 |
```

Step 2: Next to each number in the stem, write the units digit of each corresponding element of the data set in order from least to greatest. Each of these numbers is a **leaf**, and there will be as many leaves as there are numbers in the set.

```
5 | 1 3 3 5
6 | 3
7 | 0 2 5 7
8 | 2 4
```

Step 3: Make a key to show what a stem and leaf represent.

Key: 8 | 2 = 82

TRY THESE A

Write your answers in the My Notes space. Show your work.

a. Make a stem plot for Hank Aaron's home run data.

b. Make another for Harmon Killebrew's home run data.

My Notes

5. In what ways does the stem plot make the data easier to analyze?

6. Compare the home run data for both players.

7. What advantages or disadvantages do you notice when using the stem plot to analyze each player's homeruns?

Numerical data can also be organized in a **histogram**.

> **MATH TERMS**
>
> A **histogram** is a graph used to show the frequencies for a set of data. The horizontal axis is divided into equal intervals. The vertical axis shows the **frequency,** or the number of items, in each interval.

EXAMPLE 2

Draw a histogram for the set of data below.

$$\{53, 84, 55, 70, 77, 63, 51, 53, 75, 82, 72\}$$

Step 1: Draw vertical and horizontal axes, placing equal numerical intervals on the horizontal axis and **frequency** values on the vertical axis.

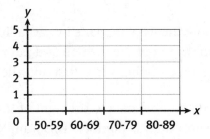

Step 2: Count the number of elements in each numerical interval and draw a vertical bar representing that frequency.

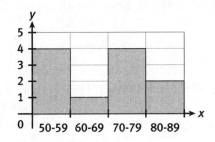

> **MATH TIP**
>
> A **histogram** is used to describe numerical data (for example, ages, heights, weights), while a **bar graph** is used to describe categorical data (for example, colors, types, qualities). The bars in a histogram always touch, but the bars in a bar graph never touch.

My Notes

SUGGESTED LEARNING STRATEGIES: Marking the Text, Question the Text, Create Representations, Group Presentation

TRY THESE B

Write your answers in the My Notes space. Show your work.
Use the home run data for Hank Aaron and Harmon Killebrew.

a. Make a histogram for Hank Aaron's data.

b. Make a histogram for Harmon Killebrew's data.

8. Look at the histograms you made for Try These B. Identify the information that you can gather about Aaron's and Killebrew's home run production using these displays.

Another display that allows for further interpretation of data is a **box plot**. Consider the following steps.

9. Construct a box plot for the following data by completing the following steps.

$$\{53, 84, 55, 70, 77, 63, 51, 53, 75, 82, 72\}$$

a. Put the numbers in order from smallest to largest and circle the maximum, minimum, and median. Leave some space between the numbers.

b. Continue using the list you made in Part a. Find the median of the data to the left of the median and put a square around this number. This number is the first quartile.

c. Find the median of the data to the right of the median and put a square around this number. This number is the third quartile.

d. Fill in the other scale marks on the number line below. Explain why 50 to 90 is chosen as an appropriate focus for this graph.

> **MATH TERMS**
>
> A **box plot**, also called a **box-and-whisker plot**, displays data organized into four sections, each representing 25% of the data.

> **ACADEMIC VOCABULARY**
>
> A **five-number summary** of data includes the minimum, first quartile, median, third quartile, and maximum. The information in the five-number summary is used in a box plot.

SUGGESTED LEARNING STRATEGIES: Marking the Text, Question the Text, Create Representations, Group Presentation, Quickwrite, Self/Peer Revision, Work Backward, Think/Pair/Share

My Notes

e. Continue working on the number line at the bottom of page 300. Plot the numbers from the five-number summary as dots above the number line.

f. Draw vertical lines above the first and third quartiles to serve as the ends of a horizontal rectangle. Draw the horizontal sides of the rectangle. Then draw a vertical line in the rectangular box for the median.

g. Draw a horizontal line to connect the dot at the maximum to the dot at the third quartile. Draw a horizontal line from the dot at the minimum to the dot at the first quartile.

10. What information does a box plot provide? What information is not provided in this display?

CONNECT TO AP

Stem plots, histograms, and box plots are among the displays used in AP Statistics.

11. Construct a box plot for Hank Aaron's home run data and another box plot for Harmon Killebrew's home run data.

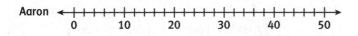

Aaron

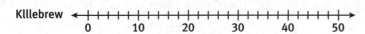

Klllebrew

12. Use the box plots in Question 12 to compare the home run data for both players. What new information can you gather using these displays?

13. Look back at the measures that you found in Question 2. Which measure do you think best describes the data for these two players? Justify your answer.

My Notes

When you want to compare part of a data set to the whole data set, you can use a circle graph.

14. These data show the percent of homeruns scored by a high school baseball team by grade level.

   Freshmen: 10%   Sophomores: 25%
   Juniors: 30%   Seniors: 35%

   Use the data and the fact that a circle has 360° to make a circle graph. Follow these steps.

   a. Determine the angle measure of the sector for Freshmen by finding 10% of 360°. Use your protractor and the circle graph template provided by your teacher to draw the sector representing Freshmen homeruns.

   b. Label the sector you drew.

   c. Repeat the steps in parts a and b for Sophomore, Junior, and Senior homeruns.

   d. Title your circle graph.

CHECK YOUR UNDERSTANDING

Write your answers on notebook paper. Show your work.

Mr. Nelson's class recently took a test. He made a list of the scores:

   66, 79, 76, 95, 55, 82, 60, 85,
   93, 76, 63, 96, 75, 82, 71

1. Find all three measures of central tendency for the test scores.

2. Create a stem plot from the test score data.

3. Create a histogram from the test score data using intervals of 5.

4. Complete a five-number summary of the test score data.

5. Use the five-number summary to make a box plot for the test score data.

6. After a student completed a makeup test, Mr. Nelson added his score, 85, to the data set. Make a box plot for the new data set.

7. These data show the attendance by grade level of students who attended high school baseball games last season.

   Freshmen: 15%   Sophomores: 20%
   Juniors: 25%   Seniors: 40%
   Create a circle graph for the data.

8. Compare the information gathered from each of the data displays.

9. **MATHEMATICAL REFLECTION** What are the advantages and disadvantages of each type of data display addressed in this activity?

Bivariate Data
Bean Counters

SUGGESTED LEARNING STRATEGIES: Activating Prior Knowledge, Marking the Text, Summarize/Paraphrase/Retell, Guess and Check, Quickwrite, Self/Peer Revision, Simplify the Problem, Role Play, Create Representations

My Notes

The culinary arts club at Lima Middle School is staging a contest to see who can guess the number of beans in a glass container. The winner of the contest gets a free bean burrito in the school cafeteria each day for a month. Fava likes burritos and is interested in winning the contest, so she measures the container. The container is in the shape of a rectangular prism and has dimensions 17 inches long, 12 inches wide, and 10 inches high.

CONNECT TO CAREERS

Culinary arts refers to the manner of preparing or presenting foods. Chefs and cooks are referred to as culinary artists.

1. What is the volume of the container in cubic inches?

2. How many beans do you think are in the container?

3. Describe methods that Fava could use to increase the accuracy of her guess in Question 2.

To help guess the number of beans in the container, Fava constructed several smaller containers out of paper and filled them with beans. By counting the beans in the small containers, Fava thinks she can predict the number of beans in the larger container.

4. Cut out Figures 1–5 on pages 307–311. Fold each one on the dotted lines and tape the sides to make a rectangular prism.

- Find and record the dimensions of each prism.
- Compute and record the volume of each prism.
- Fill each prism with beans.
- Count and record the number of beans that are needed to fill each prism.

Figure	Dimensions (in.)	Volume (in.³)	Number of Beans
1			
2			
3			
4			
5			

My Notes

ACADEMIC VOCABULARY

Bivariate data can be written as ordered pairs where each numerical quantity represents measurement information recorded about a particular subject.

MATH TERMS

A collection of data points is said to have a **positive correlation** if *y* tends to increase as *x* increases and to have a **negative correlation** if *y* tends to decrease as *x* increases.

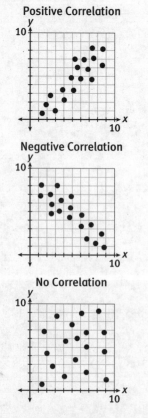

A correlation can also be called an association.

5. Compare your data table with those from others in your class. How do you explain any differences in the data collected?

6. Based on your data in the table in Question 4, would you revise your guess in Question 2? Explain your reasoning.

7. For each of the containers you constructed in Question 4, write an ordered pair (volume, number of beans) representing the **bivariate data** for that container.

Bivariate data can be organized and displayed on a graph called a **scatterplot**. To make a scatterplot, graph each of the ordered pairs for the data on a coordinate grid.

8. Make a scatterplot for your data using the ordered pairs from Question 7. Label the axes and title your graph.

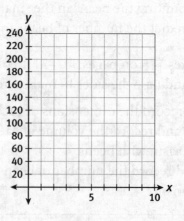

SUGGESTED LEARNING STRATEGIES: Look for a Pattern, Quickwrite, Self/Peer Revision, Marking the Text, Interactive Word Wall, Create Representations, Guess and Check

9. What patterns do you notice in the scatterplot?

10. What happens to the number of beans as the volume increases?

If the points recorded on a scatterplot appear linear, then the data can be modeled using a **trend line**.

11. Place a tool like a piece of dry spaghetti or a ruler on the scatter plot. See where you can put a line that is as close as possible to all the data points. This line will best model your data and will be your trend line. Draw it on your scatter plot.

12. Describe how to use your trend line to predict the number of beans in a container with a volume of 5 cubic inches. Explain why you can or cannot use your trend line to predict the number of beans in the contest container.

13. Fava wants to explore another method of predicting volume. Begin by completing this table.

Container	Volume	Number of Beans	Number of Beans Volume
1			
2			
3			
4			
5			

14. What patterns do you notice in the table in Question 13?

My Notes

ACADEMIC VOCABULARY

A trend line helps explain the relationship between two quantities on a graph. The trend line indicates the general course or tendency of the set of data.

CONNECT TO AP

In AP Statistics, you will use statistical calculations to find more accurate trend lines and judge how well your trend line models the data.

My Notes

© 2010 College Board. All rights reserved.

MATH TIP

A *unit rate* is a rate in which one of the quantities has a value of 1. For example, a rate of 25 miles per gallon is a unit rate that can be written as $\frac{25 \text{ miles}}{1 \text{ gallon}}$.

15. Write a *unit rate* that is represented by the patterns in the table in Question 13. Include the units in your rate.

16. Recall that the purpose in creating the small containers and gathering data was to make an educated guess in the bean container contest. Use your unit rate to make a prediction to help Fava win the contest. Explain how you made your prediction.

CHECK YOUR UNDERSTANDING

Write your answers on notebook paper. Show your work.

To raise money to buy new goals, the soccer team held a car wash. The table below shows the number of hours washing cars and the amount of money raised.

Hours washing cars	Total money raised
1	40
2	64
3	100
4	123
5	160

1. Make a scatter plot of the data in the table.

2. Does the data have a positive correlation, a negative correlation, or no correlation? What does the correlation mean?

3. On the scatter plot, draw a trend line that best models the data. Why do you think this is the best line?

4. Use the data to determine a unit rate, including units.

5. If new soccer goals cost a total of $2200, for how many hours would you estimate that the soccer team would have to wash cars?

6. **MATHEMATICAL REFLECTION** Use two examples of bivariate data to explain how the relationship between the two variables and the unit rate differs for data with a positive correlation and for data with a negative correlation.

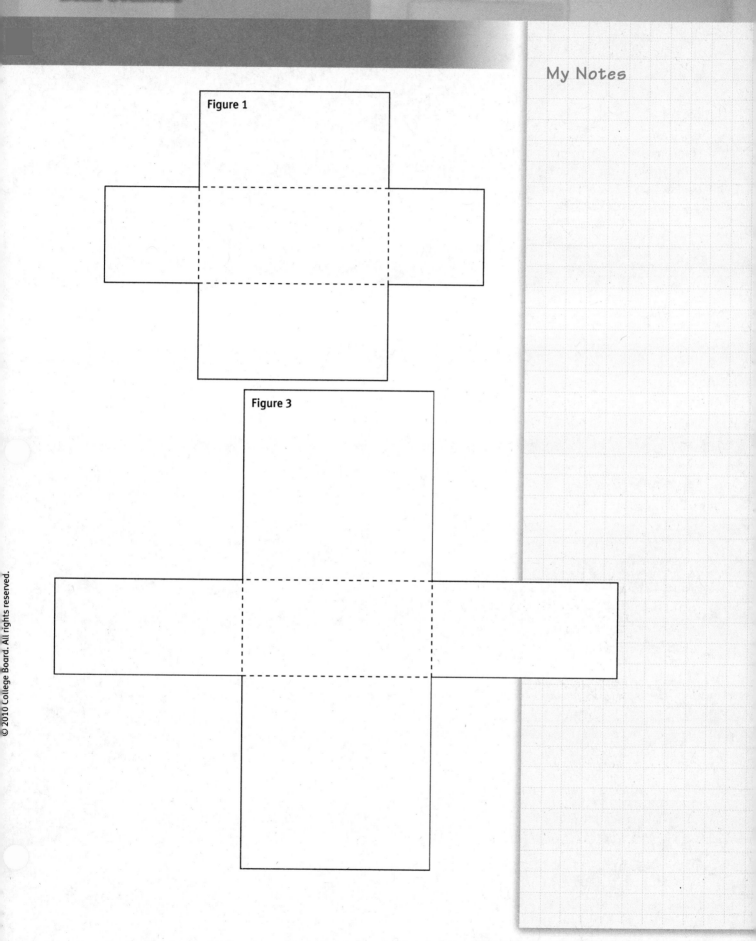

Figure 1

Figure 3

My Notes

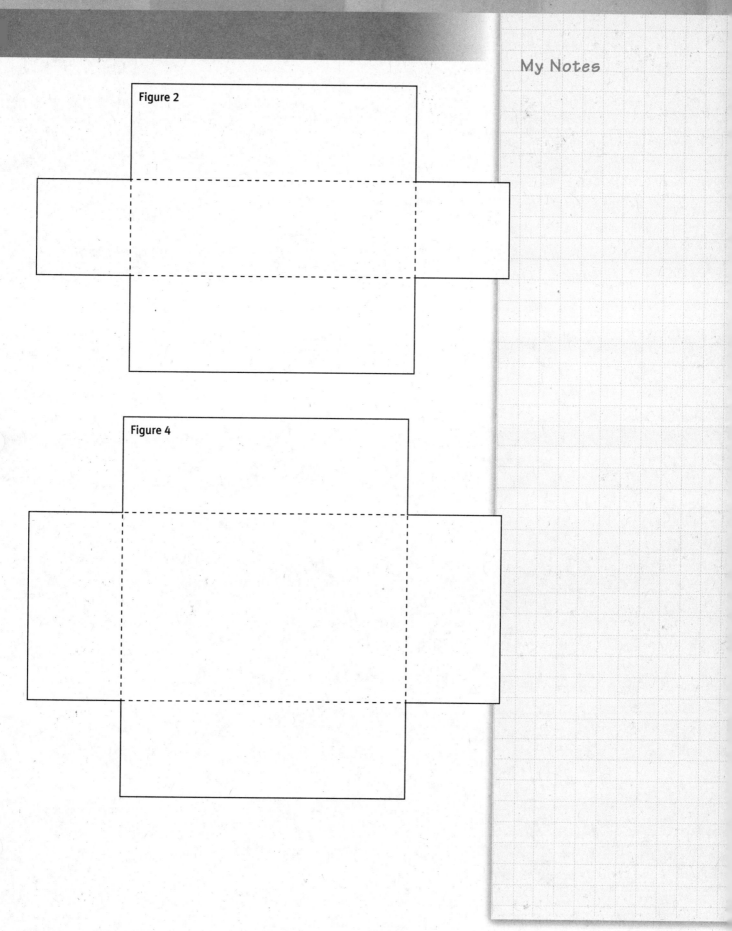

Figure 2

Figure 4

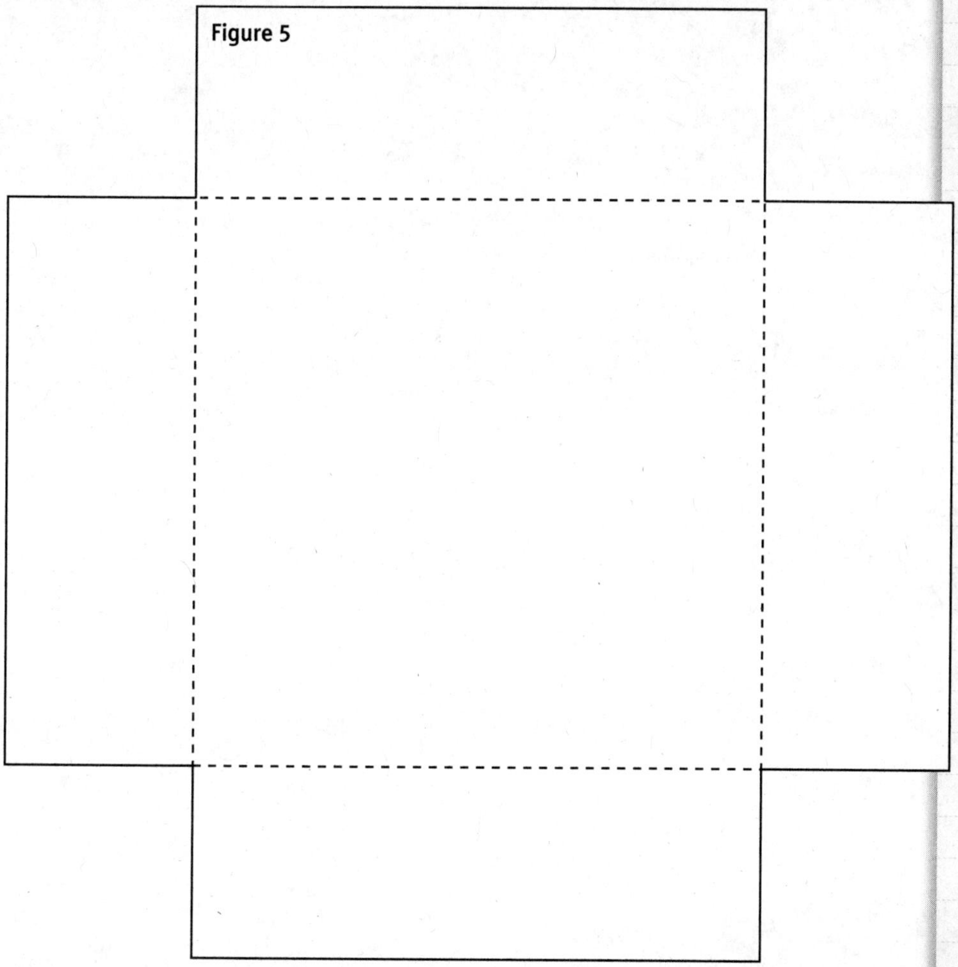

Figure 5

My Notes

Interpreting Bivariate Data Displays
Communication Breakdown

SUGGESTED LEARNING STRATEGIES: Summarize/Paraphrase/Retell,
Question the Text, Activating Prior Knowledge, Look for a Pattern,
Quickwrite, Self/Peer Revision

My Notes

Several factors contribute to the total monthly cost of using a
cellular telephone. The base cost of the service plan, taxes, talk time
usage, and text messaging all contribute to the amount of each
monthly bill. Michelle and her mother each have a phone and share
a plan with the same provider.

   Michelle quickly learned to use the text-messaging feature on
her phone. After several months, her mother collected the data
shown to the right and displayed it in the scatter plot below.

Text Messages (number per month)	Total Cell Phone Bill (dollars per month)
70	80
100	87
150	90
200	93
210	100

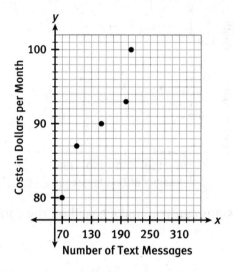

1. What conclusions can you make based on the data in the table?

2. What patterns in the table seem to agree with the patterns in the
   scatter plot?

3. What patterns in the table seem to disagree with the patterns in
   the scatter plot?

My Notes

Concerned about the meaning of the data, Michelle's mother asked Michelle to limit her use of the text feature on her phone.

4. Why might Michelle's mother make that decision?

Michelle created another scatter plot using the same data. Her scatter plot is displayed below.

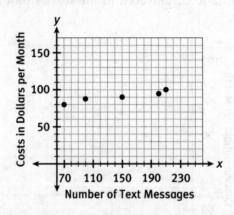

5. What conclusions can you make based on the data in the graph?

6. What patterns in the table seem to agree with the patterns in this scatter plot?

7. What patterns in the table seem to disagree with the patterns in the scatter plot?

Interpreting Bivariate Data Displays
Communication Breakdown

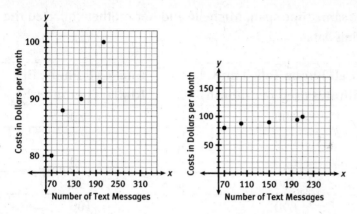

The two scatter plots are reproduced above. They both represent the same data set yet support different conclusions.

8. What features of the graphs contribute to these different conclusions? Explain below.

9. Explain how you would create a scatter plot for the text message and cost data that you think is a fair representation. After completing your explanation, draw the scatter plot.

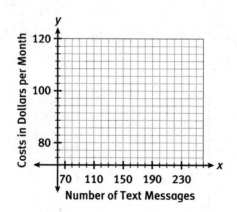

My Notes

MATH TERMS

A *biased* data display favors one point of view over another.

For the same time span, Michelle and her mother collected the following data.

Cell Phone Talk Time (minutes used per month)	Total Cell Phone Bill (dollars per month)
600	80
630	87
650	90
680	93
690	100

10. Create a scatter plot that is biased by making the increase in cost seem excessive.

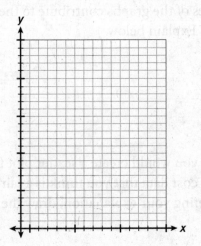

11. Create a scatter plot that is biased by making the increase seem minimal.

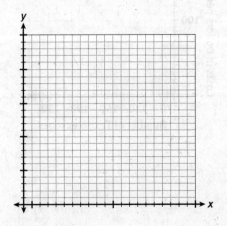

SUGGESTED LEARNING STRATEGIES: Think/Pair/Share, Look for a Pattern, Create Representations, Group Presentation, Quickwrite, Self/Peer Revision

Michelle's friend Harry collected data on his cell phone usage.

Number of Text Messages	Number of Cell Phone Minutes Used
50	300
80	275
115	200
135	195
200	140

12. Formulate a question that relates the two data sets.

13. Create a biased scatter plot for the data. Identify the intent of your bias and how the data display represents that bias.

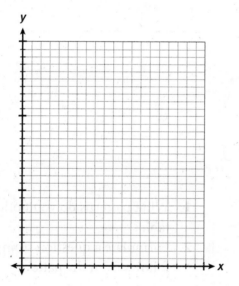

14. Create an unbiased scatter plot that is a fair representation of the data. What conclusions can you make based on this scatter plot?

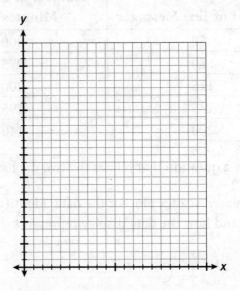

CHECK YOUR UNDERSTANDING

Write your answers on notebook paper. Show your work.

Dion began attending tutoring sessions at school in an attempt to raise his grades. He recorded the number of hours of tutoring he received and his grade point average over the course of a semester.

Hours of tutoring	Grade Point Average
3	2.6
6	2.7
9	3.0
12	3.1
15	3.4

1. What patterns do you notice from the table?

2. Formulate a question from the data that follows from the pattern.

3. Create a biased display that exaggerates the pattern that you recognized in Question 1.

4. Create a biased display that minimizes the pattern that you recognized in Question 1.

5. **MATHEMATICAL REFLECTION** Identify characteristics of graphs of bivariate data that may lead to a biased data display.

Data Display and Interpretation

DATA DILEMMA

Write your answers on notebook paper or grid paper. Show your work.

Cindy and Jan play on the Brady Middle School basketball team and were comparing their scoring prowess. The stem plots below show their scoring data after nine games. Key: 1|7 stands for 17

Cindy	
0	8 9 9
1	7 8 9
2	8 9 9

Jan	
0	3
1	1 1 2
2	0 0 1 1 4

1. List the number of points Cindy scored and the number of points Jan scored. Create a histogram for each player using intervals of 5 on the horizontal axis.

2. Using only the histograms created in Question 1, compare the scoring data for the two players.

3. Find the mean of the scoring data for each player. Does this agree with what you found in Question 2? Explain.

4. Create a box plot for each player. Use the box plots to compare the players' scoring data.

5. The scatter plot shows the total number of points scored by the team over the first eight games.

a. Draw a trend line to model the data. Then find a unit rate of points scored per game that fits the data.

b. If the team continues scoring at this rate, after how many games do you predict the team will reach a total of 600 points scored?

Data Display and Interpretation
DATA DILEMMA

	Exemplary	**Proficient**	**Emerging**
Math Knowledge #3	The student finds the correct mean scores for both players. (3)	The student finds the correct mean score for only one of the players.	The student finds the correct mean score for neither of the players.
Problem Solving #5a, b	The student: • Finds a unit rate of points scored per game that fits the data. (5a) • Makes a reasonable prediction of the number of games it will take the team to reach a total of 600 points scored. (5b)	The student: • Makes a reasonable prediction, based on an incorrect line of fit.	The student: • Finds an incorrect unit rate. • Makes a prediction that does not fit the data.
Representations #1, 4, 5a	The student: • Creates correct histograms, with the correct intervals, for both players. (1) • Creates correct box plots for both players. (4) • Draws a reasonable trend line. (5a)	The student: • Creates a correct histogram for one, but not both, of the players. • Creates a correct box plot for one, but not both, of the players.	The student: • Creates an incorrect histogram for each of the players. • Creates an incorrect box plot for each of the players. • Draws a trend line that does not fit the data.
Communication #2, 3, 4	The student: • Writes a comparison of the scoring data, based on the histograms. (2) • Explains whether the mean scores agree with the overview of the scoring data. (3) • Writes a comparison of the scoring data, based on his/her box plot. (4)	The student: • Writes an incomplete comparison of the scoring data. • Writes an incomplete explanation of the agreement between the mean scores and the overview of the data. • Writes a comparison that is incomplete.	The student: • Writes an incorrect comparison of the scoring data. • Writes an incorrect explanation of the agreement between the mean scores and the overview of the data. • Writes a comparison that is incorrect.

One-Stage Probability Experiments
Shell Identity

SUGGESTED LEARNING STRATEGIES: Marking the Text, Question the Text, Activating Prior Knowledge, Use Manipulatives, Graphic Organizer, Create Representations

My Notes

Coquina and her assistant are marine biologists who study marine mollusks. Their latest lab project is studying eight different shells they collected. In their sample box are shells of five different gastropods: a fighting conch, a lightning whelk, a banded tulip, a lettered olive, and a Sozon's cone, and shells of three different bivalves: a zigzag scallop, a lion's paw, and a calico clam.

On page 327 are Shell Information Cards with pictures of these shells and space for you to write notes. Remove the page and cut out the cards. Use them to help organize your work on this activity.

1. Coquina asks her assistant to hand her a shell. The assistant chooses one at random and hands it to her. If a selection is **random**, all outcomes are equally likely to occur.

   a. What is the probability of the event that the shell is a banded tulip? Explain.

   b. What is the probability of the event that the shell is a gastropod? Explain.

To determine the probability of each **event** in Question 1, you had to know information about all of the possible outcomes.

2. List the **sample space** for choosing a shell at random.

3. Since there are two different categories of shells in the sample box, use a Venn diagram to organize the sample space. Label both sides with the category names. Then list the shells.

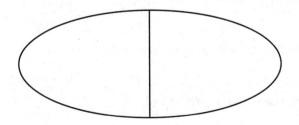

> **ACADEMIC VOCABULARY**
>
> **random**

> **ACADEMIC VOCABULARY**
>
> An **event** is an outcome (or set of outcomes) resulting from a situation involving random chance.

> **MATH TERMS**
>
> The **sample space** is the set of all possible outcomes from a situation involving random chance.

My Notes

MATH TERMS

The **probability** of an event *E* occurring, written *P*(*E*), is the ratio of the number of ways *E* can occur to the total number of different outcomes that can occur. A probability may be any rational number from 0 (meaning that the event cannot happen) to 1 (meaning that the event is certain to happen).

4. Explain how the Venn diagram can help you find the probabilities in Question 1.

Of the shells in the sample box, some are more commonly found in deep water while others are found in shallow water. Those found in deep water are the Sozon's cone and the lion's paw. The others are more commonly found in shallow waters.

5. The assistant chooses a shell from the box at random. The shells that make up the sample space each have three pieces of information associated with them. Use this table to organize the sample space. One has been done for you.

Shell Name	Gastropod/Bivalve	Water Depth Found
Fighting Conch	Gastropod	Shallow

6. Use the data in the table to answer each question about the event of selecting one shell at random from the sample box.

   a. Write the value of *P*(lion's paw).

   b. Write the value of *P*(deep water shell).

   c. Write the value of *P*(bivalve).

My Notes

    d. Explain how you used the table to determine the probabilities.

> **MATH TIP**
>
> The closer a probability is to 0, the less likely it is that the event will occur. The closer a probability is to 1, the more likely it is that the event will occur.

7. For each pair of events, identify which event is more likely and explain why.

    a. Choosing a fighting conch or choosing a gastropod.

    b. Choosing a deep water shell or choosing a bivalve.

8. Coquina asked her assistant to hand her a gastropod from the sample box. Since there were more gastropods in the box than bivalves, the assistant chose a shell at random, thinking she would probably choose the correct type of shell.

    a. What is the probability that the shell is a gastropod?

    b. Assume that the first shell chosen was put back in the box and that the assistant chose a second shell at random. What is the probability that the shell is a bivalve?

    c. Do the probabilities in Parts a and b differ from the probabilities of the same events in earlier questions? Explain why or why not.

My Notes

9. The first shell the assistant chose was a gastropod, and she gave the shell to Coquina. Coquina took the shell and asked her assistant to choose a second shell at random from the box.

   a. What is the probability of the second shell being a bivalve?

   b. Is the probability of choosing a bivalve the same in Question 8b and Question 9a? Explain why or why not.

10. The events in Questions 8 and 9 are choosing a gastropod first and choosing a bivalve second. In which question are these events independent? In which question are these events dependent? Explain.

MATH TERMS

Two events are **independent** if the outcome of the first event does not affect the probability of the second event.

Two events are **dependent** if the outcome of the first event affects the probability of the second event.

---

11. If Coquina's assistant looks into the box before choosing a shell, are all shells equally likely to be chosen? Explain.

12. The **complement** of an event E includes all possible outcomes of an experiment that are *not* outcomes of event E. The probability of the complement can be written as $P(\text{not } E)$.

   a. Describe, in words, the complement of the event "choosing a deep water shell."

   b. Evaluate $P(\text{not choosing a deep water shell})$.

   c. What do you notice about P(deep water shell) and P(not deep water shell)?

MATH TIP

$P(\text{not } E)$ is read "the probability of not E" and means the probability of event E not occurring.

My Notes

d. Write an equation using $P(E)$ and $P(\text{not } E)$.

The shells in the sample box were collected on Captiva Island, which is on the west coast of Florida. On a research trip to the beach at Captiva Island to collect more shells of these types, Coquina and her assistant collected and listed more samples.

Shell Type	Quantity
Fighting Conch	6
Lightning Whelk	12
Banded Tulip	3
Lettered Olive	10
Sozon's Cone	2
Zigzag Scallop	7
Lion's Paw	1
Calico Clam	9

13. From the samples collected at Captiva, Coquina chooses a shell at random. What is the probability that the shell is a gastropod?

14. Is the probability that you found in Question 13 theoretical or experimental? Explain.

15. A visitor to Captiva Island asked Coquina which types of shells he is most likely to find when he goes shell collecting on the same beach. Use probability to write the response that you think Coquina gave the visitor.

MATH TERMS

A **fair game** is a game in which each player is equally likely to win.

Back at the lab, two of Coquina's other assistants play a game consisting of drawing a shell at random from the sample box, whose contents are shown in the table on page 325. Assistant A wins a point if she draws a Fighting Conch, a Banded Tulip, or a Calico Clam. Assistant B wins a point if she draws a Lightning Whelk, a Sozon's Cone, or a Zigag Scallop. If a Lettered Olive or a Lion's Paw is drawn, neither assistant wins a point.

16. Are the assistants playing a fair game? Why or why not?

CHECK YOUR UNDERSTANDING

Write your answers on notebook paper. Show your work.

Use this situation for Questions 1–7: Twenty number cards are printed with the numbers 1 through 20. A card is chosen at random.

1. What is the sample space of this situation?

Find each probability based on the situation, and explain how you arrived at your answer in terms of the sample space.

2. *P*(choosing a multiple of five)

3. *P*(choosing a number greater than 13)

Identify which event is more likely.

4. Choosing an odd number or choosing a number less than 12.

5. Choosing 15, 16, 17, 18, 19, or 20 or choosing a multiple of 4.

6. What is the probability of the complement of the event "choosing a multiple of 3"?

7. Assume that a card is chosen and that the number on it is 14. If the card is replaced, what is the value for the probability of choosing a second card with an even number? If the card is not replaced, what is the value for the probability of choosing a second card with an even number?

8. Use the data in the table on page 325 to create a fair game.

9. **MATHEMATICAL REFLECTION** How is the probability of an event related to the sample space of the event? Give illustrations to support your reasoning.

My Notes

Fighting Conch

Notes

Lightning Whelk

Notes

Banded Tulip

Notes

Lion's Paw

Notes

Zigzag Scallop

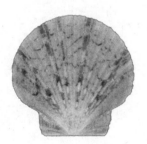

Notes

Calico Clam

Notes

Lettered Olive

Notes

Sozon's Cone

Notes

Addition Rule for Probability
Planting with Peter

SUGGESTED LEARNING STRATEGIES: Marking the Text, Summarize/Paraphrase/Retell, Activating Prior Knowledge

My Notes

Peter's Garden Center is a landscape nursery that specializes in flowering plants. To ensure quality plants, Peter and his crew grow their plants from seed and care for them until they are large enough to be used in landscaping projects. Two customers, the Garza family and the Neeper family, have hired Peter to landscape their yards with flowers. The table below lists information about the plants destined for these two projects.

Type of Flower	Color	Customer
Hyacinth	Pink	Garza
Hyacinth	White	Neeper
Hyacinth	Blue	Neeper
Hyacinth	Blue	Garza
Tulip	Pink	Garza
Tulip	White	Garza
Tulip	Pink	Neeper
Pansy	Blue	Garza
Pansy	White	Neeper
Pansy	Pink	Neeper
Pansy	Pink	Garza
Zinnia	Pink	Neeper
Zinnia	White	Neeper
Zinnia	White	Garza
Daisy	White	Garza
Daisy	White	Neeper
Daisy	Pink	Garza
Daisy	Blue	Garza
Iris	Blue	Garza
Iris	White	Neeper
Iris	Blue	Neeper
Orchid	Pink	Garza
Orchid	White	Neeper

Each plant listed above was grown in a container. Peter had labeled the bottom of the container with the flower type, color, and customer for whom it is being grown. When these plants were still young and did not have flowers, Peter put all of them on Table 1 in the greenhouse.

1. Peter asked a nursery worker to water the zinnias on Table 1. The worker knew how to identify plants only by their flowers, so he was unable to identify the zinnias. If he watered one plant at random, what is the probability that it was a zinnia?

SUGGESTED LEARNING STRATEGIES: Activating Prior Knowledge, Quickwrite, Self/Peer Revision, Create Representations, Marking the Text, Summarize/ Paraphrase/Retell, Guess and Check

2. What information did you need to find the probability in Question 1?

3. Describe the sample space for this situation, including the number of outcomes in the sample space.

4. List all of the outcomes in the event "a plant with blue flowers is watered." How many possible outcomes are in this event?

5. What is the probability of randomly watering a plant with blue flowers? Explain below.

6. Determine the probability that the worker waters a plant:

   a. that will go in the yard of the Garza family.

   b. that will go in the yard of the Neeper family.

7. Find the sum of P(plant for Garza family) and P(plant for Neeper family). Then explain how you arrived at this sum. What is the significance of this sum?

8. Consider the event "watering a plant with blue flowers" and the event "watering a plant with white flowers." In a single action, is it possible to satisfy the conditions of both events? Explain why or why not.

My Notes

9. Consider the event "watering a plant with blue flowers" and the event "watering a plant for the Neeper family." In a single action, is it possible to satisfy the conditions of both events? Explain why or why not.

10. If *A* and *B* are events in the same sample space and have no outcomes in common, then the two events are called **mutually exclusive**.

   a. If *A* and *B* are mutually exclusive, what is the probability of both *A* and *B* occurring at the same time?

   b. Which pair of events in Questions 8 and 9 is mutually exclusive? Explain why below.

11. Consider the event "watering a plant with blue flowers OR watering a plant with white flowers." Find *P*(plant with blue flowers OR plant with white flowers) and explain how you arrived at your answer.

12. Find *P*(watering a plant with blue flowers).

13. Find *P*(watering a plant with white flowers).

14. Write an equation that demonstrates the relationship between the probabilities in Questions 11–13.

My Notes

15. If events A and B are mutually exclusive events, write an equation that demonstrates the relationship between $P(A \text{ or } B)$, $P(A)$, and $P(B)$.

TRY THESE A

Write your answers in the My Notes space. Show your work.

Consider the probability experiment of rolling a fair number cube with a number from 1 through 6 on each face of the cube.

a. List the sample space for this experiment.

b. Name two mutually exclusive events of this experiment.

c. Verify that the equation in Question 15 works with this experiment. Show your work.

---

16. Consider the events "watering a plant with blue flowers" and "watering a plant for the Neeper family." You can use a Venn diagram to represent the events. Fill in the names of the flowers that belong in each of the three sections of the diagram.

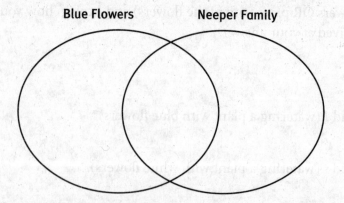

Blue Flowers   Neeper Family

17. Find P(plant with blue flowers OR plant for Neeper family). Explain how to use the information in the Venn diagram to determine this probability.

SUGGESTED LEARNING STRATEGIES: Create Representations, Guess and Check

My Notes

18. Find the following probabilities.

   a. P(plant with blue flowers)

   b. P(plant for Neeper family)

   c. P(plant with blue flowers and plant for Neeper family)

19. Complete the equation below by using the probabilities in Question 18.

   P(blue flowers OR Neeper family) $=$

20. If events A and B are not mutually exclusive events, write an equation that demonstrates the relationship between $P(A$ or $B)$, $P(A)$, $P(B)$, $P(A$ and $B)$.

TRY THESE B

Write your answers on notebook paper. Show your work.

Consider the probability experiment of rolling a fair number cube with a number from 1 through 6 on each face of the cube.

a. Name two events that are not mutually exclusive.

b. Verify that the equation in Question 20 works with these events. Show your work.

CHECK YOUR UNDERSTANDING

**Write your answers on notebook paper.
Show your work.**

**Use this situation for Questions 1–7: Index
cards are listed with the numbers 1 through 20.
A card is chosen at random.**

1. What is the probability of choosing an odd
   number?

2. What is the probability of choosing an
   even number?

3. What is the sum of these two
   probabilities?

4. Consider the events "choosing a multiple
   of 5" and "choosing a number less than 5."
   Are these events mutually exclusive?
   Explain.

5. Consider the events "choosing an even
   number" and "choosing a number greater
   than 10." Are these events mutually
   exclusive? Explain.

6. Find each of the following probabilities.

   a. P(choosing a multiple of 3)

   b. P(choosing a number greater than 11)

   c. P(choosing a multiple of 3 AND
   choosing a number greater than 11).

7. Find P(choosing a multiple of three OR
   choosing a number greater than eleven).
   How do your answers to Question 6 relate
   to this probability?

8. **MATHEMATICAL**
   REFLECTION Compare and contrast
   the terms "mutually
   exclusive" and "independent." Give
   examples to support your reasoning.

One- and Two-Stage Probability

STATE QUARTERS

Write your answers on notebook paper. Show your work.

From 1999 to 2008, the United States Mint produced commemorative quarters for each state in the United States. Each year, quarters for five different states were circulated to the public, and many people collected the coins. Steven wanted to collect these coins, so his uncle gave him a handful of the state quarters. Steven made this list of the coins that he was given.

State	Year
Tennessee	2002
Tennessee	2002
Ohio	2002
Alabama	2003
Maine	2003
Florida	2004
Florida	2004
Florida	2004
Texas	2004
Texas	2004
California	2005
California	2005
Kansas	2005

1. Steven put all the coins in his pocket and pulled one out at random.

   a. What is the probability that he selected a Texas quarter?

   b. What is the probability that he selected a quarter minted in 2002?

   c. Use the sample space to explain how you determined these probabilities.

2. After pulling out the first quarter, he put it on a table, then pulled out another quarter.

   a. Find P(first coin is a Florida quarter)

   b. Find P(second coin was minted in 2005 if first coin is a Florida quarter)

   c. Are the events in Parts a and b independent or dependent? Explain.

3. Find the probability of each compound event. Explain each answer in terms of *mutually exclusive* events.

   a. P(California quarter or Tennessee quarter)

   b. P(Florida quarter or 2004 quarter)

One- and Two-Stage Probability
STATE QUARTERS

	Exemplary	Proficient	Emerging
Math Knowledge #1a, b; 2a, b; 3a, b	The student: • Gives the correct probabilities for the two events. (1a, b) • Gives the correct probabilities for the two events. (2a, b) • Gives the correct probabilities for the two compound events. (3a, b)	The student: • Gives the correct probability for only one of the events. • Gives the correct probability for only one of the events. • Gives the correct probability for only one of the events.	The student: • Gives the correct probability for neither of the events. • Gives the correct probability for neither of the events. • Gives the correct probability for neither of the events.
Problem Solving #2c	The student correctly determines whether the events are independent or dependent. (2c)		The student makes an incorrect determination about the independence or dependence of the events.
Communication #1c, 2c	The student: • Uses the sample space to explain how he/she determined the probabilities. (1c) • Gives an explanation of why the events are independent or dependent. (2c)	The student: • Uses the sample space but writes an incomplete explanation of how the probabilities were determined. • Gives an incomplete explanation of why the events are independent or dependent.	The student: • Does not base his/her explanation on the sample space. • Gives an incorrect explanation of the relationship between the events.

ACTIVITY 5.1

1. Over a two-week period, Ms. Yule collected data on the number of customers who visited her store and then made this stem plot of the data. List the data set and find the mean, median, and mode.

```
1 | 2 9
2 | 0 3 4 9
3 | 3 4 8 8
4 | 6
5 | 2 5 7
```

A fishing guide recorded the lengths of redfish that he caught to assist in a marine research study. The lengths, in inches, of the fish that he caught during one week are listed below.

22, 18, 15, 27, 17, 19, 32, 23, 18

2. For the data listed, make a stem plot, a histogram, and a box plot.

3. To find the measures of central tendency for the data, which display would be helpful? Explain.

4. **a.** What conclusions can you make about the data using each of the data displays?

   b. Would a circle graph be an appropriate display for these data?

ACTIVITY 5.2

5. Describe a situation and draw a scatter plot that demonstrates
   a. positive correlation
   b. negative correlation
   c. no correlation

In order to repay the money his mother loaned him to buy a car, Adrian gives his mother some money every week. The table below shows the amount he owes and the number of weeks he has been paying.

Number of Weeks Paying	Amount Owed ($)
1	5700
2	5500
3	5200
4	4950

6. Make a scatter plot of the data and identify the correlation.

7. Draw a trendline that models the data. Estimate the unit rate, including units.

8. How many total weeks of payments will it be before Adrian pays off the loan from his mother for the car?

ACTIVITY 5.3

Arlene enjoys running five-kilometer races. To improve her running time, she began a training program and recorded the data below.

Weeks training	5K time (in minutes)
1	30.5
2	29
3	27
4	26.5

9. What patterns seem to result from the table?

10. Create a question from the data that follows from the pattern.

11. Make a biased data display that supports the pattern in Question 9.

12. Make a biased data display that lessens the effect of the pattern in Question 9.

13. What characteristics of the table did you change to create bias in your data display?

ACTIVITY 5.4

A vending machine for rubber bouncy balls has 11 balls inside. The balls are either solid or striped and are either blue or red. Of the blue balls, 3 are solid and 2 are striped. Of the red balls, 5 are solid and 1 is striped. One ball is chosen at random.

14. Draw a graphic organizer to represent the sample space of this experiment.

15. Make a table that represents the sample space.

16. Find each probability.

   a. P(choosing a striped ball)

   b. P(choosing red ball)

17. Describe the complement of the event "choosing a solid red ball." What is the probability of this complement?

18. A customer purchases a ball from the machine, then purchases a second ball.

   a. What is the probability that the first ball is solid?

   b. What is the probability that the second ball is red if the first ball purchased is a red striped ball?

   c. Are the two events in Part b independent or dependent? Explain.

ACTIVITY 5.5

A vending machine for rubber bouncy balls has 11 balls inside. The balls are either solid or striped and are either blue or red. Of the blue balls, 3 are solid and 2 are striped. Of the red balls, 5 are solid and 1 is striped. One ball is chosen at random.

19. Find each probability.

   a. P(choosing a red ball)

   b. P(choosing a blue ball)

   c. Are the two events in Parts a and b mutually exclusive? Explain.

20. Find each probability.

   a. P(choosing a blue ball)

   b. P(choosing a striped ball)

   c. Are the two events in Parts a and b mutually exclusive? Explain.

21. Find P(choosing a ball that is blue **and** striped).

22. Find P(choosing a blue ball **or** a striped ball).

23. Write an equation that relates P(choosing a blue ball), P(choosing a striped ball), P(choosing a ball that is blue and striped), and P(choosing a blue ball **or** a striped ball).

Reflection

An important aspect of growing as a learner is to take the time to reflect on your learning. It is important to think about where you started, what you have accomplished, what helped you learn, and how you will apply your new knowledge in the future. Use notebook paper to record your thinking on the following topics and to identify evidence of your learning.

Essential Questions

1. Review the mathematical concepts and your work in this unit before you write thoughtful responses to the questions below. Support your responses with specific examples from concepts and activities in the unit.

   - Why is it important to be able to represent data using graphs and measures of central tendency?

   - How can data and probabilities be used to predict the outcome of future events?

Academic Vocabulary

2. Look at the following academic vocabulary words:

   - bivariate data
   - five-number summary
   - random
   - event
   - measures of center
   - trend line

   Choose three words and explain your understanding of each word and why each is important in your study of math.

Self-Evaluation

3. Look through the activities and Embedded Assessments in this unit. Use a table similar to the one below to list three major concepts in this unit and to rate your understanding of each.

Unit Concepts	Is Your Understanding Strong (S) or Weak (W)?
Concept 1	
Concept 2	
Concept 3	

   a. What will you do to address each weakness?

   b. What strategies or class activities were particularly helpful in learning the concepts you identified as strengths? Give examples to explain.

4. How do the concepts you learned in this unit relate to other math concepts and to the use of mathematics in the real world?

1. Which data set is represented by the stem plot shown below?

$$
\begin{array}{c|ccc}
2 & 1 & 2 & 4 \\
3 & 3 & 3 & 7 \\
4 & 0 & 5 & 7 \\
\end{array}
$$

A. 21, 24, 33, 37, 40, 57   **C.** 42, 22, 12, 73, 33, 33, 74, 54, 4

B. 23, 41, 30, 23, 54, 77   **D.** 47, 37, 24, 22, 33, 45, 21, 33, 40

2. For two weeks Winifred recorded the high temperature for each day. The high temperature was above 83° for 6 out of the 14 days. Based on this data, what is the probability that the high temperature will be above 83° F on the fifteenth day? **Give your answer in lowest terms.**

2.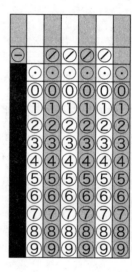

Read
Solve
Explain

3. Devin surveyed 60 people to determine whether they plan to vote for the school bond referendum. Of the people she surveyed, 35 plan to vote "yes." (**Write all answers in lowest terms.**)

Part A: Based on the survey results, what is the probability that the next person surveyed will say "yes"?

Answer and Explain

_____

_____

_____

_____

Part B: If voters are actually equally divided on the issue, what is the probability that the first person surveyed said "yes"?

Answer and Explain

_____

_____

_____

_____

Read

Solve

Explain

4. Nine coins are in Antwan's piggy bank. The coins are 5 dimes, 3 nickels, and 2 pennies. When he shakes the bank and turns it upside down, one coin drops out.

Part A: What are the possible outcomes for 1 shake of the bank? What is the probability of each outcome? **Express your answer in lowest terms.**

Answer and Explain

_____

_____

_____

_____

Part B: Antwan wants to take 15¢ from the bank. What coins does he need? What is the probability that he will get one of the coins he needs on the first shake?

Answer and Explain

_____

_____

_____

_____

Part C: Suppose that Antwan shakes the bank three times and gets a dime, a nickel, and a penny. He does not return the coins to the bank. On the next shake, what is the probability for each coin: a dime, a nickel, a penny? Which coin most likely to shake out? Explain how these probabilities compare to those in your answer in Part A.

Answer and Explain

_____

_____

_____

_____

_____

Symbols

$<$	is less than
$>$	is greater than
$\leq$	is less than or equal to
$\geq$	is greater than or equal to
$=$	is equal to
$\neq$	is not equal to
$\approx$	is approximately equal to
$\lvert a \rvert$	absolute value: $\lvert 3 \rvert = 3; \lvert -3 \rvert = 3$
$\sqrt{}$	square root
$\%$	percent
$\perp$	perpendicular
$\parallel$	parallel
(x, y)	ordered pair
$\overleftrightarrow{AB}$	line AB
$\overrightarrow{AB}$	ray AB
$\overline{AB}$	line segment AB
$\angle A$	angle A
$m\angle A$	measure of angle A
$\triangle ABC$	triangle ABC
π	pi; $\pi \approx 3.14$; $\pi \approx \dfrac{22}{7}$

Formulas

Perimeter	
P	= sum of the lengths of the sides
Rectangle	$P = 2l + 2w$
Square	$P = 4s$
Circumference	$C = 2\pi r$

Area	
Circle	$A = \pi r^2$
Parallelogram	$A = bh$
Rectangle	$A = lw$
Square	$A = s^2$
Triangle	$A = \frac{1}{2}bh$
Trapezoid	$A = \frac{1}{2}h(b_1 + b_2)$

Surface Area	
Cube	$SA = 6e^2$
Rectangular Prism	$SA = 2lw + 2lh + 2wh$
Cylinder	$SA = 2\pi r^2 + 2\pi rh$
Cone	$SA = \pi r^2 + \pi rl$
Regular Pyramid	$SA = B + \frac{1}{2}pl$
Sphere	$SA = 4\pi r^2$

Volume	
Cylinder	$V = Bh$, $B = \pi r^2$
Rectangular Prism	$V = lwh$
Triangular Prism	$V = Bh$, $B = \frac{1}{2}bh$
Pyramid	$V = \frac{1}{3}Bh$
Cone	$V = \frac{1}{3}\pi r^2 h$
Sphere	$V = \frac{4}{3}\pi r^3$

Temperature	
Celsius	$C = \frac{5}{9}(F - 32)$
Fahrenheit	$F = \frac{9}{5}C + 32$

Other Formulas	
Direct variation	$y = kx$
Inverse variation	$y = \frac{k}{x}$

Table of Measures

Customary	Metric
Distance/Length	
1 yard (yd) = 3 feet (ft) = 36 inches (in.)	1 meter (m) = 100 centimeters (cm)
1 foot (ft) = 12 inches (in.)	1 meter (m) = 1000 millimeters (mm)
1 mile (mi) = 1760 yards (yd)	1 meter (m) = 10 decimeters (dm)
1 mile (mi) = 5280 feet (ft)	1 centimeter (cm) = 10 millimeters (mm)
1 acre (ac) = 43,560 square feet (ft)	1 kilometer (km) = 1000 meters (m)
Volume	
1 cup (c) = 8 fluid ounces (fl oz)	1 liter (L) = 1000 milliliters (mL)
1 pint (pt) = 2 cups (c)	1 liter (L) = 1000 cubic centimeters (cm³)
1 quart (qt) = 2 pints (pt)	1 liter (L) = 100 centiliters (cL)
1 quart (qt) = 4 cups (c)	1 liter (L) = 10 deciliters (dL)
1 gallon (gal) = 4 quarts (qt)	1 kiloliter (kL) = 1000 liters (L)
1 gallon (gal) = 16 cups (c)	
Weight/Mass	
1 pound (lb)= 16 ounces (oz)	1 gram (g) = 1000 milligrams (mg)
1 ton (T) = 2000 pound (lb)	1 gram (g) = 100 centigrams (cg)
	1 gram (g) = 10 decigrams (dg)
	1 kilogram (kg) = 1000 grams (g)
	1 tonne (t) = 1000 kilograms (kg)
Time	
1 minute (min) = 60 seconds (sec)	1 year (yr) = 365 days (d)
1 hour (hr) = 60 minutes (min)	1 year (yr) = 52 weeks (wk)
1 day (d) = 24 hours (hr)	1 year (yr) = 12 months (mo)
	1 leap year (LY) = 366 days (d)

SpringBoard Learning Strategies

READING STRATEGIES

STRATEGY	DEFINITION	PURPOSE
Activating Prior Knowledge	Recalling what is known about a concept and using that information to make a connection to current studies	Helps establish content connections
Chunking the Activity	Grouping a set of items/questions for specific purposes	Provides an opportunity to relate concepts, assess understanding and maintain focus
Close Reading	Reading, rereading and analyzing small chunks of text word-for-word, sentence-by-sentence, and line-by-line	Assists in developing a comprehensive understanding of the text
Graphic Organizer	Arranging information into maps and charts	Builds comprehension and facilitates discussion by representing information in visual form
Interactive Word Wall	Creating an interactive visual display of vocabulary words to serve as a constant reminder of words and groups of words as they are introduced, used, and mastered over the course of a year	Provides a visual reference for reading and writing, and an ever-present tool for building word knowledge and awareness
KWL Chart (Know, Want, Learn)	Activating prior knowledge by identifying what the student **K**nows, **W**ants to know, and then reflects on was **L**earned	Assists in organizing information and reflecting on learning to increase comprehension and interest
Marking the Text	Highlighting, underlining, and /or annotating parts of the text to focus on key elements to help solve the problem or understand the text	Helps identify, examine and interact with important information from the text
Predict and Confirm	Making conjectures about what results will develop in an activity; confirming or modifying the conjectures based on outcomes	Stimulates thinking by making, checking, and correcting predictions based on evidence in the material
Questioning the Text	Developing questions about the text as it is being read.	Focuses reading, to allow the reader to form questions, seek out answers, and lead discussions
Role Play	Assuming the role of a character in the material	Helps interpret and visualize information in a problem
Shared Reading	Reading the text aloud by the teacher or a student, with other students following along silently	Helps auditory learners to decode, interpret, and analyze challenging text
Summarize/ Paraphrase/Retell	Restating, in your own words, essential information expressed in the text	Assists with comprehension, recall of text, and problem solving
Think Aloud	Describing the thinking process used to make sense of the text in order to solve a problem	Assists in processing the text, understanding the components of the problem, and thinking about possible paths to a solution
Visualization	Picturing (mentally and/or literally) what is read in the text	Increases reading comprehension and promotes active engagement with the text
Vocabulary Organizer	Using a designated format to maintain an ongoing record of vocabulary words with definitions, pictures, notation, and connections	Facilitates and sustains a systemic process of vocabulary development

SpringBoard Learning Strategies

COLLABORATIVE STRATEGIES

STRATEGY	DEFINITION	PURPOSE
Debriefing	Facilitating a discussion that leads to consensus understanding	Helps solidify and deepen understanding of content
Discussion Group	Engaging in an interactive, small group discussion	Gain information and understanding about a concept, idea, or problem
Group Presentation	Working collaboratively, students present information in a variety of formats	Allows opportunities to present collaborative solutions and share responsibility for delivering information to an audience
Think-Pair-Share	**Thinking** a problem through alone, **Pairing** with a partner to share ideas, and concluding by **Sharing** with the class	Enables construction of responses to a problem, then tests and revises ideas, and finally considers and interprets the ideas of others

PROBLEM-SOLVING STRATEGIES

STRATEGY	DEFINITION	PURPOSE
Create Representations	Creating pictures, tables, graphs, lists, equations, models, and/or verbal expressions to interpret text or data	Helps organize information using multiple representations to solve a problem or answer a question
Guess and Check	Guessing the solution to a problem, checking for accuracy, and using the information obtained to make a more reasonable guess	Allows exploration of a problem and determines a pathway to a more formal solution.
Identify a Subtask	Breaking a problem into smaller pieces whose outcomes lead to a solution	Enables organization of the work of solving a complex problem
Look for a Pattern	Observing trends by organizing data or creating representations	Helps generalize patterns and make predictions
Simplify the Problem	Using "friendlier" numbers to solve a problem	Provides insight into the problem or strategies needed to solve the problem
Work Backward	Tracing a possible answer back through the solution process to the starting point	Provides another way to check possible answers for correctness
Use Manipulatives	Using objects to examine relationships between, and among, the information given	Enables visualization information and relationships

SpringBoard Learning Strategies

WRITING STRATEGIES

STRATEGY	DEFINITION	PURPOSE
Note Taking	Creating a record of information while listening to a speaker	Facilitates active listening to record and organize ideas that assist in processing information
Prewriting	Brainstorming and refining your thoughts, reflecting and organizing your ideas prior to writing	Provides a system for beginning the writing process
Quickwrite	Writing for a short, specific amount of time about a designated topic	Enables generation of multiple ideas in a quick fashion
RAFT (Role of Writer, Audience, Format, and Topic)	Writing formally with a clearly identified **R**ole of writer, **A**udience, **F**ormat, and **T**opic	Provides a framework for formal writing
Self Revision/ Peer Revision	Working alone or with a partner to examine a piece of writing for accuracy and clarity	Provides an opportunity to edit a written text to ensure correctness of identified components

Photo Credits

Unit 3: Pentagon (pp. 207-208), Photodisc/Alamy

Unit 4: Louvre pyramid (p. 251), GlowImages/Alamy; Washington Monument (p. 251), Douglas Peebles Photography/Alamy; Flatiron Building (p. 251), Marc de Oliveira/iStockphoto; Pentagon (p. 251), Photodisc/Alamy

Unit 5: Shells (p. 327): fighting conch, Sozon's cone, and calico clam, www.seashells.org; lightning whelk, banded tulip, zigzag scallop, and lion's paw, The Bailey-Matthews Shell Museum, photos by José H. Leal; lettered olive, Matthew Ward © Dorling Kindersley

Glossary

Glosario

A

absolute value (p.14)   The distance of a number from zero on a number line. Distance or absolute value is always positive. For example, the absolute value of both −6 and 6 is 6.

valor absoluto (pág. 14)   Distancia entre un número y el cero en una recta numérica. La distancia o valor absoluto es siempre positivo. Por ejemplo, el valor absoluto de −6 y de 6 es 6.

adjacent angles (p. 153)   Angles that have a common side, but no common interior.

ángulos adyacentes (pág. 153)   Ángulos que tienen un lado en común, pero no un interior común.

alternate exterior angles (p. 155)   A pair of angles that are formed by two lines and a transversal and that are outside the two lines and on opposite sides of the transversal. When the two lines crossed by a transversal are parallel, the alternate exterior angles are congruent.

ángulos alternos externos (pág. 155)   Par de ángulos formados por dos rectas y una transversal y que están fuera de las dos rectas y en lados opuestos de la transversal. Cuando las dos rectas cruzadas por una transversal son paralelas, los ángulos alternos externos son congruentes.

alternate interior angles (p. 155)   A pair of angles that are formed by two lines and a transversal and that are inside the two lines and on opposite sides of the transversal. When the two lines crossed by a transversal are parallel, the alternate interior angles are congruent.

ángulos alternos internos (pág. 155)   Par de ángulos formados por dos rectas y una transversal y que están dentro de las dos rectas y en lados opuestos de la transversal. Cuando las dos rectas cruzadas por una transversal son paralelas, los ángulos alternos internos son congruentes.

area (p. 242)   The measure, in square units, of the interior region of a plane figure.

área (pág. 242)   Medida, en unidades cuadradas, de la región interior de una figura plana.

B

bar graph (p. 299)   A way of displaying categorical data (for example, colors, types, qualities). Each bar represents a different category. The vertical scale for the bar heights is labeled with the count or percent for each category. Also known as a **bar chart**.

gráfica de barras (pág. 299)   Gráfica que usa barras para mostrar datos por categorías (por ejemplo, colores, tipos, cualidades). Cada barra representa una categoría diferente. La escala vertical para las alturas de las barras se rotula con el conteo o porcentaje para cada categoría. También se la conoce como **gráfica de columnas**.

bias (p. 316)   A systematic error in data collection or analysis that sways the results in one direction.

sesgo (pág. 316)   Error sistemático en la recolección o análisis de los datos, que inclina los resultados en una dirección.

bivariate data (p. 304)   Data that can be written as ordered pairs, where each numerical quantity represents measurement information recorded about a particular subject.

datos bivariados (pág. 304)   Datos que pueden escribirse como pares ordenados, donde cada cantidad numérica representa información de las medidas registradas acerca de un tema en particular.

box-and-whisker plot (p. 300)   A data display organized into four sections, each representing 25% of the data. Also known as a **box plot.**

gráfica de frecuencias acumuladas (pág. 300) Representación de datos organizados en cuatro secciones, en que cada una representa un 25% de los datos. También se le conoce como **gráfica de cuadrículas.**

C

circle (p. 162)   The set of points in a plane that are an equal distance from a given point, called the center.

círculo (pág. 162)   Conjunto de puntos en un plano que están a igual distancia de un punto dado, llamado centro.

coefficient (p. 88)   A number by which a variable is multiplied. For example, in the term $6x$, 6 is the coefficient.

coeficiente (pág. 88)   Número por el cual se multiplica una variable. Por ejemplo, en el término $6x$, 6 es el coeficiente.

complement of an event (p. 324)   The complement of an event includes all possible outcomes of a probability experiment that are *not* outcomes of the event.

complemento de un suceso (pág. 324)   El complemento de un suceso incluye todos los resultados posibles de un experimento de probabilidad que *no* son resultados del suceso.

complex solid (p. 256)   In three-dimensional geometry, the result of putting two or more solids together.

cuerpo geométrico complejo (pág. 256)   En geometría tridimensional, el resultado de juntar dos o más cuerpos geométricos.

compound inequality (p. 129)   A compound inequality combines two inequalities. For example, $2 < x < 8$ is a compound inequality for the inequalities $x > 2$ and $x < 8$.

desigualdad compuesta (pág. 129)   Una desigualdad compuesta combina dos desigualdades. Por ejemplo, $2 < x < 8$ es una desigualdad compuesta para las desigualdades $x > 2$ y $x < 8$.

compound interest (p. 59)   Interest calculated on the total principal plus the interest earned or owed during the previous time period.

interés compuesto (pág. 59)   Interés calculado sobre el capital total más el interés devengado o adeudado durante el período anterior.

cone (p. 256)   A solid with one circular base and one vertex.

cono (pág. 256)   Cuerpo geométrico que tiene una base circular y un vértice.

conjecture (p. 154)   An unproved statement that seems to be true.

conjetura (pág. 154)   Enunciado no demostrado que parece ser verdadero.

constant (p. 88)   A term in an expression that does not change in value because it does not contain a variable. For example, the constant term in the expression $3n + 6$ is 6.

constante (pág. 88)   Término de una expresión que no cambia de valor, debido a que no contiene variables. Por ejemplo, el término constante en la expresión $3n + 6$ es 6.

constant of variation (p. 136)   The value k in the equation $y = kx$ represents the constant of variation, which is the ratio of y to x.

constante de variación (pág. 136)   El valor k en la ecuación $y = kx$ representa la constante de variación, que es la razón de y a x.

conversion factor (p. 195)   A ratio relating a number of units to a unit measure. For example, the ratio 12 to 1 is the conversion factor relating inches to feet, and 1 to 12 is the conversion factor relating feet to inches.

factor de conversión (pág. 195)   Razón que relaciona un número de unidades con una medida unitaria. Por ejemplo, la razón 12 a 1 es el factor de conversión de pulgadas a pies y 1 a 12 es el factor de conversión de pies a pulgadas.

coordinate plane (p. 173)   A coordinate plane is a two-dimensional system for graphing ordered pairs, formed by two perpendicular number lines intersecting at their zero points and creating four quadrants.

plano de coordenadas (pág. 173)   Un plano de coordenadas es un sistema bidimensional para graficar pares ordenados, formado por dos rectas numéricas perpendiculares que se intersecan en sus puntos cero y que generan cuatro cuadrantes.

correlation (p. 304)   A collection of data points has a *positive correlation* if it has the property that y tends to increase as x increases. It has a *negative correlation* if y tends to decrease as x increases. A correlation is also known as an **association.**

correlación (pág. 304)   Un conjunto de datos tiene una *correlación positiva* si tiene la propiedad de que y tiende a aumentar a medida que aumenta x. Tiene una *correlación negativa* si y tiende a disminuir a medida que aumenta x. Una correlación se conoce también como **asociación.**

corresponding angles (p. 155)   A pair of nonadjacent angles that are formed by two lines and a transversal such that the angles are on the same side of the transversal and one of the angles is outside the two lines while the other angle is between the two lines. When the two lines crossed by a transversal are parallel, the corresponding angles are congruent.

ángulos correspondientes (pág. 155)   Par de ángulos no adyacentes formados por dos rectas y una transversal y que están al mismo lado de la transversal, con uno de los ángulos fuera de las dos rectas y el otro ángulo entre las dos rectas. Cuando las dos rectas cruzadas por una transversal son paralelas, los ángulos correspondientes son congruentes.

cube root (p. 36)   The cube root of a number, n, is the number that when used as a factor three times gives a product of n.

raíz cúbica (pág. 36)   La raíz cúbica de un número n, es el número que usado tres veces como factor da un producto de n.

cubing a number (p. 35)   Raising a number to the third power.

elevar un número al cubo (pág. 35)   Elevar un número a la tercera potencia.

cylinder (p. 255)   A solid figure with two parallel and congruent circular bases.

cilindro (pág. 255)   Figura tridimensional que tiene dos bases paralelas que son circulares y congruentes.

D

dependent events (p. 324)   Two events are dependent if the outcome of the first event affects the probability of the second event.

sucesos dependientes (pág. 324)   Dos sucesos son dependientes si el resultado del primer suceso afecta la probabiliadad del segundo suceso.

diagonal (p. 167)   A line segment connecting two nonconsecutive vertices of a polygon.

diagonal (pág. 167)   Segmento de recta que conecta dos vértices no consecutivos de un polígono.

direct variation (p. 134)   A relationship between two variables x and y such that $y = kx$, where k is any constant other than zero.

variación directa (pág. 134)   Relación entre dos variables x e y, tal que $y = kx$, donde k es cualquier constante distinta de cero.

E

event (p. 321)   Any outcome or group of outcomes from a probability experiment.

suceso (pág. 321)   Cualquier resultado o grupo de resultados de un experimento de probabilidad.

exponent (p. 30)   An exponent is a number that tells how many times another number, called the base, is used as a factor.

exponente (pág. 30)   Un exponente es un número que expresa las veces que otro número, llamado base, se utiliza como factor.

exponential form (p. 30)   A number written with a base and an exponent.

forma exponencial (pág. 30)   Número que se escribe con una base y un exponente.

F

five-number summary (p. 300)   This summary includes the minimum, first quartile, median, third quartile, and maximum. The information in a five-number summary is used in making and interpreting box-and-whisker plots.

resumen de cinco números (pág. 300)   Este resumen incluye el mínimo, el primer cuartil, la mediana, el tercer cuartil y el máximo. La información de un resumen de cinco números se usa para hacer e interpretar una gráfica de frecuencias acumuladas.

function (p. 114)   A relation between input and output values that pairs each input value with exactly one output value.

función (pág. 114)   Relación entre valores de entrada y salida que empareja cada valor de entrada con un solo valor de salida.

H

histogram (p. 299) A graph used to show the frequencies for a set of data. The horizontal axis is divided into equal intervals. The vertical axis shows the frequency, or the number of items, in each interval.

histograma (pág. 299) Gráfica que se usa para mostrar las frecuencias de un conjunto de datos. El eje horizontal está dividido en intervalos iguales. El eje vertical muestra la frecuencia, o número de elementos, que hay en cada intervalo.

hypotenuse (p. 218) The side of a right triangle that is opposite the right angle.

hipotenusa (pág. 218) Lado de un triángulo rectángulo que es opuesto al ángulo recto.

I

image (p. 182) The position of a figure after a transformation.

imagen (pág. 182) Posición de una figura después de una transformación.

independent events (p. 324) Two events are independent if the outcome of the first event does not affect the probability of the second event.

sucesos independientes (pág. 324) Dos sucesos son independientes si el resultado del primer suceso no afecta la probabilidad del segundo suceso.

inequality (p. 127) A mathematical statement showing that one quantity is greater than or less than another. Inequalities use these symbols; > (is greater than); < (is less than); ≥ (is greater than or equal to); and ≤ (is less than or equal to).

desigualdad (pág. 127) Enunciado matemático que muestra que una cantidad es mayor o menor que otra. Las desigualdades usan estos símbolos: > (mayor que); < (menor que); ≥ (mayor o igual a) y ≤ (menor o igual a).

integers (p. 4) The set of all natural numbers, their opposites, and zero.

enteros (pág. 4) Conjunto de todos los números naturales, sus opuestos y el cero.

inverse variation (p. 137) A relationship between two variables, x and y, with the form $xy = k$ or $y = \frac{k}{x}$, where k is any constant other than zero. Inverse variation is sometimes called **indirect variation.**

variación inversa (pág. 137) Relación entre dos variables, x e y, con la forma $xy = k$ o $y = \frac{k}{x}$, donde k es cualquier constante distinta de cero. La variación inversa a veces se llama **variación indirecta.**

irrational numbers (p. 7) Numbers that cannot be written as the ratio of two integers.

números irracionales (pág. 7) Números que no pueden escribirse como la razón de dos enteros.

L

legs (p. 218) In a right triangle, the sides that form the right angle.

catetos (pág. 218) En un triángulo rectángulo, los lados que forman el ángulo recto.

M

measures of center (p. 297) Certain numbers that can represent a whole set of numerical data. These include the mean, median, and mode. Measures of center are also known as **measures of central tendency.**

medidas de centro (pág. 297) Ciertos números que pueden representar un conjunto completo de datos numéricos. Éstos incluyen la media, la mediana y la moda. A las medidas de centro también se las conoce como **medidas de tendencia central.**

mutually exclusive events (p. 331) If events A and B are in the sample space and have no outcomes in common, then A and B are mutually exclusive events.

sucesos mutuamente excluyentes (pág. 331) Si los sucesos A y B están en el espacio muestral y no tienen resultados en común, entonces A y B son sucesos mutuamente excluyentes.

N

natural numbers (p. 3) The numbers 1, 2, 3, 4, and so on. Natural numbers are also known as **counting numbers.**

números naturales (pág. 3) Los números 1, 2, 3, 4, y así sucesivamente. Los números naturales también se conocen como **números de conteo.**

net (p. 241) A two-dimensional drawing used to represent or form a three-dimensional object or solid.

red (pág. 241) Dibujo bidimensional que se usa para representar o formar un objeto tridimensional o cuerpo geométrico.

O

open sentence (p. 127) An equation or inequality with variables. An open sentence can be true or false, depending on what values are substituted for the variable.

enunciado con variables (pág. 127) Ecuación o desigualdad con variables. Un enunciado con variables puede ser verdadero o falso, dependiendo de los valores que tome la variable.

P

percent increase/decrease (pp. 54–55) The percent by which an original amount is increased or decreased. This is determined by dividing the change (increase or decrease) by the original amount.

porcentaje de aumento/disminución (págs. 54 y 55) Porcentaje en que aumenta o disminuye una cantidad original. Se determina dividiendo el cambio (aumento o disminución) por la cantidad original.

perfect square (p. 32) A number that represents the product of number multiplied by itself.

cuadrado perfecto (pág. 32) Número que representa el producto de un número multiplicado por sí mismo.

plane (p. 251) A flat surface that extends infinitely in all directions. A parallelogram is usually used to model a plane in two dimensions.

plano (pág. 251) Superficie plana que se extiende infinitamente en todas direcciones. Normalmente se usa un paralelogramo para modelar un plano en dos dimensiones.

polygon (p. 160)   A closed figure formed by three or more line segments that intersect only at their endpoints.

polígono (pág. 160)   Figura geométrica cerrada, formada por tres o más segmentos de recta que se intersecan solamente en sus extremos.

prism (p. 254)   A solid with parallel congruent bases that are both polygons. The sides (faces) of a prism are all parallelograms or rectangles. A prism is named according to the shape of its bases.

prisma (pág. 254)   Cuerpo geométrico que tiene como bases dos polígonos paralelos y congruentes. Los lados (caras) de un prisma son todos paralelogramos o rectángulos. Un prisma recibe su nombre según la forma de sus bases.

probability of an event (p. 322)   The probability of an event E occurring is written $P(E)$, which is the ratio of the number of ways for E to occur compared to the total number of different outcomes that can occur.

probabilidad de un suceso (pág. 322)   La probabilidad de que un suceso S ocurra se escribe $P(E)$, que es la razón del número de maneras en que S puede ocurrir, comparado con el número total de resultados diferentes que pueden ocurrir.

pyramid (p. 251)   A three-dimensional figure whose base is a polygon and whose other faces are triangles that share a common vertex.

pirámide (pág. 251)   Figura tridimensional cuya base es un polígono y cuyas otras caras son triángulos que comparten un vértice común.

Pythagorean theorem (p. 220)   This theorem states that the sum of the squares of the lengths of the legs of a right triangle equals the square of the length of the hypotenuse.

Teorema de Pitágoras (pág. 220)   Este teorema establece que la suma del cuadrado de las longitudes de los catetos de un triángulo rectángulo es igual al cuadrado de la longitud de la hipotenusa.

Q

quadrant (p. 186)   One of the four regions that are formed by the intersection of the x- and y-axes of the coordinate plane.

cuadrante (pág. 186)   Una de las cuatro regiones que se forman por la intersección del eje de las x con el eje de las y del plano de coordenadas.

R

random (p. 321)   If a selection is random, all outcomes are equally likely to occur.

aleatorio/a (pág. 321)   Si una selección es aleatoria, todos los resultados tienen igual probabilidad de ocurrir.

rate (p. 193)   A comparison of two different units, such as distance and time, or two different things measured with the same unit.

tasa (pág. 193)   Comparación entre dos unidades diferentes, como distancia y tiempo, o dos cosas diferentes medidas con la misma unidad.

ratio (p. 193)   A comparison of two quantities. Ratios can be written as fractions (indicating a quotient), or using the word "to," or using a colon (:).

razón (pág. 193)   Comparación entre dos cantidades. Las razones pueden escribirse como fracciones (que indican un cociente) o usando la palabra "a" o usando dos puntos (:).

rational number (p. 6)   Any number that can be written as the ratio of two integers where the divisor is not zero; for example, 8, 1.5, $\frac{2}{5}$, and -3.

número racional (pág. 6)   Cualquier número que puede escribirse como razón entre dos enteros, donde el divisor no es cero; por ejemplo, 8, 1.5, $\frac{2}{5}$ y -3.

regular pyramid (p. 269)   A pyramid with a base that is a regular polygon.

pirámide regular (pág. 269)   Pirámide cuya base es un polígono regular.

repeating decimal (p. 6)   A decimal that has one or more digits following the decimal point that repeat endlessly.

decimal periódico (pág. 6)   Decimal que tiene uno o más dígitos que se repiten sin fin después del punto decimal.

S

sample space (p. 321)   The set of all possible outcomes of an experiment.

espacio muestral (pág. 321)   Conjunto de todos los resultados posibles de un experimento.

scale drawing (p. 199)   A drawing that represents an object as an enlargement or reduction of the size of the actual object. The scale factor defines the amount of enlargement or reduction.

dibujo a escala (pág. 199)   Dibujo que representa un objeto como una ampliación o reducción del tamaño del objeto real. El factor de escala define la cantidad de ampliación o reducción.

scale factor (p. 199)   The common ratio of the corresponding side lengths in two similar figures.

factor de escala (pág. 199)   Razón común de las longitudes de los lados correspondientes de dos figuras semejantes.

scale model (p. 203)   A model that represents an object as a three-dimensional enlargement or reduction of the size of the actual object. The scale factor describes the amount of enlargement or reduction.

modelo a escala (pág. 203)   Modelo que representa un objeto como una ampliación o reducción tridimensional del tamaño del objeto real. El factor de escala describe la cantidad de ampliación o reducción.

scatterplot (p. 304)   A graphic display of bivariate data on a coordinate plane that may be used to show a relationship between two variables.

diagrama de dispersión (pág. 304) Representación gráfica de datos bivariados sobre un plano de coordenadas, que puede usarse para mostrar una relación entre dos variables.

scientific notation (p. 64)   A number is written in scientific notation when it is expressed in the form $a \times 10^n$, where $1 \leq a < 10$ and n is an integer.

notación científica (pág. 64)   Un número se escribe en notación científica cuando se expresa en la forma $a \times 10^n$, donde $1 \leq a < 10$ y n es un entero.

sector of a circle (p. 270) A pie-shaped part of a circle formed by two radii and an arc of the circle.

sector de un círculo (pág. 270) Parte de un círculo con forma de trozo de tarta, formada por dos radios y un arco del círculo.

set notation (p. 3) In set notation, the elements or members of the set are listed in brackets and separated by commas. For example, the set of natural numbers can be written as $N = \{1, 2, 3, 4, \ldots\}$.

notación de conjuntos (pág. 3) En notación de conjuntos, los elementos o miembros del conjunto se escriben entre corchetes y se separan con comas. Por ejemplo, el conjunto de los números naturales puede escribirse como $N = \{1, 2, 3, 4, \ldots\}$.

similar figures (p. 209) Figures in which the lengths of the corresponding sides are in proportion and the corresponding angles are congruent.

figuras semejantes (pág. 209) Figuras en las que las longitudes de los lados correspondientes están en proporción y los ángulos correspondientes son congruentes.

similar solids (p. 285) Solids that have the same shape but not necessarily the same size.

cuerpos geométricos semejantes (pág. 285) Cuerpos geométricos que tienen la misma forma, pero no necesariamente el mismo tamaño.

skew lines (p. 252) Lines that not parallel but do not intersect.

rectas que no se cruzan (pág. 252) Rectas que no son paralelas, pero no se intersecan.

slant height of a regular pyramid (p. 268) The height of a triangular face of a pyramid.

altura inclinada de una pirámide regular (pág. 268) Altura de una de las caras triangulares de una pirámide.

slope (p. 111) The slope of a line is the ratio $\frac{\text{change in } y}{\text{change in } x}$ between any two points that lie on the line.

pendiente (pág. 111) La pendiente de una recta es la razón $\frac{\text{cambio en } y}{\text{cambio en } x}$ entre cualquier par de puntos que yacen sobre una recta.

solid (p. 253) A three-dimensional figure having length, width, and height.

cuerpo geométrico (pág. 253) Figura tridimensional que tiene longitud, ancho y altura.

solution (pp. 102, 128) Any value that makes an equation or inequality true when substituted for the variable.

solución (págs. 102, 128) Cualquier valor que hace verdadera una ecuación o desigualdad al reemplazar la variable.

sphere (p. 263) The set of all points that are the same distance from a given point, called the center.

esfera (pág. 263) Conjunto de todos los puntos que están a igual distancia de un punto dado, llamado centro.

square root (p. 31) The square root of a value is the number you can square to get that value. For example, $\sqrt{25} = 5$ because $5^2 = 25$.

raíz cuadrada (pág. 31) La raíz cuadrada de un valor es el número que elevado al cuadrado da ese valor. Por ejemplo, $\sqrt{25} = 5$, ya que $5^2 = 25$.

stem-and-leaf plot (p. 298) a data display that shows each data value in two parts according to its place value. The stem represents the first digit or digits, and the leaf represents the last digit of the number. A legend or key shows how to read the values.

Examples:　　$1|4$ represents 14
　　　　　　　$21|0$ represents 210

Also called a **stem plot.**

diagrama de tallo y hojas (pág. 298) Representación de datos que muestra cada dato en dos partes de acuerdo con su valor posicional. El tallo representa el primer o primeros dígitos y la hoja representa el último dígito del número. Una leyenda muestra cómo leer los valores.

Ejemplos:　　$1|4$ representa 14
　　　　　　　$21|0$ representa 210

También se lo denomina **diagrama de tallo.**

subset (p. 7) A set whose elements are all in another set. Every set is a subset of itself.

subconjunto (pág. 7) Conjunto cuyos elementos están todos en otro conjunto. Todo conjunto es un subconjunto de sí mismo.

surface area (p. 242) The sum of the areas of the faces of a solid figure.

área superficial (pág. 242) Suma de las áreas de las caras de un cuerpo geométrico.

T

terminating decimal (p. 6) A decimal that has a finite or limited number of digits following the decimal point.

decimal exacto (pág. 6) Decimal que tiene un número finito o limitado de dígitos después del punto decimal.

tetrahedron (p. 285) A solid with four faces, each of which is an equilateral triangle.

tetraedro (pág. 285) Cuerpo geométrico que tiene cuatro caras, cada una de las cuales es un triángulo equilátero.

transversal (p. 154) A line that intersects two or more lines at different points.

transversal (pág. 154) Recta que interseca dos o más rectas en diferentes puntos.

trend line (p. 305) A line drawn on a scatterplot to show the general direction of the association or correlation between two sets of data.

línea de tendencia (pág. 305) Línea dibujada sobre un diagrama de dispersión para mostrar la dirección general de la asociación o correlación entre dos conjuntos de datos.

two-dimensional figure (p. 159) A figure which lies completely in a plane.

figura bidimensional (pág. 159) Figura que yace completamente sobre un plano.

U

unit rate (p. 306) A rate in which one of the quantities represented has a value of one. For example, a rate of 25 miles per gallon is a unit rate that can be written as $\frac{25 \text{ miles}}{1 \text{ gallon}}$.

tasa unitaria (pág. 306) Tasa en la que una de las cantidades representadas tiene un valor de uno. Por ejemplo, una tasa de 25 millas por galón es una tasa unitaria que puede escribirse como $\frac{25 \text{ millas}}{1 \text{ galón}}$.

V

Venn diagram (p. 3)   A graphic organizer used to show relationships among sets of numbers or objects using overlapping shapes.

diagrama de Venn (pág. 3)   Organizador gráfico que se usa para mostrar las relaciones entre conjuntos de números u objetos usando figuras que se traslapan.

vertical angles (p. 154)   Pairs of angles formed when two lines intersect. Vertical angles share a common vertex but no common rays.

ángulos opuestos por el vértice (pág. 154)   Pares de ángulos que se forman cuando dos rectas se intersecan. Los ángulos opuestos por el vértice comparten un vértice en común, pero no rayos comunes.

volume (p. 245)   The measure of the space occupied by a three-dimensional figure. Volume is measured in cubic units, such as cubic inches (in.³).

volumen (pág. 245)   Medida del espacio que ocupa una figura tridimensional. El volumen se mide en unidades cúbicas, como pulgadas cúbicas (in.³).

W

whole numbers (p. 4)   The numbers 0, 1, 2, 3, 4, and so on.

números enteros (pág. 4)   Los números 0, 1, 2, 3, 4, y así sucesivamente.

Definition in Your Own Words	Important Elements

Academic Vocabulary Word

Visual Representation	Personal Association

Eight Circle Spider

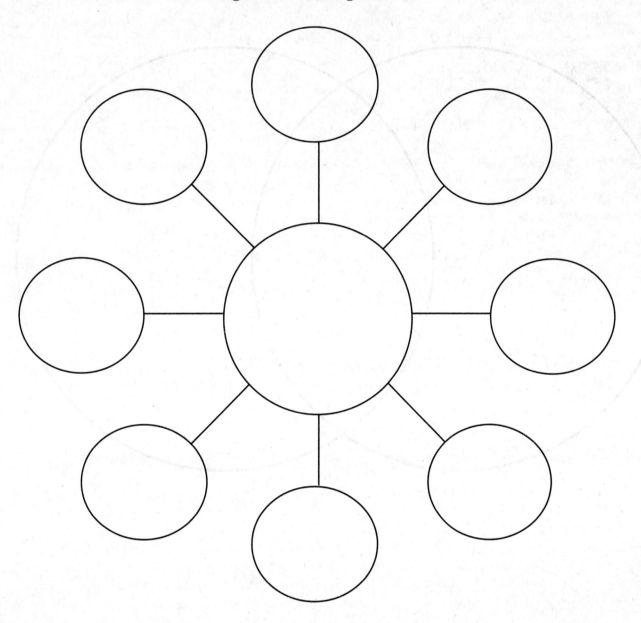

Venn Diagram

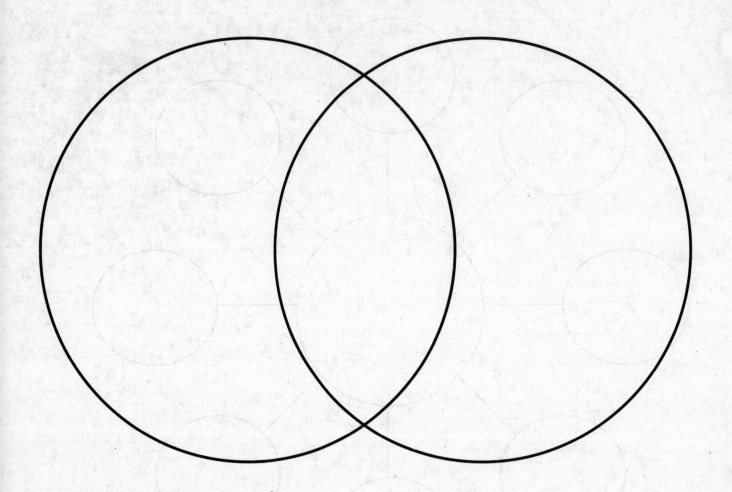

Vertical/Horizontal T-Table

Name: _____ Date: _____ Class: _____

Quarter Inch Grid Paper

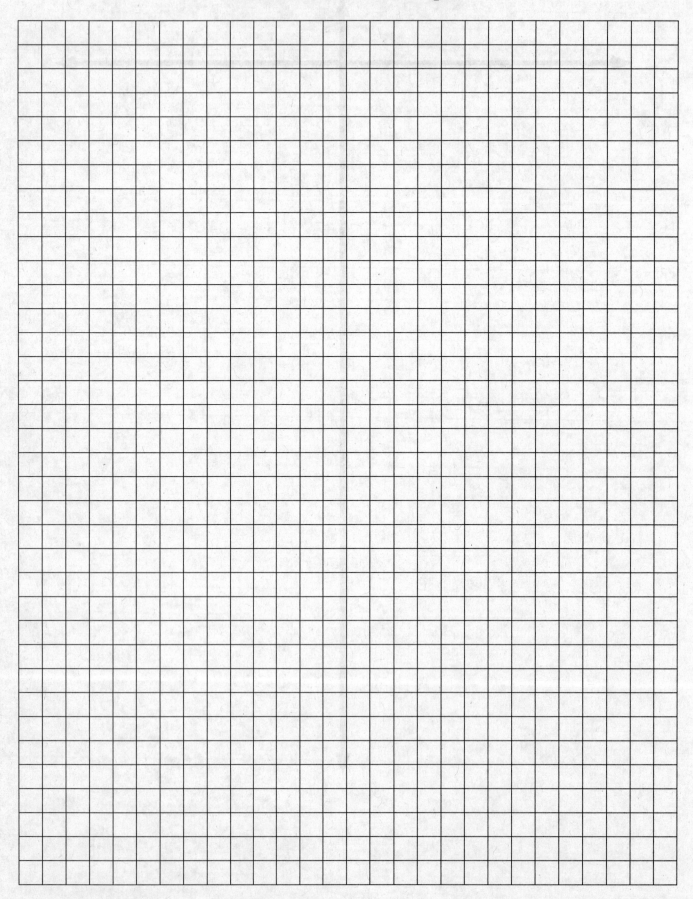

Centimeter Grid Paper

Tables and Coordinate Grids

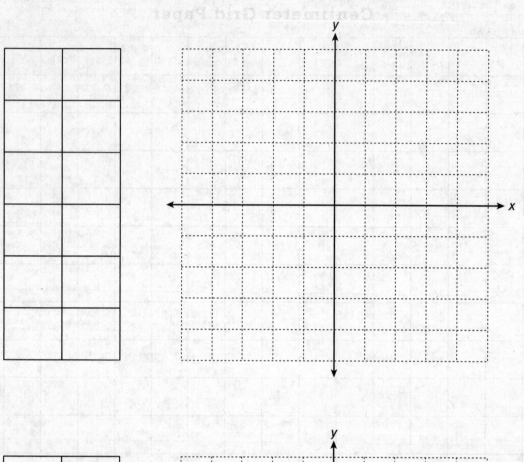

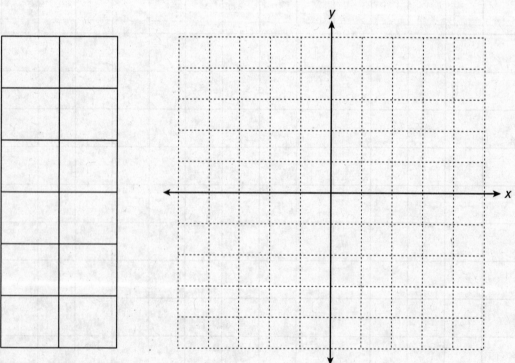

Circle Graphs

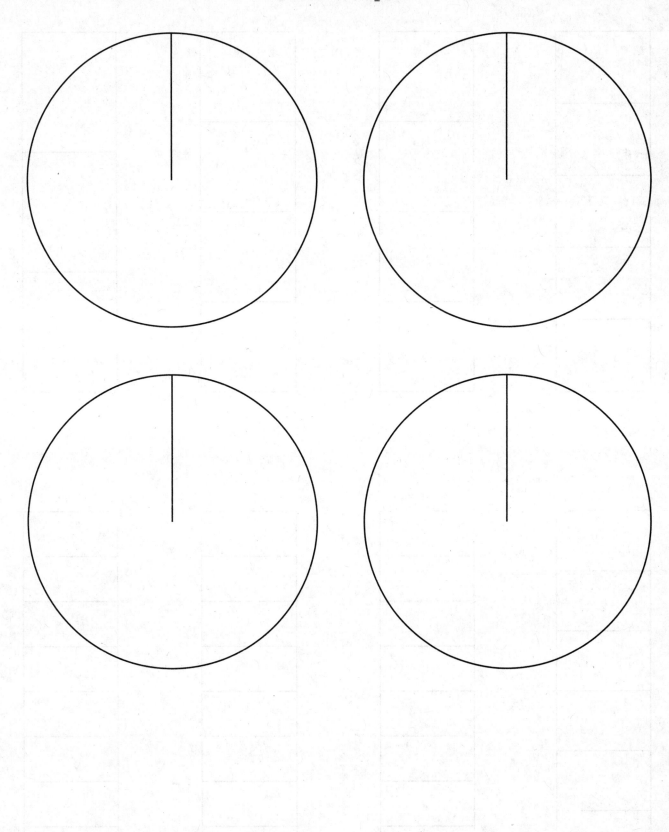

Fraction Strips

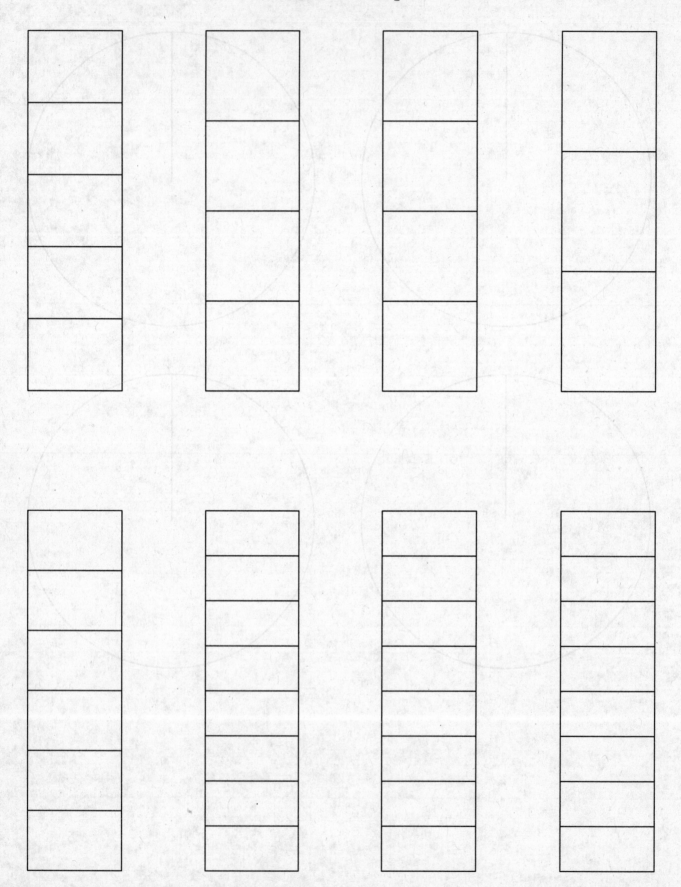

Index

A

Absolute value, 14
Acute angle, 151
Addition
  decimals, 42–46
  fractions, 47–51
  integers, 16–21
  of probability, 329–333
Adjacent angles, 153
Algorithm, 42
Alternate exterior angles, 155
Alternate interior angles, 155
Angles
  acute, 151
  adjacent, 153
  alternate exterior, 155
  alternate interior, 155
  complementary, 152–154
  corresponding, 155
  naming, 151
  obtuse, 151
  right, 151
  sum of triangle, 166
  supplementary, 152–154
  vertical, 154
Area
  circle, 162
  composite figure, 163
  parallelogram, 163
  plane figure, 242
  rectangle, 162
  square, 29–30, 163
  surface, 242
  trapezoid, 163
  triangles, 163
Associative Property, 9

B

Bar graph
  uses of, 299
Base, 30
Bias
  data display, 316–318
Bivariate data
  bias and, 316–318
  defined, 304
  negative correlation, 304
  positive correlation, 304
  scatterplot, 303–306, 313–318
  trend line, 305
Box plot, 300–301

C

Circle
  area, 162
  circumference, 162
  sector, 270–271
Circle graph, 302
Circumference, 162
Coefficient, 88
Commission, 58
Commutative Property, 9
Complement of an event, 324
Complementary angles, 152–154
Complex solid, 256–257

Composite figure
  area, 163
  perimeter, 163
Composition of transformations, 174
Compound inequality, 129
Compound interest, 59–61
  compared to simple interest, 60
Concave polygon, 165–166
Cone
  surface area, 270–271
  volume, 273
Congruency, 183–186
Constant, 88
Constant of variation, 136
Constructions, 223–226
Conversion factor
  defined, 195
  proportional reasoning and, 195–197
  scale drawings and, 201–202
Convex polygon, 165–166
Coordinate plane
  defined, 173
  quadrants, 186
  transformations, 173–190
Correlation
  negative, 304
  positive, 304
Corresponding angles, 155
Corresponding parts, 187–189
  similar figures and, 209
Counting numbers, 3–5
Cube
  net, 241–249
  surface area, 242–243, 281–286
  volume, 35–36, 245–246, 281–286
Cube root
  defined, 36
  symbol for, 36
Cylinder
  net, 269–270
  sketching, 255
  surface area, 269–270
  volume, 260–261

D

Data display
  bivariate data, 303–306, 313–318
  box plot, 300–301
  circle graph, 302
  histogram, 299–300
  negative correlation, 304
  positive correlation, 304
  scatterplot, 304–306, 313–318
  stem plot, 298–299
  trend line, 305
Decimals
  addition, 42–46
  division, 42–46
  multiplication, 42–46
  as rational number, 6
  repeating, 6–7
  subtraction, 42–46
  terminating, 6
Dependent events, 324
Direct variation
  constant of variation, 136

  defined, 134
  equations, 134–136
  form for, 136
Discount, 53–54
  defined, 53
  percent of, 55
Distributive Property, 9
  two-step equations and, 100–101
Division
  decimals, 42–46
  fractions, 47–51
  integers, 27–28
  power of ten, 68–69
  scientific notation, 68–69

E

Ellipses, 3
Entrepreneurs, 53
Equations
  direct variation, 134–136
  equivalent, 104
  inverse variation, 137–140
  open sentences, 127
  two-step, 93–105
  writing, 119–123
Equilateral triangle, 160
Equivalent equations
  defined, 104
  two-step equations, 102–105
Equivalent fractions, 197
Estimation strategies
  decimal computation, 44–46
  fraction computation, 50
Euclid, 223
Event
  complement of, 324
  defined, 321
  dependent, 324
  independent, 324
Experimental probability, 325
Exponent, 30
Exponential form
  defined, 30
  scientific notation, 63–72

F

Figures
  transformations, 173–190
Fractions
  addition, 47–51
  division, 47–51
  equivalent fractions, 197
  multiplication, 47–51
  as rational number, 6
  subtraction, 47–51
Frequency
  histogram, 299
Function, 114

G

Geometry
  angles
    acute, 151
    adjacent, 153
    alternate exterior, 155

Prism
    defined, 243
    net, 267–268
    sketching, 254–255
    surface area, 267–268
Probability
    addition of, 329–333
    defined, 322
    event, 321
    experimental, 325
    independent events, 324
    mutually exclusive, 331–332
    one-stage probability experiment,
        321–325
    random, 321
    sample space, 321
    theoretical, 325
Profit
    defined, 54
    percent of, 55
Properties
    Associative, 9
    Commutative, 9
    Distributive, 9
    Identity, 9
    Property of One, 197
Property of One, 197
Proportional reasoning
    conversion factor, 195–197
    sampling method and, 193–198
    scales drawings, 200
Pyramid
    defined, 251
    net, 268–269
    regular, 269
    square, 268–269
    surface area, 268–269
    volume, 262–263
Pythagoras, 220
Pythagorean Theorem, 217–222
    defined, 220
    using to estimate distance, 220–222

Q
Quadrants, 186
Quadrilateral
    sum of interior angles, 167

R
Random, 321
Rate
    unit rate, 306
Ratio
    conversion factor, 195–197
    defined, 193
    proportional reasoning and, 193–198
    scale factor, 212–214
Rational numbers
    computation with, 41–51
    defined, 6
    symbol for, 6
Reading Math, 15, 151, 159
Real numbers, 8–10
    defined, 8
    properties of, 8–10
    symbol for, 8
Rectangle
    area, 162
    defined, 162

Rectangular prism
    net, 241–249, 260–261
    surface area, 243–245
    volume, 246–247, 259–260, 303–306
Reflection, 173
Regular pyramid, 269
Repeating decimal, 6–7
Rhombus, 162
Right angles, 151
Right triangle
    hypotenuse, 218
    legs, 218
    Pythagorean Theorem, 217–222
Rotation, 173

S
Sale price, 54
Sales tax, 54
Sample space, 321
Sampling method
    proportional reasoning and, 193–198
Scale, 199
Scale drawing, 199–202
    enlarging, 205
    scale factor, 199–200
Scale factor
    defined, 199
    similar figures and, 212–214
Scale model, 203–205
Scalene triangles, 160
Scatterplot, 304–306
    bias, 316–318
    negative correlation, 304
    positive correlation, 304
    trend line, 305
Scientific notation, 63–72
    converting to standard form,
        65–66, 70
    defined, 64
    division, 68–69
    multiplication, 67–68
Sector, 270
Set notation, 3
Similar figures, 207–215
    changing dimensions, 285
    corresponding parts and, 209
    defined, 209, 285
    determining, 210–211
    scale factor, 212–214
    similar triangles, 215
Simple interest
    compared to compound interest, 60
    defined, 58–59
Sketch, 224
Skew lines, 252
Slope
    defined, 111
    as rate of change, 109–111
Solids
    complex, 256–257
    defined, 253
    sketching, 252–257
Sphere
    changing dimensions, 281–286
    surface area, 281–286
    volume, 263, 281–286
Square
    area, 29–30, 163
    defined, 162
    exponential form of, 30

perfect, 32
perimeter, 163
Square pyramid, 268–269
Square root
    defined, 31–32
    finding, 33–34
    symbol for, 31
Standard form, 64–72
    converting to scientific notation,
        65–66, 70
    defined, 64
Stem-and-leaf plot, 298
Stem plot, 298–299
Subset, 7
Subtraction
    decimals, 42–46
    fractions, 47–51
    integers, 16–21
Supplementary angles, 152–154
Surface area
    changing dimensions, 281–286
    cone, 270–271
    cube, 242–243, 281–286
    cylinder, 269–270
    defined, 242
    prism, 267–268
    rectangular prism, 243–245
    regular pyramid, 269
    sphere, 281–286
    square pyramid, 268–269

T
Terminating decimal, 6
Tetrahedron
    similar figures, 285
Theoretical probability, 325
Three-dimensional geometry
    area, 242
    changing dimensions, 281–286
    cube
        changing dimensions, 281–286
    net, 241
        cube, 241–249
        prism, 267–268
        rectangular prism, 241–249, 260–261
    pyramid, 251
    solids
        sketching, 251–257
    sphere
        changing dimensions, 281–286
    surface area
        cone, 270–271
        cube, 242–243
        cylinder, 269–270
        prism, 267–268
        pyramid, 268–269
        rectangular prism, 243–245
    volume
        cone, 273
        cube, 245–246
        cylinder, 260–261
        pyramid, 262–263
        rectangular prism, 246–247, 259–260
        sphere, 263
        triangular prism, 260
Transformations, 173–190
    composition of, 174
    congruency, 183–186
    corresponding parts, 187–189
    image, 182